THE HANDY BOOK OF

Indoor Games

THE HANDY BOOK

OF

Indoor Games

BY GEOFFREY MOTT-SMITH

Permabooks

14 WEST 49TH ST., NEW YORK

PREFACE

This book shows how to play the principal indoor games of skill. The games have been selected, first of all, according to popularity as shown by a recent survey. The most-played games are Contract Bridge, Rummy, Poker, Chess, and Checkers. Also high on the list are Pinochle, Hearts, Russian Bank, and Backgammon. Some new games have been presented here because, though they have not yet made great headway against the perennial favorites, they show signs of so doing. This is particularly true of Oh Hell and Canasta.

Popularity was not the only criterion. I have wished also to do justice to certain games of real skill that are often underrated. For example, Casino is usually regarded as strictly a juvenile pastime; yet it is harder to play well than Gin Rummy. Other juvenile favorites that give adults opportunities for skill are Eights, Dominoes, Salvo, and Quadrangles. The inclusion of Skat may call for explanation, for this game is little known in the Atlantic and Pacific coast states. But it is widely known in the Midwest, where there are many Skat clubs and a national Skat league. The game is at least on a parity with Pinochle as regards skill.

To round out the book with a selection of games suitable for all occasions, I have also included such popular pastimes as Euchre and Solitaire.

The games are grouped in three classes according to the equipment used—playing cards, boards and pieces, pencil and paper. The explanatory text is intended to be of interest to the experienced player as well as to the beginner. All the basic rules of the game are first given under the heading, "How to play . . ." The experienced player may, if he wishes, skip this and go at once to the information given under the heading, "Strategy."

It is manifestly impossible, in the space available, to give a complete account of the theory of the major games, such as Chess, Checkers, Contract Bridge, etc. I have, therefore, aimed to state the important principles and to give a distillation of experience, rather than a manual of detailed precepts. I have played every one of these games for years, and the advice set down in this book is what I have found most useful to me. Of course, I have checked its soundness with whatever precise analysis has been published.

In many of the "minor" games, I have mostly had to blaze my own trail. This is particularly true of Quadrangles, which seems to have completely escaped the attention of game analysts and mathematicians.

I am indebted to my brother, Kenneth O. Mott-Smith, for expert advice on Chess; to Alfred P. Sheinwold for valuable suggestions on Pinochle; to Albert H. Morehead for checking the entire manuscript.

G. M-S.

Contents

PART TWO

BOARD AND PIECE GAMES

PART THREE

WORD GAMES AND PENCIL-AND-PAPER GAMES

PART ONE

Card Games

CONTRACT BRIDGE

Contract Bridge is the pre-eminent card game of skill. It is played by four, in partnerships of two against two.

Contract Bridge is the latest and in every way the most varied and interesting of the succession of related games which started with Whist and continued through Bridge Whist and Auction Bridge. Every hand of Contract is challenging and full of possibilities. The Contract player gains in skill and judgment through increasing experience and knowledge of the game.

How to Play Contract Bridge

The Deck. Use a regular deck of 52 cards. It is customary to use two decks alternately, one being shuffled by the dealer's partner while the other is dealt. The cards in each suit rank: A (high), K, Q, J, 10, 9, 8, 7, 6, 5, 4, 3, 2. The suits rank: spades (high), hearts, diamonds, clubs. (When referring to individual cards or to suits in hands, we shall represent the four suits by their pips, as follows: ♠, spades; ♥, hearts; ♦, diamonds; ♣, clubs.)

Preliminaries. Determine the partnerships, if you wish, by drawing cards from a deck spread face down. The two drawing the highest cards are partners against the other two. Partners sit opposite each other. The player drawing the highest card has choice of seats and (if two decks are used) cards.

The deck to be dealt is shuffled by the opponent at the left of the dealer. The dealer also may shuffle, if he wishes. When a shuffled deck is idle, it should be placed at the left of its dealer. When ready to deal, the dealer transfers the deck to his right, and the opponent on that side *cuts* it. To cut, the right-hand opponent divides the deck into two parts, each of at least four cards. The dealer then closes the cut by placing the former bottom part on top.

The Deal. The dealer distributes the whole deck, one card at a time in clockwise rotation, beginning with the opponent at his left. Each player thus receives thirteen cards.

The players deal in turn, in clockwise rotation.

The Auction. The dealer makes the first *call,* which must be a *pass* or a *bid.* Thereafter, each player calls in rotation until the auction *closes.* If all four players pass at the outset, the deal is abandoned without score; the cards are thrown in and the next dealer deals with the other deck. If any bid is made in the first round, the auction continues until three players in succession pass, whereupon the auction closes.

After any bid has been made, additional calls (besides pass and a bid) that may be made are *double* and *redouble.*

Bids. A bid is an offer to contract to win a certain minimum number of tricks, in return for the privilege of naming the *declaration.* As the least that may legally be bid is seven tricks, a bidder specifies only the *odd tricks,* that is, those beyond six. A bid of "one" is thus an offer to win seven tricks.

Together with a number of odd tricks, the bidder must specify his intended declaration—a trump suit or no trump. The five *denominations* rank: no trump (high), spades, hearts, diamonds, clubs. To be *sufficient,* a bid must be higher than any previous bid—higher either as to number of odd tricks or rank of denomination. For example: to bid over "one no trump" a player must bid at least "two"; "three diamonds" may be *overcalled* by "four clubs" or by three of any other denomination.

Doubles and Redoubles. The call "double" is legal only if the last previous bid was made by an opponent and if no calls other than passes have intervened. The effect of a double is to increase certain scoring values if the bid so doubled becomes the *contract*.

The call "redouble" is legal only if the last previous call, other than a pass, was a double by an opponent. Its effect is further to increase the scoring values if the bid doubled and redoubled becomes the contract.

Neither a double nor a redouble affects the rank of a bid for *sufficiency*. For example: "one no trump" being sufficient to overcall one of any suit, it is also sufficient to overcall one of a suit, doubled or redoubled. Any bid made after a double or redouble nullifies it (since that bid can no longer become the contract).

Review. A player is entitled to have all previous calls restated for his information (a) at any time that it is his turn to call; (b) after the auction is closed, but before the opening lead has been made. After the play has begun, a player is entitled to be told what the contract is (and whether doubled or redoubled), but is not entitled to any other information about the auction.

Commencement of Play. After the auction closes, the highest bid becomes the *contract*. The side that made the bid becomes the *contractors,* and the other side the *defenders.* The player of the contracting side that first bid the denomination named in the contract becomes the *declarer.* Note that this is not necessarily the last bidder. For example: South, one no trump; West, pass; North, three no trumps; all pass. Although North made the winning bid, South is the declarer, for he first named no trump. The declarer's partner becomes *dummy.*

The opening lead is made by the defender at declarer's left. He may lead any card (if not constrained by a penalty).

After the lead is made, dummy lays his entire hand face up on the table. It is customary to sort the dummy hand into suits, with the trumps (if any) at dummy's right.

The Contractors. Declarer plays the cards from both his own hand and the dummy hand. Dummy may assist by pushing out cards from his hand as directed by declarer, but must not suggest any plays or in any other way advise his partner on matters of strategy. Dummy may also protect the legal rights of his side, as by drawing attention to irregularities by the defenders. But he loses even these conditional privileges if he voluntarily looks at a card in any other hand. In social games, the dummy often asks for a look at declarer's entire hand, so that he may make advance estimate of the prospects of success. This practice is frowned upon in tournament play. Even in social play, dummy should never lean over to peek at the hand of a defender.

The Play. After a lead, each other player in rotation plays a card and the four cards constitute a *trick*. A lead calls upon each other hand to follow suit if able; if unable, the hand may play any card. A trick is won by the highest trump, or, if it contains no trump, by the highest card of the suit led. The winner of a trick leads to the next. Declarer and one defender gather all the tricks won by their respective sides. The tricks should not be lumped in a heap, but kept in overlapping packets so that their number can be ascertained at a glance.

The object of play is solely to win tricks. Declarer tries primarily to *make contract* by winning at least as many tricks as his side has bid; *overtricks* beyond the contract also have scoring value. The defenders try primarily to *set* the contract; the more *undertricks* they win (tricks by which declarer falls short of his contract) the greater the gain.

A side is *vulnerable* when it has won a game toward the rubber. It is *not vulnerable* when it has won no game. Where scoring values differ according to vulnerability, this always refers to the contractors; vulnerability of the defenders is immaterial.

Scoring. The regular Bridge scoresheet is divided into

two columns by a vertical line, one column labeled "WE" and the other "THEY." There is also a horizontal line

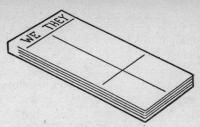

Fɪɢ. 1—Bridge score pad.

somewhat below the middle. Under this line, in the appropriate column, are entered only the points for *odd tricks* earned by a declarer who fulfills his contract. All other scoring items are entered *above the line*.

When declarer fulfills his contract, his side scores *below the line* as follows:

ODD TRICKS

Trump		Undoubled	Doubled	Redoubled
Clubs	each odd trick	20	40	80
Diamonds	each odd trick	20	40	80
Hearts	each odd trick	30	60	120
Spades	each odd trick	30	60	120
No Trump	first odd trick	40	80	160
	each subsequent	30	60	120

If declarer wins more tricks than his contract, the overtricks are scored *above the line* as follows:

OVERTRICKS

		Not vulnerable	Vulnerable
Undoubled	each overtrick	same as odd trick value	
Doubled	each overtrick	100	200
Redoubled	each overtrick	200	400

For making a doubled or redoubled contract, with or without overtricks, declarer receives a bonus above the line of 50 (regardless of vulnerability).

If declarer fulfills a contract of six odd tricks (*little slam*) or seven odd tricks (*grand slam*), he scores a bonus above the line, additional to all other scores due, as follows:

SLAMS

	Not vulnerable	Vulnerable
Little slam	500	750
Grand slam	1000	1500

If declarer is *set*, the defending side scores above the line for *undertricks* (each trick by which declarer falls short of his contract) as follows:

UNDERTRICKS

		Not vulnerable	Vulnerable
Undoubled	each undertrick	50	100
Doubled	first undertrick	100	200
	each subsequent	200	300
Redoubled	first undertrick	200	400
	each subsequent	400	600

When there is a trump suit, the *honors* are the five highest trumps. At no trump, the honors are the four aces. If one hand (not merely one side) is dealt four or five honors, that side scores a bonus above the line as follows:

HONORS

Four trump honors	100
Five trump honors	150
Four aces at no trump	150

Note that honors are credited to the side, contractors or defenders, regardless of whether the contract is made. As to all other scoring items, only the contractors score when the contract is made and only the defenders when the contract is set.

Game is won by the side that first reaches a total of 100 or more points *below the line*. Any *part score* recorded below the line for the opponents is "wiped out" so far as concerns the next game, which begins at 0-0 odd-trick score. Such lost "partials" remain on the scoresheet, however, and are added into the grand total.

Rubber is won by the side first to win two games. The ensuing rubber then commences at 0-0 game score. For winning a rubber, a side scores a bonus above the line as follows:

RUBBER BONUS

Rubber in two games	700
Rubber in three games	500

A session of play, or a partnership arrangement, is preferably terminated only at the end of a rubber. Whenever there is to be settlement, the columns for each side are totaled—all items above and below the line being added together. The side with the larger total "wins the rubber" by the difference. (It has been legally decided that a bet as to who will "win a rubber" is decided by reference to the final totals; the side that wins two games out of three may still have the smaller total.)

STRATEGY OF CONTRACT BRIDGE

We bring together here the most important points in Contract Bridge strategy.

Hand Valuation. The Culbertson table of *honor tricks* (hereinafter abbreviated to HT) is given on page 8. Requirements for bids are given, in part, by HT.

CULBERTSON HONOR TRICK TABLE

2+	A K Q		1	A
2	A K J			K Q
	A K			K J 10
1½	A Q J		½+	K J x
	A Q		½	K x
1+	K Q J			Q J x
	A J x			

The "x" indicates any indifferent low card. Two "plus" values are considered the equivalent of ½ HT.

The HT valuation gives the probable number of actual tricks that high cards can be expected to win in the most unfavorable circumstances, that is, on defense against an adverse suit contract. That is why A K Q is rated at 2+, not 3. If all hands follow to three leads of this suit, the combination will win all three tricks; but a suit is distributed 4-3-3-3 only 10% of the time. In 90% of cases, some hand will be able to trump the third round, and the odds are at least 2 to 1 that this hand will be an opponent rather than partner.

Pattern. The number of tricks that a hand can be expected to win at its own or partner's best declaration is the HT count plus its *distributional values*. The latter arise from the *pattern* of the hand, the count of the number of cards held in each suit. The weakest pattern is 4-3-3-3; the only distributional trick it could develop would be a *long card* in the four-card suit. (A long card is one that wins a trick, not by reason of its rank, but because all other cards of the suit have been played.) All *balanced* patterns are necessarily weak, such as 4-4-3-2, 5-3-3-2. The patterns become stronger as they become *unbalanced*, as 5-4-3-1, 5-4-4-0. A very rough method of counting distributional values is to count ½ for the fourth card of length, and 1 for each card over four. Examples of *playing trick* valuation (expected number of actual tricks as a contractor):

(1) ♠ A x x   ♥ A x x   ♦ A x x   ♣ x x x x

3 HT; 3 playing tricks. The ½ trick in clubs is negligible.

    (2) ♠ A Q x x x ♥ x ♦ x x x ♣ A x x x

2 and ½ HT plus 2 in distributional values; 4½ playing tricks.

With patterns so unbalanced as to be *freak,* or with fairly solid top holdings, a direct count can be made of fairly sure playing tricks.

    (3) ♠ K Q J 10 x x ♥ x ♦ x ♣ A K Q x x

If spades are trumps, this hand will probably lose only three aces, thus winning 10 tricks.

Opening Bid. An opening bid of one is only secondarily an offer to assume a contract. Primarily, it shows partner a certain minimum HT strength in support of future operations. As a rule, 3 HT are too much to pass, and should be bid regardless of other considerations. But 2½ or even 2+ HT make a correct opening bid if the hand is sufficiently fortified with playing tricks. For example:

    (4) ♠ A Q x ♥ K x ♦ A x x x ♣ x x x x

Bid one diamond. Too much to pass.

    (5) ♠ A Q x ♥ x x ♦ A x x x ♣ x x x x

Pass. Too weak for a 2½ HT opening.

    (6) ♠ J x x x x x ♥ K x ♦ K J x ♣ A x

Bid one spade. The six-card suit is "all velvet" over the 2+HT.

    (7) ♠ A x ♥ Q x ♦ Q J 10 x ♣ K J 10 x x

Bid one club. The "plus" values promote the playing strength to about six tricks.

Choice of Opening Bids. The modern tendency is open with a no trump bid only on pattern 4-3-3-3 or 4-4-3-2. The hand should have a *stopper* (A, or K x, or Q x x) in each of at least three suits. The no-trump bid, unlike a suit bid, shows a *maximum* strength as well as a minimum. It guarantees 3½ HT (possibly 3 with strong intermediate cards) and not more than 4 HT. The point is that there is no object in bidding only one no trump if able to bid two or three—the inordinate top strength will support any operation partner wishes to undertake.

With any less balanced, and therefore stronger, pattern, an opening suit bid is preferred. The systemic rules as to choosing between two suits are intricate; the following is a broad summary:

1. With suits of unequal length, bid the longer first.

2. With suits of equal length, five cards or more, bid the higher-ranking first.

3. With two or three four-card suits, bid first the one that ranks below the shortest suit in the hand.

Here are some examples:

(8)   ♠ A K Q J x   ♥ Q 10 x x x x   ♦ x   ♣ A

Bid one heart. Length of the heart suit governs.

(9)   ♠ J 10 x x x   ♥ K Q J x x   ♦ x   ♣ A x

Bid one spade. Rank of the suit governs.

(10)   ♠ A K x x   ♥ x   ♦ K x x x   ♣ A Q x x

Bid one diamond. The idea is "preparedness" for partner's most probable response, one heart—the suit of which this hand is shortest.

Opening Two-bid. By convention, an opening bid of two in a suit is *forcing* to game. That is, it commands partner not to let the auction close until the side has reached a game bid. (For game in one hand, 100 points in odd tricks are required. Such a score can be made by a contract of three no trumps, four spades or hearts, five diamonds or clubs. Because of the superiority enjoyed by spades and hearts, they are called *major* suits, while diamonds and clubs are *minor*.)

The two-bid is of course designed for hands so strong that they need little more than a "fit" with partner's cards to make game. But for the force, the partner might be unable to make any response. The normal minimum is 4½ HT, together with great playing trick strength; a rule-of-thumb is that the hand is worth a two bid if the HT are greater than the *losers*. Losers are the tricks the hand must expect to lose if partner has no high card whatsoever.

(11) ♠ A Q J x x x ♥ A K x x x ♦ A x ♣ —

Bid two spades. The HT count is 4½; the expected maximum loss is one trick in spades, one or two in hearts, one in diamonds.

Responses to Opening Bids. After an opening no-trump bid, partner should *raise* to two no trumps with 2 HT or with 1½ and a five-card suit. (Although 5 HT in the combined hands give expectation of game-in-hand, there is no need for the responding hand to jump to three. The original bidder will almost never pass two no trumps, if three are needed for game.) With an extra HT, jump to three no trumps. (If the original hand has more top command than his bid guarantees, slam is in sight.) The *takeout* of one no trump by a suit bid of two is a warning of lack of support for no trump—less than 2 HT—but of course shows a five-card or longer suit. With strength sufficient to raise the no trump, but a preferable suit bid (five spades or hearts), jump to three of the suit. This *jump* is a force to game.

It will be noted that the responses to an opening no trump bid show the strength of the hand at once. But the minimum responses to a suit bid of one are equivocal—the hand may be a minimum or very strong—and current practice is to construe any such response as a *one-round force*. That is, the original bidder must not let the response die as the contract.

Fortified by this convention, the responder should use his opportunity primarily to show *pattern*. He should prefer showing a five-card major to all else. If the original bid was a major, he should prefer to raise it if he has positive trump support (any four trumps, or three headed by queen or better). A no-trump takeout shows a fairly balanced pattern, certainly with no five-card major. A minor suit takeout shows either inability to make a more forward bid or extra strength that will be clarified by a *rebid*.

The strength required for a response to partner's opening suit bid is as follows:

With no more than ½ HT, usually pass (possibly bid a major suit of freak length).

With 1 HT, bid one in a five-card suit or raise with four trumps.

With 1 or 1½ HT, bid one in a five-card suit or raise with as good as Q x x in partner's suit or bid one no trump.

With 2 HT or more raise or take out with a bid of two, if necessary.

With 3 to 3½ HT, there is probably a game; give a double raise, or bid two no trumps, or temporize with a minimum suit bid. The first two courses are clearly strength-showing; the suit takeout is equivocal, but you will clarify it by a rebid on the next round.

With 4 HT, slam becomes a possibility, and an unequivocal forcing bid should be made. The clearest procedure is a jump takeout in another suit, which forces partner to keep the auction open at least to game.

Response to Opening Two-bid. Since this is a forced response (you must not pass if the intervening hand has passed), the problem is what to do with a weak or destitute hand. Current practice is to reserve two no trumps to show a "bust." Real support for no trump (1½ HT or more) is shown by a jump to three no trumps. A simple raise to three of partner's suit requires about 1 HT; a suit takeout requires a five-card suit with 1½ HT or any longer suit with about 1 HT.

Rebids. A *free rebid* by the original bidder (after a response that the system permits him to pass, or after an adverse bid has kept the auction open) should of course be made on solid values over those already guaranteed by the opening bid. These values need not be extra HT, they may be partly or wholly extra playing tricks. For example, suppose South holds:

(12)   ♠ K Q x x x   ♥ A Q x x x   ♦ x x   ♣ x

The bidding is South, one spade; West, pass; North, one
no trump; East, pass. South is free to pass, but should bid
two hearts. North is not entirely destitute, and it is extremely likely that two spades or two hearts will be a better
contract than one no trump. South has only the minimum
of 2½ HT, but the rebid is justified by the strong pattern.

But suppose that the bidding has been: South, one spade;
West, two clubs; North, pass; East, two no trumps. Now
South should pass. The strength shown by the opponents
makes a rebid very risky.

When the bidding goes: South, one in a suit; West, pass;
North, one in a higher suit or two in a lower suit; East,
pass; South is systemically compelled to rebid. He should
announce the most important fact about his hand from the
point of view of distribution and "fit," e.g., show a second
long suit, rebid a long strong major suit, raise his partner's
major takeout, bid no trump to indicate strength in the
three suits other than the takeout. Systemic refinements
aside, none of these choices shows any extra strength over
the original bid, except for certain cases of second-suit bids.
The tendency is to treat every showing of a new suit,
hitherto unbid by the side, as strength-showing; and, when
the new suit is bid by the responding hand, as a *one-round
force*. Thus, South, one heart; North, two clubs; South, two
diamonds, practically precludes a pass by North. South in
rebidding must therefore be careful not to show a new suit
unless (a) he has the extra strength necessary to cover
North's probable response, or (b) the suits are such as to
permit a low *sign-off*.

The foregoing bidding is reasonable when South holds

(13)   ♠ x x   ♥ Q J 10 x   ♦ A Q 10 x   ♣ K x x

Although South has a weak pattern and no HT over his
original bid, he is justified in showing the second suit
because the partnership should not be in trouble if North
next calls two hearts, three diamonds, or three clubs. Show-

ing the diamonds may enable North, with strength only in the black suits, to bid two or three no trumps.

As a matter of both convention and common sense, *reversal* in bidding two suits must show extra strength. For example: South, one heart; North, two diamonds; South, two spades. If North prefers hearts to spades, he has to bid one level up to show the fact; likewise he must go to three if his pattern calls for confirming the spades; since he is pushed up in either case, South must have the extra strength to cover. Many players use a reversal as forcing to game. Suppose that South holds

(14)   ♠ x x   ♥ A J x x x   ♦ J x   ♣ A K x x

The bidding: South, one heart; North, two diamonds. In analogy with Example 12, there is some temptation to bid three clubs, hoping that North will have spades adequately stopped and can bid three no trumps. But suppose he has only a minimum response, with or without a spade stopper. South's unwarranted reverse will have pushed the partnership out on a limb. South's correct rebid is two hearts—which guarantees nothing more than a five-card suit. True, he has 3 HT instead of the 2½ that North might expect, but this is not sufficient margin for a strength-showing rebid.

Defensive Overcall. All bidding by the opponents of the opening bidder is called *defensive,* although it may quickly develop that this side has the stronger cards. In making the first defensive bid, the player faces a definite tactical situation, and there is little compulsion to bid even when able. The requirement for his overcall is primarily the assurance that he cannot be slaughtered at his bid—he should have within two or three *playing tricks* of his contract in his own hand. He should also have a minimum of about 1½ HT, else he forfeits the actual defensive value of the initial overcall (i.e., information to partner that he can win one or two tricks against any adverse contract).

With better than an original bid, say 3½ HT up, with playing tricks to match, make some effort to show the extra strength at once, to cover a response by partner. The choices here are: (a) a *negative double* (explained below); (b) a *jump* overcall, appropriate with a suit of extra strength and length; (c) a no-trump bid. The last is not a forcing bid, but still operates to invite a response more strongly than a suit overcall, because it shows positive stoppers in the adverse suit (usually two stoppers) and entire willingness to be left in. A hand strong enough for such a bid must necessarily give good protection to a response by partner, made on a strong pattern though weak in HT.

Negative Double. A double is interpreted as *negative* if it applies to not more than one no trump or three of a suit, if it was made at first opportunity of the doubler to make a double, and if the partner has previously made no call other than pass.

A negative double asks partner to make a response if the intervening opponent passes. It must therefore show values necessary to cover a forced response at the necessary level. The double is used for either or both of these purposes: (a) to find out at once the distributionally best suit of the partnership, when the doubler has a balanced pattern; (b) to advertise a better-than-minimum HT count.

Here are examples of what to do in making the initial defensive overcall.

South bids one heart, and West holds

     (15)   ♠ Q J 10 x x x x   ♥ x   ♦ x x x   ♣ x x

Pass. An immediate overcall would lie about the HT count. The spades may be bid later if the tactical situation that develops makes the bid necessary and expedient.

     (16)   ♠ K Q x x x   ♥ x   ♦ A x x x   ♣ x x x

Bid one spade. A normal minimum overcall.

     (17)   ♠ x x x   ♥ x x   ♦ A J x x x   ♣ K J x

Pass. A minor overcall at the two-level ought, in all common sense, to show either (a) too many HT to pass; or

(b) strong distributional support for an unbid major suit. Here the support for spades is too feeble to warrant inducing East to make a spade bid that he would not make freely.

(18) ♠ Q x ♥ x x ♦ A x x ♣ A K Q x x x

Bid three clubs. The idea is to induce partner to bid three no trumps if he has a heart stopper. Of course this bid is risky, for if East has a bust the partnership may take a licking at a high club contract.

(19) ♠ K J x x ♥ x ♦ A J x x ♣ K Q J x

Double. This is the ideal pattern (next to 5-4-4-0) for a negative double, as it is distributionally prepared to raise any suit takeout.

(20) ♠ A x ♥ x ♦ Q J 10 x x ♣ A K x x x

Double. East may have the right cards to produce even a minor game, without being able to respond unless forced. Double to show real strength, so that after you have shown both minor suits East will appreciate the value of some such hand as ♠ Q x x x ♥ x x x ♦ K x ♣ Q x x x.

Response to Negative Double. The first principle of responding is never to pass from fright. The weaker the hand, the more imperative it is to bid. The second principle is to prefer a major suit, even of four cards, to a minor suit, even of five or more. Relative strength of suits is of no moment—the important thing is that the double may be an effort to find a major split 4-4 between the partners. A long strong minor can be shown by a rebid later.

With no major suit, bid a minor suit unless having real strength for positive action. This may involve bidding a three-card minor. For example: South, one heart; West, double; North, pass; East holds

(21) ♠ x x x x ♥ x x ♦ x x ♣ A Q x x x

Bid one spade.
Or if, with the same bidding, East holds

(22) ♠ x x x ♥ J 10 x x ♦ x x x ♣ Q x x,

bid two clubs.

A response of one no trump shows at least one stopper in the suit doubled, with at least 1 HT. But few players will make this bid with the bare minimum, preferring to wait at least for plenty of plus values in order to support a continuation of no-trump bidding. For example:

(23) ♠ x x x ♥ J 10 x x ♦ x x x ♣ A x x

Two clubs looks better than one no trump. The idea is to feign great weakness, but then to double any heart rebid for business. Actually, the pattern is the weakest possible for offensive purposes.

The pass of a negative double turns it into a *positive* or *business* double. The pass should be made only with reasonable assurance of setting the contract, *plus* the conviction that the doubling side cannot make a game of greater value. When the bid doubled is one of a suit, these requirements are fulfilled only by extraordinary length or strength or both in the suit, with little else. For example, pass one heart doubled with

(24) ♠ x x ♥ K J x x x ♦ K x x ♣ x x x

When one no trump is doubled, pass if you possibly can, unless you have a strong pattern and little HT count. Making game against a sound opening no-trumper usually takes a great deal in the way of unbalance, plus most of the rest of the high cards. But defeating one no trump is relatively easy when a sound double is faced by a good sprinkling of intermediate cards. For example: South, one no trump; West, double; North, pass; East holds

(25) ♠ x x x ♥ x x x ♦ Q J x x x ♣ x x

Bid two diamonds. Too weak for anything else.

Or if, with the same bidding, East holds

(26) ♠ J x x x x ♥ x ♦ A Q x ♣ Q x x x,

bid three spades. The hand is strong enough to warrant a try for game, if West has spade support. West might pass two spades, believing East to be weak in HT because he did not pass the double.

(27)   ♠ J x x   ♥ Q 10 x x   ♦ K J x   ♣ J 10 x

Pass. The intermediate strength has good chance of defeating the contract, opposite a sound double.

Slam Bidding. The combined hands of a partnership, having no void suit, normally require at least 7 HT to make a slam. The ground for a slam bid is usually laid by a game-forcing bid at some stage, such as a forcing takeout or an opening two-bid. The final stage is usually concerned with discovering the *controls,* i.e., aces or ability to trump the first round of a plain suit. Various systems of slam bidding are in use. Most prevalent is the Blackwood System, as follows:

A bid of four no trumps is a slam try, and asks partner to make a conventional response:

> Five clubs to show no aces.
> Five diamonds to show one ace.
> Five hearts to show two aces.
> Five spades to show three aces.
> Five no trumps to show four aces.

If the four-no-trump bidder bids five no trump after the response, he asks for a showing of kings, on the same principle. (The bid of five no trump for this purpose is rare, since it can only be made when small slam is sure and only grand slam is in question.)

The partners must usually agree on what the declaration is to be, before either can well bid four no trump, but sometimes one partner, having extraordinary support for a late suit bid by his partner, can advertise his certainty of a "landing spot" by four no trumps in lieu of a raise. Of course the four-no-trump bidder must also have assurance, from the earlier bidding, that the hands have "body" for at least 11 tricks: four aces do not make a slam. And there is no point in using the convention when a "sign-off" is precluded. For example, if the agreed suit is clubs, and the bidder hopes to find two aces in his partner's hand for a small slam bid, there is no point in bidding four no trumps. With even one ace, partner will respond at least five diamonds, and the partnership will have to go back to its real suit at six anyhow.

Declarer's Play. You have won the contract; the opening lead is made; dummy goes down on the table. Before playing a single card, make a count of your two hands. Total the sure and highly probable tricks: is the contract sure, possible, or impossible? What resources do the hands hold for developing additional tricks? The cards fix what you *can* do, but the count in relation to the contract fixes what you *should* do.

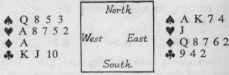

♠ Q 8 5 3
♥ A 8 7 5 2
♦ A
♣ K J 10

♠ A K 7 4
♥ J
♦ Q 8 7 6 2
♣ 9 4 2

East is declarer at four spades; no adverse bidding. South opens the ♠ 10. Declarer counts as follows:

In spades, five tricks. Normal expectancy (about 70%) is that the five outstanding spades will split 3-2. After three leads of trumps, declarer will have one trump left in each hand, and these can surely be made separately.

In hearts, one trick.

In diamonds, one trick.

In clubs, one trick.

The total is eight sure tricks, minimum. The resources for additional tricks are many. Six or seven tricks might be won with spades, through *cross-ruffing* the red suits. (To cross-ruff is to trump plain suits alternately in two hands, as diamonds and hearts, each hand being void of one suit.) Or a long heart or long diamond might be developed by ruffing that suit alone. Two tricks may develop in clubs through finding the queen in the South hand.

All of these resources are at the mercy of the breaks in the red suits and the location of the club queen. The right plan is to plumb them in an order that conserves all so long as possible.

In the play below, the card in italics wins the trick, and the card below it is the lead to the next trick.

Trick	South	West	North	East
1	♠ 10	♠ 3	♠ 6	♠ *A*
2	♣ 5	♣ 10	♣ *Q*	♣ 2

The clubs are tackled first because (a) they may provide the ninth trick at once; (b) East must utilize his *entries* to lead up to dummy's clubs for a *finesse* (see below); (c) declarer will not have enough tricks if he takes out the adverse trumps, so must develop the clubs in the hope that the split is 4-3.

3	♠ 2	♠ 5	♠ J	♠ *K*

As the club queen was offside, and the unkind trump leads have killed the cross-ruff, the only remaining hope is to set up a red suit. The better candidate is hearts, since West has most of the entries. East therefore puts up the ♠ K to save his two small trumps for ruffs.

4	♥ Q	♥ *A*	♥ 3	♥ J
5	♥ 4	♥ 2	♥ 6	♠ *4*
6	♦ 5	♦ *A*	♦ 3	♦ 2

Giving up command of the diamonds is risky, but what can he do? If he tries to force entry in clubs, the defender with the club ace may lead the last trump, and kill the second heart ruff.

7	♥ 9	♥ 5	♥ *K*	♠ 7
8	♣ 7	♣ *J*	♣ A	♣ 4
9	♦ *9*	♥ 7	♦ 4	♦ Q

North has made a nice try by *underleading* his ♦ K. The point is that if he lets West in cheaply, say by a club,

West will take out the last trump with the ♠ Q, then lead a heart to force out the ten. Then West will win the last two tricks with the long trump and the long heart. The only defensive hope is to force out West's long trump before the long heart becomes established. If North had laid down the ♦ K, West would have trumped, *cashed* the ♠ Q, and then led a heart. Although out of trumps, he would win the rest by virtue of having command of both diamonds and clubs. On North's underlead, declarer put up the ♦ Q because his only chance for contract was that North held the ♦ K.

Declarer finishes the play by leading a diamond for West to ruff, cashing the ♠ Q, then the ♣ K, and conceding the last trick to the adverse ♥ 10.

Timing. The order in which declarer should develop the various suits depends usually on what is called *timing*. This is the race between declarer to establish and cash his contract-making tricks and the defenders to establish and cash their contract-setting tricks. Not every hand involves a race—the problem for one side may be merely to develop *enough* tricks, given unlimited time. But declarer must always keep track of how many times he must or may lose the lead, and calculate what damage if any the defenders can do with their leads.

East is declarer at four hearts, with no adverse bidding. South opens the ♦ K.

Declarer counts: four heart tricks in the East hand, four top tricks on the side, total 8. For additional tricks there is the chance of establishing one or two long spades and the chance to make one of West's trumps separately from East's by ruffing the third diamond.

The correct play is as follows:

Declarer *ducks* the ♦ K by *holding up* the ace. The point is that he must lose one diamond anyhow, and wants to lose it now so that he can pick his own time to lead the third diamond. South continues diamonds and East wins. East cashes the ace and king of hearts. It would be a great mistake to lead the third diamond at this juncture—the ruff is a vital *re-entry* to dummy that may be needed later. East leads a spade; West cashes the tops, then leads a third spade for East to ruff. If the adverse spades split 3-3, this ruff sets up two long cards, to which the ♣ A will give re-entry. But North discards on the third spade, showing the split to be 4-2. It is because of this possibility that declarer has saved up the trump re-entry. He now goes back by ruffing his last diamond with dummy's last trump. A fourth spade is led, North again discards, and East ruffs. Then East leads a club to the ace, and West leads the long spade, on which East discards a club. Declarer makes ten tricks. Note that it does not matter if the long spade is ruffed by the last adverse trump. Losing the inevitable trump trick that way gives East five trump tricks, instead of four as originally counted.

Timing is largely concerned with *entries* and *re-entries* —commanding cards whereby partnership hands can pass the lead to each other—and *stoppers*—high or intermediate cards that eventually win tricks against adverse leads of the suit. It must never be overlooked that the whole advantage in naming the trump suit is in the possession of *long trumps* that act as "wild stoppers," applicable to any suit of which the hand is void. These trump stoppers must be manipulated as carefully as side aces.

Development Plays. Declarer usually has only a few *top* or *solid* tricks; most have to be *established* by forcing out adverse stoppers. Long cards in plain suits, to take tricks, have to be established by forcing out all other cards of the suit. In the course of such development play, any of the following devices may be required:

THE FINESSE. A *finesse* may be defined broadly as a lead

toward rather than *away from* a high card or combination, in the effort to increase the number of high-card tricks or to win earlier rather than later tricks. Example: declarer holds ♣ A Q, dummy ♣ x x. If he leads from his own hand, declarer will win only one trick. If he leads from dummy, and the next hand plays low, the queen has a 50% chance of winning the trick. Another example is ♣ A J 10 in one hand, ♣ x x x in the other. A *double finesse* may be taken by leading the low toward the honors and playing the 10; if this loses to K or Q, a second lead is made toward A J and a second finesse taken. There is a 75% chance to win two tricks by this process.

THE HOLD-UP. The refusal to put up the master card of the suit, on an adverse lead, may have any of several purposes. One is to preserve a favorable *tenace* (combination of high cards not in sequence). Example: opening lead is ♣ K; dummy holds ♣ x x x, declarer ♣ A J x. Declarer *holds up* the ace, playing the x. If the leader continues clubs, declarer will win two tricks with his *major tenace*. At worst, the leader is compelled to shift suit. Another frequent purpose in holding up is to void one defender of a suit before losing command, so as to reduce to 50% the chance that when declarer later loses the lead this suit can be led again.

THE DUCK. This is in effect a hold-up on one's own lead. The commonest purpose is to retain command until a later round, for reasons of entry. Example: dummy holds ♣ A K Q x x x, declarer ♣ x x. Dummy has no possible side entry, and declarer must win five club tricks for contract, but does not need six. Declarer leads a low club and *ducks* by holding up the top honors; this assures five club tricks against a 4-1 split, whereas to lead the top clubs at once would lose contract against a split worse than 3-2.

Trump Manipulation. When he can afford to do so, declarer should lead trumps enough times to *bail out* the adverse small trumps that might otherwise capture his side tricks. But many reasons can arise why it is advisable to defer leading trumps, or avoid leading them until no other suits are left. Among such reasons are:

1. Trump leads are deferred to utilize for ruffing the small trumps of the *shorter* holding (as between declarer and dummy).

2. Trump leads are entirely avoided, the plan being to *cross-ruff*.

3. As a matter of timing, certain plain suits must be developed before the adverse trump stoppers are knocked out.

4. Trump leads are deferred until entry is gained to the right hand for opening the trump suit, or until the splits found in plain suits have revealed some probabilities about the trump split.

5. Declarer does not have enough trumps, or enough top trumps, to tackle the suit directly, and must accept the risk of having side cards trumped, or must actually *force* the defenders with plain suits to weaken their trumps.

Defenders' Play. Declarer sees both hands of his partnership, and therefore is able to estimate how he stands in relationship to his contract. He is able to form a general plan, subject perhaps to modification as he gains information about the unseen hands. The situation of a defender is markedly different. He sees one hand of each side, his own and dummy. To make any estimate of how either side stands, he must rely on *inferences* as to the unseen hands. Furthermore, he is often forced to make a crucial decision at a very early stage, when the available information is minimal. It is proverbial that the opening lead makes or breaks the contract more often than any other single factor.

The principles of defensive play are grounded on a negative motive—to do the least possible damage to the defensive chances. The defender, much more than declarer, is concerned with problems of *exit*—getting out of the lead at lowest cost. At the same time, the defender must be alert to realize when positive action is called for, when direct attack must supplant mere passivity.

The Opening Lead. At no trump, the strongest offense by

either side is often to develop its own longest suit. The fate of the contract is often decided by which side first establishes and cashes one or more long cards. At a suit contract, leads of their long suit by the defenders are less likely to develop remote tricks, but usually have the negative merit of providing safe exit. The normal rule for the opening lead, against either a suit or no trump, is therefore to seek a suit in which the defenders are long.

The leader should normally open a plain suit of which he has four or more cards, or a suit bid by his partner (unless such bid may be made systemically on three cards or less).

In opening his own suit, the leader selects the card according to the following standard conventions:

1. The fourth-highest card is led from any holding that lacks top strength for a high-card lead. All high-card leads are listed below.

2. Against no trump, a high lead is made only from three honors, at least two of them in sequence. The correct lead is the top of the sequence. Example: K *J* 10 x; *Q* J 10 x: K *10* 9 x. (Lead the card in italics.) But from A K J x, A K Q X, and other sequences of ace and king, lead the king first: lead of the ace against no trump is reserved to ask partner to follow with his highest card of the suit. Example: from A K x x x x x the ace might be led so that from sight of dummy and his partner's highest card the leader can estimate whether the suit is solid. Naturally, it is always a matter of judgment whether to lead ace or king first.

3. Against no trump, a high lead from only two honors in sequence may be made if the suit is longer than five cards—this is a matter of judgment.

4. Against a suit contract, usually lead high when the suit is topped by any two honors in sequence. Lead the king from A K or K Q; but the lead from Q J x x is a matter of judgment, and from lower sequences (of only two) the fourth-best is preferred.

5. Against a suit contract, usually do not *underlead* an

ace, even in a suit bid by partner. The lead of an ace, by rule 4, denies having the king, except that the lead of ace and king in this order is reserved to show a *doubleton* and ability to trump a third round of the suit.

In opening a suit that partner has bid, observe these rules:

1. Lead the fourth-best from four or more, except that high may be led from an honor-sequence, and an ace should not be underled against a suit contract.

2. Lead the highest card from three or less, except that against no trump the third-best may be led from three topped by at least the jack. The object in so underleading even a low honor is to hold it over a possible low stopper in declarer's hand.

With choice between one's own long suit and a suit bid by partner, prefer the latter where it seems important to lead *toward* rather than *away from* high cards. Own suit is preferable if it has powerful top strength that makes an intrinsically desirable lead, as A K Q, A K J, K Q J, Q J 10. Against no trump, the choice should usually fall on the suit whose length is held by the defender who also holds, probably, the greater number of side re-entries.

The long-suit opening is normal, against either no trump or a suit. But special circumstances often indicate the desirability of an abnormal *short-suit* lead. The commonest cases are:

1. A plain singleton, or worthless doubleton, or ace from A x, is led against a suit contract in the hope of getting a ruff.

2. A strong short sequence is opened in preference to a long but broken suit, as jack from J 10 9 in preference to fourth-best from K J x x. There is a well-founded but overworked prejudice against underleading kings against suit bids.

Responses to Leads. Observe that in *leading* from a sequence, the convention is to lead the top card (except as to A K). In *following suit* from a sequence, the convention is to play always the bottom card.

How high to play, on a low lead by partner, of course depends upon dummy's holding in the suit. As a rule, the defender playing third to the trick should make the best possible effort to win it. Example: the ♣ 4 is led, dummy holds ♣ 10 7 5; third hand holding ♣ K J 2 should play the king. But third hand should duly *finesse* against the dummy when there is prospect of gain by doing. Example: the ♣ 4 is led; dummy holds ♣ Q 7 5 and plays the 5; third hand holding ♣ K 10 2 should play the 10.

In following to partner's lead, when making no effort to win the trick, a player is expected to indicate a preference by his *response*. The play of the lowest card held in the suit, as the 3 from 9 7 3, is *negative* or *discouraging*. It carries the message, "Shift to another suit" or "I have no tops in this suit" or "I have no reason to request continuation of this suit." The play of any card but the lowest, as the 7 from 9 7 3, is *positive* or *encouraging*. Completion of the signal by the subsequent play of a lower card of the same suit is called an *echo, come-on,* or *down-and-out*. The positive response requests a continuation of the suit or shows a high card in it. The request for continuation may be based on shortness plus ability to ruff. Example: opening lead against four spades is the ♥ K and third hand has the ♥ 4 2; he plays the 4, so that if the leader continues with ♥ A he will read by the echo that his partner can ruff the third round of hearts.

GIN RUMMY

One in every two adult Americans knows how to play some game of the Rummy family, if we are to believe the surveys. Certainly, no other family of games is so widely-known, and few other families have been so prolific. Happily, though—if you like to keep up to the minute and play the variant that is "all the rage"—all the offspring have a strong resemblance to the parent stock. Once you have learned the simple rudiments of any Rummy game, you are equipped to learn any other in short order.

Gin Rummy is a fast-moving variant for two players. It can be and often is played by three or more, even by teams of two or more on a side, but this is all a matter of scheduling—the game itself is fought out between just two opponents at a time.

How to Play Gin Rummy

The Deal. A regular deck of 52 cards is used. Most people like to speed up the mechanics by using two decks, one being shuffled while the other is dealt. It is important to shuffle thoroughly. Both players may shuffle the deck if they wish, but the dealer has the right to shuffle last.

When you begin a session, decide the first dealer by drawing cards from the deck, spread face down. The cards rank: K (high), Q, J, 10, 9, 8, 7, 6, 5, 4, 3, 2, A (low). The suits rank: spades (high), hearts, diamonds, clubs, for purposes of the cut; in the play, the suits have no relative rank. The player drawing the higher card has choice of everything, including the deal. Since he usually requires his opponent to deal first (the dealer being at a slight disadvantage), the rule is often stated that "lower card deals first."

After the first deal, the winner of each deal or *box* deals next. If you play several games at one sitting, the winner of a game deals first for the next game.

The dealer gives cards alternately, one at a time, until each player has ten cards. He turns the twenty-first card of the deck face up on the table; this is the *upcard*. The rest of the deck is put face down beside the upcard, forming the *stock*.

Drawing and Discarding. The non-dealer has first turn, and thereafter the turn alternates. Each turn comprises two stages, a *draw* followed by a *discard*. In *drawing,* the player has choice of taking the face-up card (the *upcard* or *dis-*

card of his opponent) or the face-down card on top of the stock. Having thus taken an eleventh card into his hand, the player reduces it again to ten by *discarding* one card face up. All discards are put in one pile—on top of the upcard, if it was rejected. Local practice differs as to whether the discard pile must be kept squared up or may be spread for inspection of the past discards. Before you commence play, agree with your opponent as to which rule you will follow.

There is one exceptional point about the first turn of all. The non-dealer may take the upcard if he wishes, but if he rejects it he may not at once draw from the stock. He must say "No" or "Pass," whereupon the dealer has a chance to take the upcard if he wants it. If the dealer takes it, he in effect gets first turn. If he rejects it, the non-dealer draws from the stock.

Sets. Your object, in drawing and discarding, is to form your hand into *sets*. (A set is also called a *meld,* a *spread*.) There are two types of sets: (a) three or four cards of the same rank; (b) three or more cards of the same suit in sequence. For example, the following are valid sets.

♠ A-♥ A-♦ A   ♣ 7-♠ 7-♦ 7-♥ 7

♥ 10-♥ 9-♥ 8   ♦ 6-♦ 5-♦ 4-♦ 3-♦ 2

Note well that a set must include at least three cards. A set of type (a) cannot include more than four; a set of type (b), a *sequence,* can theoretically extend to ten cards—but try and get it!

Remember that ace ranks low. It is not in sequence with the king. Therefore A-K-Q is not a valid set in Gin Rummy (though it is in some types of "round-the-corner" Rummy). A card may not be used in more than one set. For example, with ♥ 9-♣ 9-♦ 9-♠ 9-♠ 8-♠ 7 you can form a set of nines or a spade sequence, but not both.

Deadwood. The cards included in valid sets are called *matched*. The *unmatched* cards taken together are often called *deadwood*. The purpose in forming sets is really to *reduce the count of deadwood*.

By the *count of deadwood* we mean the numerical total of all the unmatched cards. Each card has a point value as follows:

Each king, queen, jack, and ten counts . . . 10
Each ace counts 1
Each other card counts its nominal value

For example, if your deadwood comprises ♠ J-♣ 7-♦ 7-♥ A, you have a count of 25.

Knocking. The cardinal rule of Gin Rummy—the feature in which it differs from all other Rummy variants—is:

You may *knock* if your count of deadwood is 10 or less.

To *knock* (also called to *go down*) is to end the play of a deal. You signify that you knock, preferably, by making a discard *face down*. But knocking is also signaled by saying "Knock" or "Down" or simply by laying one's hand face up on the table.

The knocker must immediately expose his whole hand, arranged in sets, with the deadwood segregated. If he fails to segregate his sets, his opponent may and should demand that he do so. (There may be choice in the way the sets are formed, and the knocker must commit himself before the opponent exposes his own hand.)

If you knock with no deadwood at all, all your cards being matched, you *go gin*. Strictly, you must say "Gin" to get credit for it.

Laying Off. Following a knock other than gin, the opponent of the knocker may *lay off* on his sets. To *lay off* is to add cards that are valid—the fourth of a rank on three-of-a-kind, or additional cards in suit and sequence on a sequence. The player's object in laying off is to get rid of cards that would otherwise be counted in his deadwood.

The opponent may not lay off on a gin hand. Here we follow the prevalent rule, but you should be warned that a fierce controversy rages over it. Before playing Gin Rummy with a stranger, ask him what rule he prefers on this point (and also, as mentioned, on spreading the discard pile).

Limit of Play. The last two cards of the stock must not be drawn. If neither player has knocked by the time the player who draws the fiftieth card of the deck has discarded, the deal is abandoned without a score. The same player redeals for the next box.

Scoring a Deal. If the knocker has a lower count than his opponent (after the latter has reduced as he can by laying off), the knocker scores the difference of the counts.

For example, suppose that you knock and lay down this hand:

♠ K-♠ Q-♠ J   ♥ 8-♣ 8-♦ 8   ♣ 4-♦ 3-♠ 2-♣ A

Your opponent's hand is:

♦ 10-♠ 10   ♣ 9-♦ 9-♥ 9   ♠ 8-♦ 6-♠ 6-♠ 5-♥ A

He lays off the ♠ 10 on your sequence and the ♠ 8 on your eights. The nines being matched, his deadwood then comprises: ♦ 10-♦ 6-♠ 6-♠ 5-♥ A. His count is 28, while yours is 10; you score the net of 18.

If the opponent of the knocker has an equal or lower count, he is said to *undercut* the knocker. For undercut, he scores a bonus of 25 plus the difference of the counts (if any).

For example, suppose you knock and lay down:

♠ K-♠ Q-♠ J   ♥ 8-♣ 8-♦ 8   ♣ 4-♦ 3-♠ 2-♣ A

Your opponent's hand is:

♦ J-♦ 10-♦ 9   ♣ 6-♦ 6-♠ 6   ♠ 8-♥ 4-♦ 4-♦ 2

After he lays off the ♠ 8 on your eights, his count is 10, the same as yours. You score nothing, and he gets 25 for undercut.

If the knocker goes gin, he cannot be undercut, and he scores a bonus of 25 plus the count of his opponent's deadwood. Notice that by this rule there is a check on "sandbagging." That is, if you fail to knock with a count of 1, waiting for your opponent to knock so that you can undercut him, you do indeed "sandbag" him if he goes down with any deadwood, but if he goes gin you are hoist with your own petard.

Scoring a Game. Keep score with pencil and paper. Divide the paper into two columns, one for each player. Enter the score of each deal in the proper column, and keep a running total of each player's score. The usual practice is to write down only this running total, but if you don't like mental addition, write down the separate scores also. Here is a sample scoresheet.

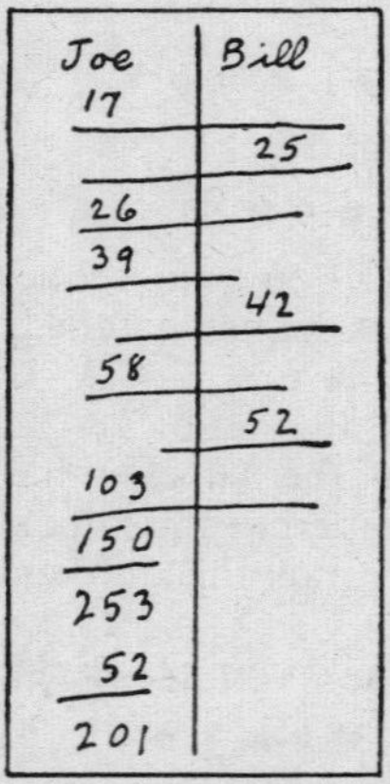

Fig. 2—Gin Rummy scoring. Each horizontal line crossing the center marks a "box" won by one player or the other.

The first player to reach a total of 100 or more points wins a *game*. To his score is then added the *game bonus*. This is 100 points, unless the loser has scored not a single point (called *shutout, schneider, whitewash,* or *skunk*), in which case the game bonus to the winner is 200.

For each deal he has won during the game, each player is now credited with 25 points, the *box* score. (Some call it the *line* score. Both names come from the way of setting up the scoresheet.) A shortcut is to count the number of deals won by each player, subtract, and award 25 for each deal only to the player who has won the preponderance.

Each player's final score for the game is the total of points won during the play, plus any due box scores, plus (for the winner) game bonus. If you play for a monetary stake, settle each game on the difference of the two final scores.

Hollywood Gin. This is a method of scoring that allows three games to be played simultaneously. The scoresheet is laid out with double columns (one for each player) for each of Game 1, Game 2, and Game 3. The first time a player wins a deal, the score is entered in Game 1. His second win is entered in Game 1 and also in Game 2. His third and subsequent wins are entered in all three games. Each game is terminated independently under the usual rules (including shutout), and after a game is finished the subsequent deals are of course scored only in the games still open.

STRATEGY OF GIN RUMMY

Combinations. Before you can complete a *set*, which comprises not less than three cards, you must have two cards that form a pair or a sequence in suit. Such an incipient set we will call a *combination*. A card that will promote a combination to a set is a *filler*. A hand is said to be *calling* certain specific cards when these cards would be fillers.

A combination calls at most two cards. For example, ♦ Q-♣ Q can be filled by ♠ Q or ♥ Q; ♣ 8-♣ 7 can be filled by ♣ 9 or ♣ 6. But some combinations are manifestly inferior, because they call only one card. For example, ♥ J-♥ 9 calls only the ♥ 10. Likewise inferior is any other combination, calling two cards, when one of these cards is already *dead*, i.e., buried in the discard pile.

When both fillers of a combination are dead, "combination" becomes a misnomer. These are just a couple of odd cards.

A basic point of skill is to keep track of what are two-way combinations, what are one-way, and what are mere odd cards. If the discard pile is open for inspection, you

need remember only what discards your opponent has
picked up; if the discard pile is closed, you must remember
all the discards too.

A *double combination* is a pair plus a card in sequence
with one of the pair, for example: ♥ J-♣ J-♣ 10. This is
intrinsically open four ways, (can be filled by any of four
cards), and therefore is more economical than two isolated
combinations, which entail holding four cards.

Interlocking combinations call a common card and are
therefore less economical than isolated combinations. For
example: ♥ 9-♠ 9 and ♣ 8-♣ 7 together call three cards,
♦ 9, ♣ 9, and ♣ 6. This is one less than two isolated combinations would call.

Offensive Play. Such choice of play as you have has to be
exerted primarily in the discard, secondarily on the choice
of draw. In discarding there are two objectives to be served,
each fairly clearly defined, and sometimes antithetical. You
play *offensively* when you are dealt a good hand, or when
you think your chances of knocking are greater than your
opponent's; you play *defensively* when you are dealt a poor
hand, or when you think your opponent may knock ahead
of you.

When you are on the offensive, choose your discard
primarily to preserve the maximum *places open* in your
hand. This term, places open, is borrowed from Pinochle;
it means in Gin Rummy terms, keep the ten cards that make
the number of cards you are *calling* a maximum.

You should keep track of what cards are dead and base
your count on the actual cards that are still *live*. Where
everything is still live, you can short-circuit this count by
the general propositions set forth in the foregoing section:
a double combination is the most economical of all (four
places open in three cards), two isolated combinations
(four places open in four cards) are preferable to two inter-
locked combinations (three places open in four cards).

Defensive Play. Without at this time going in to the whys
and wherefores, be it said that at some stages of a deal you
may have to base your discard primarily upon *safety*.

Experienced players recognize at least three degrees of *safety* in a discard: *wild, protected,* and *safe*.

A card other than an ace, two, queen, or king, can conceivably be used to fill any of six combinations. For example, the ♣ 7 can fill any of the following:

♥ 7-♠ 7   ♥ 7-♦ 7   ♠ 7-♦ 7   ♣ 9-♣ 8   ♣ 8-♣ 6   ♣ 6-♣ 5

Cards of extreme rank cut out one or more possibilities. Thus, a king cannot be used in an upward sequence, but only in one of four remaining ways.

A card is *wild* when all its possible uses as a filler are still open. For example, the ♥ 6 is wild if none of the following cards has been discarded or remains in the hand of the player who contemplates discarding it: ♠ 6, ♦ 6, ♣ 6, ♥ 8, ♥ 7, ♥ 5, ♥ 4.

A card is *protected* when one or more of such "near" cards is dead or in one's own hand. For example, the ♥ 6 is a protected discard when you hold the ♥ 5, because two of the six intrinsic ways that the ♥ 6 might be used by your opponent are impossible.

A card is completely *safe* when it cannot possibly be a filler, all other near cards being dead.

Not until the play is well advanced—say, until the stock is half-gone—can you expect to have any completely safe cards to discard. At the beginning, all your cards may be wild, unless you choose to split a combination for the degree of protection so attained. But this supine course is rarely good; you don't *split* combinations early unless you have no *off* cards at all. (Off cards are those not included either in sets or combinations.) In fact, the probability that every early discard is an off card provides you with some inferences as to relative safety in discarding.

When your opponent refuses to pick up, say, the ♦10, or discards the ♦10, you can be sure he does not have a pair of tens left. Therefore, you can discard a ten with assurance that he cannot use it for three-of-a-kind, though he might use it for sequence. The best single-card protection you can have is knowledge that *another card of same rank* is dead.

Similarly, the discard of the ♦ 10 is protected when your opponent has discarded the ♦ 9. Oddly enough, the degree of protection is greater if he has discarded a ninespot of any other suit! To grasp this fundamental fact, visualize what we have called the six "intrinsic possibilities" of using the ♦10. These are to fill any of the following combinations:

1. ♠ 10-♥ 10   2. ♠ 10-♣ 10   3. ♥ 10-♣ 10   4. ♦ Q-♦ J

5. ♦ J-♦ 9   6. ♦ 9-♦ 8

If your opponent discards the ♦ 9, he eliminates 5 and 6, but he still might hold any of the combinations 1, 2, 3, 4.

If he discards, say, the ♣ 9, you infer that he does not hold a pair of nines, nor ♣ 10-♣ 9, nor ♣ 9-♣ 8 (always assuming that this is an early stage where you do not expect him to split a combination). Now, if he lacks both the ♣ 10 and ♦ 9, the combinations 2, 3, 5, 6 are all eliminated; he could use your ♦ 10 only for 1 or 4. In other words, you can infer that your discard of the ♦10 is twice as safe after he discards the ♣ 9 (or ♠ 9 or ♥ 9) than after he discards the ♦ 9.

The Upcard. Now let us apply the foregoing principles to cases. The first problem that may confront you is, should you take the upcard?

If the upcard is a filler, of course you take it. If it is a low card, and if all you need in order to knock is to reduce your count, of course you take it. For example, as non-dealer you hold:

♥ J-♦ J-♣ J   ♠ 9-♠ 8-♠ 7   ♦ 6-♣ 5-♥ 3-♠ 2

The upcard is the ♥ A. Take it, and discard the ♦ 6 or ♣ 5. Then you can knock as soon as you get a four or lower card.

Should you take the upcard merely because it is low? As a general proposition, no. Lacking two sets, and therefore needing one or more fillers, go after the fillers first. Draw from the stock—you may get a filler. Now how about the position of dealer, who never gets first draw from the stock anyhow? For example, as dealer you hold:

♥ J-♦ J-♦ 10   ♠ 9-♠ 8-♦ 8   ♦ 6-♣ 5-♥ 3-♠ 2

The upcard is the ♥ A. Your opponent refuses it. Should you take it, on the principle that you thereby gain a reducer, at no cost?

With this particular hand, strong in the possession of two double combinations, you should take the ♥ A, discarding the ♣ 5. But don't overlook that you do actually pay something for this card. You compel yourself to make your first discard wholly "blind," whereas if you refuse the upcard it is your opponent who has to make the first blind discard. His discard may help you to pick a discard of your own that is not wholly wild. This defensive aspect is paramount if your hand is notably poor. For example, as dealer you hold:

♦ Q-♥ J-♦ 10-♠ 9-♦ 8-♣ 7-♦ 6-♣ 6-♥ 3-♠ 2

The upcard is the ♥ A. Don't take it! With such a miserable hand, there is no percentage in grabbing reducers. Until your hand improves, you have got to play defensively, picking the safest discard at each turn in the hope of staving off a knock by your opponent. For this purpose, the sight of *his* first discard is more valuable to you than the ♥ A.

Should you take the upcard merely to make a combination? As a general proposition, no. Further, as a general proposition, don't take *any discard* merely to make a combination. Prefer to draw from the stock—you might get a filler. However, exceptional situations do arise. For example, as non-dealer you hold:

♦ Q-♥ J-♦ 10-♠ 9-♦ 8-♣ 7-♦ 6-♣ 6-♥ 3-♠ 2

The upcard is the ♠ 10. You might well take it so as to make a double combination, thereby improving your poor hand. True, you will then have to make the first discard—but you will have to anyhow if the dealer refuses the ♠ 10.

Holding this same hand as dealer, you should refuse the ♠ 10, to preserve the defensive edge of making your opponent discard first.

What to Discard. If there is any golden rule about discarding, it is this: Pick the safest discard consistent with offensive action warranted by your hand. This is not necessarily the safest discard in the hand. To put it extremely, the safest blind discard would be from a matched set, and next to that, from a combination. But you will rarely want to press "protection" this far! Most of the time, you can afford to limit your choice of discard to off cards.

After drawing from the stock, as non-dealer, you hold:

♠ K-♥ K-♣ K   ♦ J   ♣ 9-♥ 9-♥ 7   ♠ 5-♦ 5-♣ 3-♥ A

The upcard was the ♠ 7, and you both refused it. Now, the ♥ 7 is a safe-looking discard; the combination it makes with the ♥ 9 is an inferior "inside straight." Which is more important, safety or the combination? With such a good hand, the answer is—the combination! Discard the wholly wild ♦ J, simply to keep maximum chances of filling a second set.

Suppose that in the same situation your hand after the draw is:

♣ K-♠ K   ♥ Q   ♦ J   ♣ 9-♥ 9-♥ 7   ♠ 5-♦ 5-♣ 3-♥ A

The hand is middling-good, but would cost plenty if your opponent knocked before you filled those kings. Before you can think of unloading the kings (discarding them), you have to unload two other 10-point cards, which at the moment are wild. The indicated policy is defense: stave off a knock until the topheavy end of your hand improves. Hence, discard the ♥ 7. Safety is more important than the combination.

The Player. When your opponent takes a discard, you must assume that he thereby fills a set (or adds to a set). Ask yourself, what kind of set is it: three-of-a-kind or a sequence? The dead cards, or the cards in your hand may supply the answer. In any event, you must thereafter avoid (but there are exceptions!) discarding another card that could surely or possibly be added to his set.

A card in your hand, which you have to keep for this

reason, is a *player,* so-called because if he knocks this card can (presumably) be laid off on his set. Now, a player is a pleasant card to have as concerns reducing your deadwood, but mighty inconvenient as concerns knocking. If it is high, say a fivespot or higher, it may prevent you from ever knocking with only two sets.

If saddled early with a player, try to build it into a combination and then a set of your own. If you cannot do so, or if the play is too far advanced for this process, reduce your deadwood by saving low cards and play for undercut. Of course, your opponent may cross you up by going gin —when you cannot lay off—but what else can you do? Well, to answer a rhetorical question, there *is* something you can do. You can discard the player early; he may grab it and go down for less than gin, and you may thereby save a greater loss. Such a "might-have-been" is rarely calculable, but sometimes at an advanced stage you can see that giving up a player is better than another discard—where this other discard would fill a new set for him. He reduces more by filling a new set than by adding to an old.

When to Knock. A large majority of deals are won by hands that knock with only two sets, plus four or less unmatched cards. Remember this fact in discarding; don't keep so many combinations that you need three sets to knock at all; save a sufficiency of low cards, when you can, even though they form no combinations.

Suppose that at an early stage, your hand after you have drawn from the stock is:

♠ K-♥ K   ♦ 10-♦ 9   ♣ 7-♥ 7   ♠ 5-♦ 5-♦ 4   ♣ 2   ♥ A

In order to keep all combinations, you would have to discard the deuce or the ace. But this would be foolish play. You would then have to fill three sets to knock, or else draw low cards to replace the low card you wantonly threw away. The right discard is to break a combination, saving above all the three lowest cards.

Should you knock as soon as you can? Yes, unless you have clear evidence that you will probably be undercut.

Such evidence would be your reading of the adverse hand, from the discards, the number of cards he has picked up, what cards he has refused, what cards he has *not* discarded, and so on. If your powers of memory and inference are not sufficiently developed so that you know what your opponent has, after most of the stock is gone, skip it. Go down at first opportunity, and you will win more often than you are undercut.

Playing for Gin. When should you play on, hoping for a gin hand? Playing for gin, as a way of increasing your take, is a losing proposition. You will gain more in the long run by knocking every time as soon as you can. But you may have to play on for gin to avoid being undercut. This situation commonly arises only when your opponent is stuck with one or more players on your sets—and you read the fact. But the issue here is not whether to try for gin but whether to risk undercut. So the same answer must be made as above—if your powers of inference tell you there is danger of undercut, play on, either to reduce or go gin. If you cannot read the cards that closely, knock quickly—"take the cash and let the credit go."

CONTRACT RUMMY

The basic idea of Contract Rummy is that a game comprises a prefixed number of deals, and that the requirements as to melding vary from deal to deal. These requirements, the *contract,* are not at all standardized. You may write your own contract, if you choose—and many Rummy players have so chosen, generating a flock of variants under various names, Liverpool Rummy, Joker Rummy, Zioncheck, and so on.

The game as here described includes the commonest features found among these variants, but omits special frills. It can be played by any number of players from three to about eight, each for himself. It is best for three to five.

How to Play Contract Rummy

The Deck. With three or four players, use two regular decks of 52 cards, plus one joker. With five or more players, use three regular decks plus two jokers.

All jokers and deuces (twospots) are *wild*. A wild card may be designated to be of any suit and rank, at the pleasure of the owner, to complete a meld.

The Deal. The dealer distributes cards one at a time to the left (clockwise), beginning with the player at his left and ending with himself. A game comprises seven deals. In each of the first four, ten cards are dealt to each player, and in each of the last three deals, twelve cards. These numbers remain the same regardless of how many players participate.

The undealt remainder of the deck is placed face down on the table to form the *stock*. The top card is turned face up beside the stock to start the *discard pile*.

Drawing and Discarding. The player at left of the dealer has first turn, and thereafter the turn rotates clockwise as usual. To begin his turn, a player may draw the top card of the stock or take the top card of the discard pile. He may then, if able and willing, *meld* cards, that is, put cards from his hand face up on the table in accordance with rules given below. He ends his turn by discarding one card face up on the discard pile.

There is a special proviso about drawing. If the in-turn player wants the discard, he takes it, and that's that. But if he doesn't want it, he is not free to draw at once from the stock. He must say "No" or otherwise indicate his rejection. Then each other player in turn to the left has a chance to take the discard. The first who wants it may take it, but he must also take one card from the stock, and he may not at that time either meld or discard. The fate of the discard being settled, the in-turn player draws from the stock—he is not entitled to take the next card of the discard pile, uncovered when another player claims the top card he has rejected.

As distinguished from certain other Rummy games, in Contract Rummy a player can take the discard without immediately melding it, and a card once buried in the discard pile is forever dead.

Sets. The objective in drawing and discarding is to form *sets*. There are two types of sets: (a) a *group*, three or more cards of the same rank, regardless of suits; (b) a *sequence*, three or more cards of the same suit in sequence.

GROUPS

♥ 5-♣ 5-♠ 5   ♥ 8-♦ 8-♠ 8   ♣ K-♦ K-♠ 2

SEQUENCES

♥ A-♥ K-♥ Q   ♣ 7-Joker-♣ 5

Note that the ace ranks high, above the king. Unless you have a special agreement to the contrary, the following are not valid sequences: 3-2-A, 2-A-K.

The Contract. In each deal, the first meld made by a player must comprise certain prefixed sets, called the *contract*. The contracts are as follows:

    1st deal: Two groups.

    2nd deal: One group and one sequence.

    3rd deal: Two sequences.

    4th deal: Three groups.

    5th deal: Two groups and one sequence.

    6th deal: One group and two sequences.

    7th deal: Three sequences, with no unmatched card.

In each of the first six deals, every set called for by the contract must comprise just three cards—no more. Additional cards may be laid off later, as described below. In the last deal, the entire hand must be melded at once, with no unmatched card; consequently one or all of the sequences must include more than three cards.

Laying Off. Once a player has melded the contract, he is free on subsequent turns to *lay off*—and that is the only way he can get rid of his remaining cards, for he may not initiate any more melds.

To *lay off* is to add cards to existing melds, consistent with their character. A player may lay off on all melds, his opponents' as well as his own. A sequence may not be extended, by laying off, beyond thirteen natural cards plus one wild card.

Wild Cards. As is illustrated in the foregoing examples, any deuce or joker may be designated to be of any suit or rank to complete a set. If melded with a group, a wild card is immovable, but if melded with a sequence it can be claimed in exchange for the natural card it represents. For example, if the meld is ♣ 7-Joker-♣ 5, the joker stands for the ♣ 6 and can be claimed by the holder of a natural ♣ 6. Claim to a wild card may be made at once, without waiting for one's turn (as when one player melds his contract and another has a natural card for which a wild card was used in the contract). If two or more claim the wild card simultaneously, it goes to the first player at the left of him who melded it.

Having obtained a wild card in exchange for a natural card, the player must wait his turn to meld it.

Going Out. A player *goes out* when he gets rid of his last card, by melding or laying off. Play ends, and the deal is scored.

The entire stock may be drawn. If no player has gone out by the time it is exhausted, there is no winner and the deal is scored as below.

Scoring. The winner of a deal (the one who goes out) scores the point value of all cards remaining in the other hands. The point values are:

Each wild card	20
Each ace	15
Each king, queen, jack, ten	10
Each lower card, its nominal value	

If no one wins, the points remaining in each player's hand are subtracted from his score.

The winner of the game is the player with the highest cumulative score after the seven deals.

STRATEGY OF CONTRACT RUMMY

The sixty-four-dollar question is, should you meld the contract as soon as you can, or hold up as long as you can?

Perhaps when you first learn the rules, you will think that it is difficult to collect the right cards to form the contract. Especially if your only previous acquaintance with Rummy is through Gin, where good defensive play by your opponent will often frustrate your would-be sets, you may decide, "Well, if I can ever scrape the contract together I will slap it down immediately!" So you try out that policy, only to find that the other fellows go out first by laying off on the melds you have kindly provided.

It dawns on you that you give the opponents a lot of help by melding. So you decide to play it cagey—you will hold up your first meld until all or most of your hand is ready to lay off right afterward. When you try out this stratagem, you find that some other fellow beats you to the draw—he melds his contract, and next turn lays off the rest of his hand on it.

Now you see the true light—you will hold up until someone else "cracks," then meld your contract and at least limit your loss. After you have done this faithfully a few times, the other fellows catch on, and now they begin to trap you by going down as soon as they can. You go down as promptly as you can afterward—and find them laying off on your melds but not their own. Thus you have helped them reduce your potential winnings.

It is useless to look for a sure-fire rule among these conflicting experiences. All that can be said is that it certainly is useless to meld your contract if you have not a single additional card to lay off on it. If you want a rule of thumb, do go down as soon as you can, if you have any extra meldable card other than a wild card. What to do about the wild card is a real puzzle. Should you wait for a natural card so as to save the wild card in your hand? Use your best judgment, and read the play of the opponents for every possible inference.

During the first six deals, it certainly is easier to make the contract than the novice thinks. There are at least nine wild cards to help out, and the privilege of taking the discard out of turn is often a lifesaver. Of course you can earn this privilege only at the cost of taking extra cards, but there are many occasions when you welcome them—when you are short in combinations, when you desperately need a wild card. It is rarely advisable to take a discard out of turn merely to make a combination, but think twice about passing up a filler to a meld.

The picture changes radically with the seventh deal. Here, where you have to meld your entire hand at once, every added card you take over the twelve is a headache. Sooner or later you have got to draw a replacement for it, a wild card or a natural card that connects with one of your melds. Every extra card decreases geometrically the chance of success. Yet if you pass up a filler to a meld, you may have to reform a large part of your hand to make any sequence at all. The saving clause is that your right-hand opponent finds life as hard as you do; the exigencies of fulfilling the contract largely deprive him of the luxury of defensive play. If he holds up cards you want, he may simply wreck his own hand. Therefore you can often ease your own situation by planning your contract melds in accordance with what he rejects in the discards and what he discards in the early stages. You can well afford to pick up his early discards merely to make combinations, knowing that if he draws from the stock cards helpful to you they will be squeezed out of his hand sooner or later.

CANASTA

Developed in Argentina, Canasta (the word means *basket*) has spread to metropolitan centers in South and North America. It is an elaboration of Rummy, best for four players in two partnerships.

How to Play Canasta

The Deck. Use two regular decks of 52, shuffled together; also four jokers.

The Deal. Decide partnerships and the first dealer, if you wish, by drawing cards from the deck, spread face down. The pair drawing highest cards are partners against the other two, and highest card deals first. For purposes of the draw only, the cards rank: A (high), K, Q, J, 10, 9, 8, 7, 6, 5, 4, 3, 2. A player drawing a joker must draw again.

After the first deal, the job of dealing rotates to the left, clockwise.

The dealer gives cards one at a time, clockwise, beginning with the player at his left, until each has eleven cards. The rest of the deck is put face down in the center of the table to form the *stock*. The top card is turned over and placed beside it, to start the *discard pile*.

Red Treys. Any player to whom a red trey (threespot) is dealt must, in his first turn, put it face up on the table and draw a replacement for it from the stock. At any later time, a red trey drawn from the stock must be at once shown and the next card taken instead. The red treys are bonus cards, having value in scoring, but they are not used in play.

Drawing and Discarding. Each player in turn, beginning with the player at the left of the dealer, draws one card, then discards one card face up on the discard pile. The player may always draw the top card of the stock, but he may instead, under rules given below, take the top card of the discard pile.

After drawing and before discarding, the player may *meld* under rules given below. If a player (legally) gets rid of his last card, the play ends. He need not at this last turn make a discard; he may meld all his remaining cards. All of the stock may be drawn; the rules for termination in this case are given later.

Melds. The general object in drawing and discarding is to form *melds*. A meld is three or more cards *of the same rank,* which may include wild cards, as explained below. Sequences are not valid sets, as they are in Gin and other variants of Rummy. A set has a plus scoring value only when properly *melded,* i.e., placed face up on the table in a proper turn of the owner. A set of, say, three jacks, left in the hand when some other hand *goes out,* is not a meld—the cards count minus against the owner, like all other cards left in the hand.

Jokers and deuces may never be melded as sets of three or more. Black treys (threespots) may be melded only in his last turn by a player who *goes out.* Red treys are, in effect, melded singly as they turn up. All other ranks may be melded.

A player may meld any number of cards in one turn, subject to the restrictions on going out.

Wild Cards. The four jokers, and also the eight deuces (twospots), are *wild.* A wild card may be designated to be of any rank the owner chooses, for purpose of completing a meld. But the use of wild cards is limited by these two rules: (a) Every meld must contain at least two *natural* cards; (b) no meld may contain more than three wild cards.

Laying Off. Once a player has made a proper meld of three or more cards, both he and his partner may add other cards of the same rank to it, singly or in any number. By custom, one player collects all the cards melded by his side in front of himself, putting all of each rank in an overlapping line.

Canastas. A meld of seven or more cards of the same rank is a *canasta*. Each canasta earns a bonus, and a side may not *go out* until it has built up at least one canasta. (Some play that a side may not go out until it has two canastas.)

A canasta of seven or more natural cards is a *natural canasta;* one that includes one to three wild cards is a *mixed canasta*. When a meld is built to a canasta, the cards are by custom squared up in a pile, with a red card on top to indicate that it is natural or a black card to show that it is mixed. Additional cards may be laid off on a canasta, and add their numerical count to the score, but do not increase the canasta bonus.

The Initial Meld. The first meld made by a side during play of one deal is its *initial meld*. The initial meld must answer to a certain *minimum count,* which varies according to the total cumulative score of that side as a result of all previous deals in the game. The schedule is as follows:

Score to date	Minimum count
Any minus	None
From 0 to 1495	50
From 1500 to 2995	90
3000 or more	120

The *count* of a meld is the total of the numerical values of its component cards. The (invariant) values of the cards are as follows:

Joker	50
Deuce	20
Ace	20
King to 8, inc.	10
7 to 4, inc.	5
Black 3	5

At the beginning of a game, the minimum requirement can be met by the meld of any of these: A-A-A, A-A-2, 8-8-8-2. The count may be satisfied by melding two or more sets at once, and this course is practically forced when the minimum is 120.

Once a side has made its initial meld, it may make additional melds (and lay off additional cards) without restriction as to count.

The Discard Pile. A player may draw the top of the discard pile, instead of the top of the stock, only when he can immediately meld that card. But this is not the only condition.

At the beginning of a deal, the pile is *frozen* for each side. Whenever the pile is frozen, the top card may be taken only for a meld with two *natural* cards of the same rank. It may not be taken to be laid off. The initial meld unfreezes the pile for that side only. When the pile is not frozen, the top card may be taken to be laid off, or to form a new meld with a natural pair or one natural card and one wild card.

Whenever the top of the discard pile is taken, the player must first show the cards (if any) necessary to establish his right to it. Having melded it, he must then take *all the rest of the discard pile*.

The pile is frozen at any time that a wild card is discarded (rare, but it happens). The freeze evaporates after the pile is taken.

Should the card turned up to start the discard pile, after the deal, be a red trey, a second card must be turned upon it, and the pile is frozen until taken. (The effect of this rule is that, even though a player makes the initial meld entirely from his hand, the discard pile remains frozen until the red trey is removed.) On capturing a red trey this way, a player must face it on the table but does not draw a replacement from the stock.

On taking the discard pile, a player may use the cards to make such additional melds as he pleases, but only the top card may be counted in determining his legal right to take the pile at all.

The effect of discarding a black trey or a wild card is to prevent the left-hand opponent from taking the pile at this juncture.

There is one more limitation on taking the discard: while

any card remains in the stock, a player may not take a discard pile of only one card (to lay off) when he himself holds only one card.

Going Out. A player *goes out* when he gets rid of his last card, by discard or meld. Neither partner may go out until his side has melded at least one canasta. He may go out with a *concealed hand*—having made no previous meld whatsoever—provided that it contains a canasta, or his partner has previously melded a canasta. The hand does not count as concealed if any card is laid off on partner's previous melds.

Forcing. If the last card of the stock is reached, and it is a red trey, play ends forthwith. If it is another card, the player who drew it discards. If the opponent at his left can legally pick it up (to lay it off) he must do so. Play continues, by *forcing,* until some hand is unable, under the rules, to pick up the last discard. The force operates as to laying off on sets already melded, but not as to cards concealed in the hand—if a player can use a discard with cards from his hand, he may do so, but is not so compelled.

Scoring. The side that goes out scores 100 therefor. If play ends by exhaustion of the stock, with none going out, this bonus is not counted.

Each red trey counts 100, plus to the side that held it if that side made a meld, but minus if it made no meld. However, if all four red treys were drawn by one side, they count 200 each.

Each natural canasta scores 500; each mixed canasta, 300.

A player who goes out concealed scores 100, additional to the bonus for going out.

The net score of a side for a deal is the total of its due bonuses for going out, for red treys and canastas, plus the numerical value of all melded cards, less the numerical value of all cards left in both hands of the partnership.

Keep the running total of the scores on paper, one column for each side. The scorekeeper should announce, at the beginning of each deal, the count required for the initial meld of each side.

A game is won by the side first to reach 5000 points. But there is no "counting out." If a side knows that it has reached 5000 during the course of a deal, the deal is nevertheless played out. If both sides reach 5000, the higher total wins. There is no bonus for winning a game. Settlement of monetary stakes is made on the difference of final totals.

STRATEGY OF CANASTA

When minimum count for your opponents is 50, possibly when it is 90, aim to build up a high score in melds rather than to go out fast. But when they need 120, try to go out in a hurry.

The more cards you have in your hand, the better your chances of melding. Therefore, at the beginning of a game, weigh the potential advantage of making your initial meld against the cost in cards it may take from your hand. It goes without saying that when you can make the initial meld in a minimum of cards, say three or four, you should do so pronto. If you are dealt the required cards, you may do well to hold off a few rounds, both to see if your partner can make an initial meld and to let the discard pile build up. But do not wait too long—you may crucify your partner.

If you would have to meld six cards to make 50, or nine cards to make 90, put on your thinking cap! Will it pay to wreck your hand, in order to open up the discard pile for your partner? Many considerations have to be weighed. The risk of deferring the initial meld increases as the play advances. A thin discard pile may be valueless, but the game may hinge on a thick pile containing several canastas and near-canastas of low cards. Wrecking your own hand may be a good investment by providing a place for your partner to park several otherwise useless cards. As a rule-of-thumb, make the initial meld, no matter how many cards you have to use, if one of your melds is aces. You not only provide a parking place for one or two aces with which your partner may be stuck, but you also "fix" the opponents as regards discarding aces.

The picture changes when the opponents need 120. This is actually a colossal demand; barring exceptional situations, it is met only by the possession of two jokers or a joker and two deuces. You have a good chance to set the opponents back. Try to go out in a hurry, and therefore meld everything and as quickly as you can.

After your partner has made the initial meld, at once lay off on his cards everything you can that is eightspot or higher. The only case for not laying off everything you can is this: Perhaps at some later stage, when the discard pile is frozen, your right-hand opponent will discard a card that you could otherwise take to lay off; if you have a pair of this rank in your hand, you can foil his effort to sneak the card by. Experience shows that hope of this eventuality is plausible as concerns cards worth 5, but not cards worth 10. So, if you have a mind to, hold up your low cards, but certainly you should lay off your high cards at once, so as to make clear at once to your partner which melds are the best candidates for canastas.

After your side has made its initial meld, the next objective is to make a canasta. If you have captured a discard pile replete with the low cards that are regularly spewed out by all hands at the beginning of a deal, you probably do not have to worry. But if your melds are few, and especially if you and your opponents have melds of the same rank— aces are often split this way—watch your management of whatever wild cards you draw. Don't use a wild card to capture the discard pile unless you get some helpers to your longest melds. You may bitterly regret not having laid off a wild card on a set of six. Contrariwise, if you have an excess of wild cards, don't treasure them for their looks. Take the strain off your partner by laying off, say, all but one, on the melds that can most benefit thereby.

The defensive value of black treys is greatly over-rated. Don't hoard them with the notion that they will ultimately turn defeat into victory. All that a black trey does is to estop your left-hand opponent for one turn; a discard he cannot use has the same effect. If you want to save cards on remote speculation, save a low pair rather than a black trey.

POKER

Poker is the most universal of all card games. It is played in every country where playing cards are known. It is essentially a "money" game; Poker played merely "for buttons" is ludicrously far from the real thing. But even at trifling stakes, Poker makes an exciting pastime for a social group, and it has the advantage of being elastic as to the number of players. It can actually be played by any number from two to about eight; most variants are best for five or more.

Poker is not a single game, but a vast family of related games. Even the best-known variants are played with many minor differences of rules in different localities. Fortunately, the principal rules are the same for all variants and the local practices can be learned in a few minutes. All Poker games can be classed in four general types: Draw, Stud, Lowball, and mixtures such as High-Low. We will discuss these four types after describing the features common to all Poker games.

GENERAL RULES OF POKER

The Deck. The regular deck of 52 cards is used. The cards in each suit rank: A (high), K, Q, J, 10, 9, 8, 7, 6, 5, 4, 3, 2. There is never a relative ranking of suits. For small games (two or three players) the deck is usually *cut* by discarding some of the lower cards.

Wild Cards. In some games, certain cards of the deck are designated as *wild* cards. The holder of a wild card can specify it to be of any rank and suit that he pleases, for purpose of making the best possible hand. The usual choices for wild cards are deuces or "one-eyed" jacks (spades and hearts) or both.

The *joker* is sometimes added to the deck as a wild card. Alternatively, the joker may be added as the *bug,* a limited wild card. The bug may be designated of any rank to complete a *straight,* or of any suit to complete a *flush,* but may stand only for an ace in any other type of hand.

Poker Hands. The winner of a pot or round is the player who shows the *best Poker hand,* among those who have *stayed in.* The hand (in almost all variants) comprises just five cards, but in some variants the player holds a greater number from which he may select the best five.

The following is the list of recognized Poker hands, in order from highest to lowest.

STRAIGHT FLUSH. Five cards of the same suit, in sequence, as: ♥ J-10-9-8-7. As between straight flushes, the one headed by the highest card is highest. The unbeatable hand, A-K-Q-J-10 of the same suit, is called a *royal flush.*

FOUR OF A KIND. Four cards of the same rank, with any fifth card, as ♠ 8-♥ 8-♦ 8-♣ 8 ♠ J. As between fours of a kind, the set of highest rank is highest.

FULL HOUSE. Three cards of one rank, with two cards of another rank, as ♦ 3-♣ 3-♥ 3 ♠ Q-♦ Q. As between full houses, the one with the triplet of highest rank is highest.

FLUSH. Five cards of the same suit, not all in sequence, as ♣ A-10-8-7-5. As between flushes, the one with the highest card or highest several cards is highest. The foregoing example is higher than ♠ A-9-8-7-5 but lower than ♥ A-J-4-3-2.

STRAIGHT. Five cards in sequence, not all of the same suit, as ♣ A-♦ K-♠ Q-♥ J-♣ 10. For purposes of a straight only, an ace may be ranked below the deuce; hence 5-4-3-2-A is a legitimate low straight. As between straights, the one headed by the highest card is highest.

THREE OF A KIND. Three cards of one rank, with one card of a second rank and one card of a third rank, as ♦ 10-♣ 10-♠ 10 ♦ 7 ♥ 3. As between threes of a kind, the one with the highest triplet is highest.

TWO PAIRS. Two cards of one rank, with two cards of another rank, and one card of a third rank, as ♣ K-♥ K

♠ 9-♦ 9 ♣ 4. As between hands of two pairs, the highest is determined by comparing first the higher pairs, then (if these are the same), the lower pairs, then (if both pairs are the same) the fifth card. A hand of two pairs is customarily described by its higher pair, as "kings up."

ONE PAIR. Two cards of one rank, with three cards of different ranks, as ♠ A-♥ A ♦ Q ♣ 9 ♥ 2. One-pair hands rank first of all according to the pair, and if the pairs are the same, according to the first of the next-lower cards that are not the same. The foregoing example is higher than ♦ A-♣ A ♥ J ♦ 10 ♠ 7 but lower than ♦ A-♣ A ♠ K ♥ 3 ♦ 2.

HIGH CARD. Any hand not containing any of the higher combinations. Such a hand is customarily described by its highest card, as "I have a queen." A colloquial term for a no-combination hand is *runt*. Among runts, the one with the highest card is highest, the comparison being carried right down to the fifth card, if necessary, when all higher cards are the same.

When the deck contains any wild card, there is one possible hand in addition, *five of a kind*. This ranks highest of all, above a royal flush. In wild-card games, between identical forms of a kind, or identical triplets, unmatched cards decide.

The Deal. The preliminaries of shuffling, cutting, etc., are the same as in most other card games. With few exceptions, the cards are dealt one at a time in rotation, beginning with the player at the left of the dealer. The chief exception is that in Draw Poker after the *discard* from the original hands, the dealer *serves* each hand with whatever is needed to restore it to five, in one packet.

As in most other games, the rotation of the deal, turn to play, etc., is to the left or clockwise, beginning always with the player at the left of the dealer.

Banking. Each deal is settled immediately (there being no *games* or *rubbers*). Settlement in cash being awkward, the custom is to use *Poker chips* as tokens. In a gambling casino, the management acts as *banker*, selling chips to the players and redeeming chips for cash. In home games, one person (usually the host) is appointed to be banker, with the same duties.

Sets of Poker chips are made in three or four colors. Custom fixes the relative values of the colors as follows: white, 1; red, 5; blue, 10 or 20; yellow, 25 or 100. What this means in terms of cash is, of course, decided by the casino, or by the participants in private play.

Betting. For each deal, a *pot* of chips is built up that will eventually go to the winner. In most variants the pot is begun before the cards are distributed, by an *ante*. The ante may require all players to contribute equal amounts (as, one white chip), or may require the dealer to make an extra contribution, or may require only the dealer to contribute.

Thereafter, the nature of the variant fixes certain intervals during which players may *bet*. The first such interval is after the original deal, whether it comprises five cards to each player (as in Draw Poker) or two (as in Stud Poker).

A player *bets* by adding chips to the pot, in excess of his ante. Each hand in turn after a bet must *drop, call,* or *raise*. When a player drops, refusing to make a total contribution to the pot equal to that of the last previous bettor, he places his hand face down on the table and is out of the subsequent play—receiving no more cards and being ineligible to win the pot. To *call* is to contribute a number of additional chips equal to the last previous bet; to *raise* is to put more than this number into the pot. The general principle is that a player may remain eligible to win only by making a total contribution at least equal to the highest amount previously contributed by any other player, and when he raises he compels all other players still in either to drop or to stay in by calling or reraising.

After the last betting interval, there is a *showdown*. This means the exposure of all hands still eligible to win the pot, to determine which is highest. The showdown is compulsory if a bet or raise has only been *called* by each other player still in (i.e., having been called, a bettor may not now increase the amount of his bet). If a bet or raise has not been called by anyone, the bettor takes the pot without showing his hand (unless he must *prove openers*).

In most variants, it is permissible for a player at the beginning of a betting interval to *check,* i.e., stay in the pot without betting. This right squares with the general principle stated above, because at the moment all players have contributed equally to the pot. But of course a player may not check if there has been a bet ahead of him. If there is a bet after his check, he must then in turn drop or call; usually he may raise if he wishes, but in Lowball the check-and-raise is barred.

Betting Limits. A limit is almost invariably placed upon the amount any player may bet or raise at one turn. For example, a casino provides several tables with different *fixed limits,* as "1 and 2" and "2 and 4." By "1 and 2" is meant, in Draw Poker, that a player may bet or raise one white chip in a turn, before the draw, and two white chips after the draw. Similar fixed limits are often agreed in private play.

Among other ways of fixing limits, the chief is *table stakes.* The limit for a bet or raise is the number of chips the player happens to have at the moment. All participants purchase equal stacks of chips at the outset; none may be cashed in until the game ends, and the purchase of additional stakes is strictly regulated, e.g., no purchase may be made while a deal is in progress. A player may call by putting all his remaining chips in the pot, even if he does not thereby equal the total contribution of a previous player. The pot is then split into two parts. The *main pot* contains the contributions from all active players, up to the total put in by the short caller. The excess goes into a *side pot.* The short caller remains eligible to win the main pot, despite any future raises and calls. If he wins it, the side pot then goes to the best hand among the other active players. (In theory, there might be a series of pots, due to several short calls in the same deal.)

Irregularities. Certain errors in dealing may be corrected at the time, e.g., giving a hand too few cards, dealing too many hands. Otherwise, a misdeal deprives the player of the right to deal (position of dealer is an advantage), and the turn passes to his left.

A player must on demand make good any deficiency in his contribution to the pot, for his ante or for an announced bet, call, or raise. In social play, a player is usually allowed to retract the excess if he puts in too many chips and the error is noticed at once. But in no other case may chips once put in the pot ever be withdrawn (except as the pot is won). If there is a misdeal, the ante stays in the pot and there is a second ante for the proper deal by the next player. If a player puts chips in the pot out of turn, to bet, call, or raise, the chips stay there. The offender may count these chips to determine how much it will cost him to call or raise in rightful turn, but if he chooses to drop the chips are lost to him.

The most serious breach of ethics is dropping out of turn. It is manifestly unfair to the other active players to let a bettor or caller know in advance how many players after him are going to drop. Although the rules provide a penalty for this breach—the premature dropper must pay a penalty equal to what a call would have cost in his turn—it is often waived in private games.

If a player holds too many cards, at any time after he has looked at his hand, the hand is dead and the player is out of the pot.

Each player should be careful not to expose his own cards to the other players, especially after he has dropped out of a pot.

In a game that requires *openers* (e.g., jackpots), the player who has opened must *prove* his right, by exposing his hand when he drops out of the pot, or at the showdown. In social play, it is often required to show only the openers, e.g., the pair of jacks or better, but in casinos the opener must show all five cards.

At the showdown, every player still in must show all five cards.

DRAW POKER

Preliminaries. The best game is with six or seven players. In the casinos the game is played by eight. Before the deal, every player antes one white chip. Every player receives five cards, dealt one at a time.

First Betting. After the deal, each player in turn *checks* if unable or unwilling to *open*. Any in turn may open if he has a pair of jacks or a better hand. He signifies the fact by making a bet. If no one opens, the cards are thrown in and the deal passes to the left, a new ante being added to that already in the pot.

When any hand opens, each other player in turn may drop, call, or raise. If there is any raise, all remaining active players in turn must drop, call, or reraise—and so on, until there are no more raises.

The Draw. There being two or more active players left in, the dealer now *serves* each in turn. But before distributing the cards, the dealer *burns* the top card. This means that he exposes it, then places it face-up at the bottom of the deck. The function of the burned card is to show when the deck has been exhausted (also, to conceal the face of the bottom card). This matter is important in large games, where the deck is likely to be exhausted before all players have received all the cards to which they are entitled. When the burned card is reached, the dealer must gather it together with all previous *discards,* shuffle thoroughly, burn a new card, and continue dealing with the reconstituted stock. The player may *stand pat* by keeping his original five cards, or may *discard* one, two, or three of them. (In small games, it is sometimes permitted to discard any number, up to all five.) The dealer gives the player as many cards as he discards, thus restoring his hand to five cards. If the dealer is himself active, he must announce orally the number of cards he serves himself.

Discards should be put in one heap face down and should

not be touched unless they must be gathered to replenish the stock.

Second Betting. Beginning with the first active player at left of the dealer, each in turn may check or bet. If all check, all active hands are exposed to determine the winner. If any bets, the betting proceeds as during the first interval, until there are no more raises. There is a showdown (if necessary) and the winner takes the pot.

Openers. The player who opens must show his whole hand (or, if allowed, merely his openers) at the time he drops out, or at the showdown if he stays. If it is found that he did not have valid openers, or had a foul hand (more than five cards), all contributions to the pot except the ante and the false opener's bet are withdrawn. Any hands that elected to stay may then play again, if any chooses to open. If none stayed or none opens, the cards are thrown in and the next dealer deals.

A player may *split* his openers for the draw, e.g., having J J 10 9 8 he may discard a jack and draw to his possible straight. He need not announce that he is splitting, but must segregate his discard from all others and see that it is held out of the stock so that he may later prove his openers.

Strategy of Draw Poker. As in most "money" games, skill consists primarily in knowing the "percentages" and adhering to them with the utmost fidelity, so as to gain by whatever slight "edge" they yield. Unlike most other "money" games, Poker also gives scope for jockeying the bets so that on occasion an inferior hand will induce a superior hand to drop, or a superior hand will induce an inferior hand to bet against it.

In most other games, it is considered unethical to try to infer what cards a player holds by his mannerisms, etc. But in Poker the utilization of all such extraneous information is not only ethical—it is the very life of the game. The proper effort of the player is to create false impressions about his hand, through every possible means, and to read correctly the clues dropped by his opponents.

The greatest thrill of Poker, to many players, is to succeed in a bluff. But it is a great mistake to imagine that bluffing is the whole game. The expert player attempts no more than two or three outright bluffs in a session. His superiority manifests itself mainly in a high "batting average" in reading the hands of the other players. He discovers that he is beaten in time to limit his loss; he knows how to build up a large pot when he has the best hand.

The following suggestions are intended for competition against strong players; if the competition is mediocre, you may do better to play more "wide open":

1. Do not open "under the guns" unless you are strong enough to reraise any raise, or to stay in against two raises.

2. Rarely open when the chances are that someone behind you will open. The opener puts himself at an immediate disadvantage, since he must bet first after the draw.

3. Speculate if you will on going into a pot opened ahead of you, when you hold one pair, a four-flush or four-straight. Maybe you will get a cheap opportunity to draw. But never stand a raise with such hands. Never pay more than the minimum to draw when you know you are beaten before the draw.

4. Raise before the draw with a pat straight or flush.

5. Raise with two low pairs only when you are the next active player to the left of the opener; drop if the opening bet has already been raised. With queens up or better raise if only one player has stayed in after the opener. Do not stand a raise with less than kings up. Do not stay in on two pairs when there have been two raises.

6. Watch the players back of you at all times. The chief use of the raise before the draw is to squeeze out a hand that is not so good as yours before the draw but that has a better chance to improve.

7. Before you call a raise before the draw, or reraise, decide how you are going to play the hand through. Beware of starting something you can't finish—betting strongly before the draw, then checking after the draw.

8. The big hands take care of themselves, if you regularly and consistently bet according to *position* rather than *cards*.

Don't make the first raise or bet when you think another player will raise or bet if you don't. Reraise before the draw only when you have got to make what you can out of one or two surviving customers. The ideal is to "let everybody in." Reserve your heavy play until after the draw.

9. After the draw, don't call out of curiosity, or because you are "already in for so much." Call because you are convinced you have the best hand.

10. Raise or reraise after the draw, if you believe that you can thereby squeeze out a better hand back of you. But don't try to bulldoze the man ahead of you this way, except as the concluding act of a bluff started before the draw.

STUD POKER

The Deal. The dealer first gives each player one card face down, his *hole* card. Then he distributes four additional rounds of one card to each active player, face up, with due pauses for betting as explained below. All cards must be left on the table, not picked up, but each player may look at his hole card at any time after it is dealt. The dealer also has the duty of drawing attention to the hand that must bet first in each betting interval.

Betting. There is no ante in Stud Poker except by special agreement. The first pause for betting occurs after each hand has received its hole card and one card face up. The highest face-up card marks the first bettor; if there is more than one card of this rank showing, the hand nearest the dealer clockwise is the bettor. At this first interval, the first bettor *must* make a bet: he may not check. Each other hand in turn then drops, calls, or raises, and the betting continues until there are no further raises. A player signifies that he drops by turning his face-up card or cards face down.

After each of the three additional rounds of the deal, there is a betting interval. The first bettor is the one whose face-up cards show the highest Poker combination, e.g. A 6 is higher than K Q, and 2 2 3 is higher than J 10 9 (potential straights and flushes rank lower than actual pairs, threes, etc.). In these later rounds, the first bettor may bet or check, as he pleases.

At the showdown, a player called must show his hole card. No other player need reveal his entire hand except to claim the pot.

Variants. The foregoing is the basic five-card Stud game. There have been many elaborations, e.g., each player receives six, seven, or eight cards, or chooses any five of them for his hand. Wild cards are frequently introduced, usually the deuces.

Strategy of Stud Poker. Action is rare in the final betting interval; with most of each active hand in sight, it is usually obvious which is the best hand. The pot usually goes by general concession. Where there is action, the following precepts are suggested.

1. The hand best on the table, but not improved by its hole card, should check not bet. No one will call a bet unless his hole card gives him the better hand, in which case he wins willy nilly. After the check, the best-on-table must usually call any bet, if only to protect himself from larceny, but of course should drop if he has had clear indication in previous rounds that the bettor's hole card makes a better hand.

2. The hand best on table, when promoted to a sure winner by its hole card, should check or bet according to the known temper of the other active players. The question is which course is more likely to pull a few more chips from a player whose hole card gives him a hand better than that best-on-table.

3. It is folly to try to steal a pot by betting with a hand of five cards that is beaten by another hand of four cards in sight.

4. When another player has a pair showing, drop unless you have a higher pair.

LOWBALL POKER

Lowball Poker follows all the rules of Draw Poker with these exceptions:

1. The pot is won by the *lowest* hand.

2. The ace always ranks low, below the deuce. Straights and flushes are ignored. The lowest hand, called a *bicycle* or *wheel,* is therefore 5-4-3-2-A.

3. Any player may open the pot, regardless of his hand.

4. A player who has checked before the pot is opened may *back in,* but may not raise before the draw.

These differences make Lowball of necessity much more "wide open" than straight Draw Poker. The no-check-and-raise rule destroys opportunity for "sandbagging" before the draw. Allowing any hand to open makes it more difficult to estimate what the unseen hands are. The chances of improvement by the draw are sufficiently greater so that they play a large part in deciding whether to stay in or drop. While a player can find some opportunity to apply the niceties of Draw Poker skill, he is likely to find more opponents in every pot and therefore to suffer a greater chance that another hand will "draw out" and beat him.

OTHER POKER GAMES

High-Low. The valid hands and their ranking are the same as at all forms of high-hand Poker. The pot is split equally between the highest and lowest hands at the showdown, any odd chip being left in the next pot. The lowest possible hand is 7-5-4-3-2, not all of the same suit. The ace ranks high, except that 5-4-3-2-A is a low straight. High-Low may be played as Draw or Stud.

Spit in the Ocean. Each player receives four cards face down. Then one card is dealt face up on the table. This card is wild, and is construed to be the fifth card of each player's hand. There are betting intervals between rounds of the deal and after the complete hands are dealt. The first bettor is always the player at the left of the dealer. The draw principle may be introduced by letting each player discard any number of his four hidden cards and receive an equal number from the stock.

Cincinnati. Each player receives five cards face down. An extra hand is dealt face down in the center of the table. The cards of this hand are turned up one at a time, with a betting interval after each turn. After the final betting, each survivor for the showdown selects the best hand of five cards he can make out of his own five plus the five on the table. The game can be made even more kaleidoscopic by use of wild cards.

Dealer's Choice. As the name implies, this game permits the dealer to designate what Poker variant is to be played. Dealer's Choice is popular in private games, especially when hilarity rather than the redistribution of wealth is the objective. Favorite choices are of course the wild and woolly variants where the hand is selected from more than five cards, and where wild cards are plenteous. Not a few of the widely-played variants have developed from spur-of-the-moment improvisations at Dealer's Choice.

MICHIGAN

Michigan has ideal qualifications as a "family" game and as an "icebreaker" on social occasions. Any number of players up to about eight may participate—and the more, the merrier. No skill is required, and only a minimum of attention. Children can play, on a parity with adults. Poker chips are used; there is all the excitement of spot settlement of winnings and losses, which need no translation into dollars and cents to preserve the "action"—everybody plays in every deal.

How to Play Michigan

The Cards. Use a regular deck of 52 cards. From a second deck take the following four cards: ♥ A, ♣ K, ♦ Q, ♠ J. Put them in the center of the table, face up, forming the *layout*. The cards in the full deck, corresponding to the four in the layout, are often called *boodle cards* or *money cards*.

Chips. If the game is all in fun, supply all players with equal quantities of poker chips. The simplest way to do this is to deal out the chips of each color, one at a time, as far as they will go evenly. With the usual set of chips in three colors, call white chips 1, red 5, blue 10.

The Deal. The job of dealing rotates as usual to the left. It is a good idea to end a session of Michigan at a juncture when all participants have dealt an equal number of times, since the dealer has an advantage.

The dealer gives cards one at a time, beginning with a *widow* (an extra hand) at his immediate left. The whole deck is dealt out, as far as it will go. Unless the number of players is exactly four, some players will receive fewer cards than others; this does not matter.

The Ante. Before or during the deal, each player other than the dealer must *dress the layout* by putting one white chip on each card. The dealer puts two chips on each, paying for his advantage.

The Widow. The extra hand belongs to the dealer. If he does not like the hand dealt to himself, he may discard it face down and take the widow instead—sight unseen, for he may not look at the widow before making up his mind.

If the dealer does not choose to take the widow, he must sell it at auction to the highest bidder. The purchaser, if any, pays his chips to the dealer, discards his original hand face down, and picks up the widow. After the disposition of the widow is decided, the play begins.

The Play. The cards played are not put together in tricks. Each player faces his card on the table near himself, at the same time announcing its rank; if it is the first card of a new suit, he also announces the suit. This oral accompaniment is necessary to expedite the play, for the turn to play does not rotate regularly but skips here and there according to the vagaries of the hands.

The first play is made by the player at the left of the dealer. He may play any suit, but must put down the lowest card he holds in the chosen suit. Suppose he starts with the ♦ 4 (saying "Four of diamonds"). Now the hand holding the next-higher card of the same suit—in this case the ♦ 5 —must play it. And so on: cards must be played in ascending sequence in the same suit as long as possible. The ace is high, ranking above the king.

Presently a *stop* is reached, either because the sequence has been built up to the ace, or because the next-higher card lies in the widow or the discarded hand, or because the next-higher card was played at some previous time. Whenever an apparent stop occurs, the player of the last card should say "Stop," and unless there is prompt response he is entitled to assume that it is a real stop. The same player then plays again, provided that he can *change suit*. If all his remaining cards are of the same suit as that just run up to a stop, he must pass, and the turn goes to the player at his left. If no player holds a card of another suit, the last player begins with his lowest card of the stopped suit. In starting a new suit, the player begins with the lowest card he holds in it.

Money Cards. Whenever a money card is played, the player collects all the chips lying on its duplicate in the layout.

If, at the end of play, the chips on any layout card have not been won, they remain there, to be increased by subsequent antes, until they are won.

Settlement. Play continues until some player gets rid of his last card. Each other hand then pays the winner one chip for every card remaining in his hand. (Some follow the rule that a player must pay five for an unplayed money card.

STRATEGY OF MICHIGAN

Although Michigan is largely a game of luck, there are a few things you can do to better your fortunes.

Keep track of what cards in your hand become stops, by reason of the fact that a new suit has been opened by the next-higher card of the same suit. For example, if you have the ♣ 5 and a club series is at some time begun with the ♣ 6, the ♣ 5 is a stop card. Knowledge of your stop cards may enable you, if you gain a stop with only a few cards left, to lay them all down without pause—the stop cards first, then any doubtful card last.

The privilege of taking the widow is worth something, if only because you know every card in the discard, and therefore start with a knowledge of every stop card in the deck. To what extent this knowledge avails, however, is a matter of chance. The widow you pick up may contain none of the stop cards. Certainly, buy the widow cheaply when you can, if only for this potential advantage. But don't give up a good hand for this purpose. Any hand with two aces or three kings is "good"; high cards, generally, make a hand worth saving. Don't bid high for the widow merely in the hope of buying a money card. If you feel like speculating, do so when you have no high cards—say, nothing above a jack.

In starting a new suit during the early stages, as a rule pick your longest suit. This is often good policy in later stages, even if it means by-passing a short suit in which you have a money card. Suppose your only diamonds are Q-2. The notion of playing the ♦ 2 with a view to having the sequence built up to your queen is a snare and a delusion. All that you do is increase the chance that someone will go out *before* you have a chance to play the money card. Much better is to let someone else start the diamonds—necessarily at a higher level—and the lower diamonds left in play may block the potential winner until you have cashed your ♦ Q.

TWO-HAND PINOCHLE

Pinochle, like Poker and Dominoes, is not the name of one specific game but of a whole family of games having some features in common. The hallmark of the Pinochle games is the Middle-European ranking of cards—ten next to ace—and the basic melds. Having learned the rules of one Pinochle game, you are happily able to pick up the rules of another quickly. But don't assume that the objectives and the strategy are the same. For example, two-hand Pinochle and three-hand Pinochle differ more widely than do the innumerable variants of Rummy that go by different names.

How to Play Two-Hand Pinochle

The Deck. The regular Pinochle deck contains 48 cards, two duplicates of each rank in each of the four suits. The cards in each suit rank: A (high), 10, K, Q, J, 9. When duplicate cards are played to the same trick, the first-played ranks higher. The suits have no relative rank, though in some games a special scoring value is attached to Spades.

The Deal. Decide who is to deal first by drawing cards from the deck, spread face down. Lower card deals. If equal cards are drawn, draw again.

If you play each deal a separate game, the winner of a deal is the next dealer. If you play for a fixed game, as 1000 points, the deal alternates after the first dealer is decided by drawing.

The dealer gives each player twelve cards, in batches of three at a time. The next card is turned face up; this is the *trump card.* It fixes the trump suit for the deal. The rest of the deck is put face down in the center of the table to form the *stock.* By custom, the trump card is put crosswise below it, still face up.

The Play. The non-dealer leads to the first trick. A trick is won by the higher trump, or by the higher card of the suit led if neither is a trump, or by the leader if identical cards are played. The winner of a trick leads to the next.

The foregoing rules apply throughout the play. During the first twelve tricks (i.e., so long as the stock is not exhausted), the second player to a trick need not follow suit to a lead, even when a trump is led—he may play any card whatsoever. The winner of a trick draws the top card of the

stock to restore his hand to twelve cards, and his opponent
then draws the next card. The winner of the twelfth trick
draws the last face-down card, and he must expose it. His
opponent takes the trump card, and thus each player knows
one card in the other's hand (in addition to melded cards).

In the last twelve tricks (i.e., after the stock is exhausted), the second player to a trick must follow suit to
the lead if able, and if unable to follow to a plain-suit lead,
must trump if able. When a trump is led, he must if able
play a higher trump.

Objectives of Play. There are three objectives in the play:

(a) To *meld* (place certain combinations of cards face
up on the table);

(b) To win high cards in tricks;

(c) To win last trick.

Melding. All the valid melds, together with their scoring
values, are shown in the following table:

SEQUENCES

A-K-Q-J-10 of trumps, called *flush*	150
K-Q of trumps, called *royal marriage*	40
K-Q of a plain suit, called *marriage*	20

GROUPS

Four aces, one of each suit, called *100 aces*	100
Four kings, one of each suit, called *80 kings*	80
Four queens, one of each suit, called *60 queens*	60
Four jacks, one of each suit, called *40 jacks*	40

SPECIAL

♠ Q and ♦ J, called *pinochle*	40
9 of trumps, called *dix* (pronounced deece)	10

A player may meld only after winning a trick and before
drawing from the stock. He may make only one meld in a
turn. The same card may be used in two or three melds, if
they are of different classes. For example, the king of
trumps may be used in a flush and also in 80 kings; the
queen of spades may be used in pinochle, 60 queens, and
also in a marriage. The same card may be used in a different

meld of the same class, provided that the second meld scores higher than the first. For example, a royal marriage may be melded, and later the other three cards may be added to make a flush, but if the first meld is a flush, the royal marriage is lost, nor can it be scored by adding one queen or one king to the five cards already on the table. The same card may never be used in two identical melds. For example, if a heart marriage has been melded, a second cannot be scored merely by adding the duplicate king or queen of hearts; both duplicates would be needed to score a second heart marriage.

In any case, at least one new card from the hand must be placed on the table to score a meld. For example, suppose that a player melds pinochle, already having shown 80 kings. Having elected pinochle, he may not score the spade marriage also—no more than one meld per turn—nor may he circumvent this rule by pointing out the marriage at his next turn and claiming score for it. But he could score both melds by adding the spade queen for a marriage at one turn, and later melding the diamond jack to make pinochle.

At the time that either player melds a dix, he may exchange it for the trump. The dix (or exchanged trump card) need not be left on the table as other melds are. If a dix is turned for the trump card, the dealer scores 10 for it.

Though placed on the table, melded cards still belong to the player's hand. He may lead and play them just as he does his concealed cards. After the twelfth trick, it is usual for both players to pick up all their melded cards and hold them concealed.

Point Values. All cards won in tricks, except ninespots, have a point value as follows:

Each ace	11
Each ten	10
Each king	4
Each queen	3
Each jack	2

The winner of the last trick scores 10 points therefor.

The total of points to be won other than by melding is thus 250.

Scoring. The score is usually kept on paper, with one column for each player, only the cumulative total being entered. Every meld is scored at once. The melder should claim its value orally, even though he himself is the only scorekeeper, to avoid misunderstandings. The points for cards won in tricks are reckoned after the last trick. Custom is for the winner of the last trick to count his point values while the opponent watches. The total (with 10 for last trick) is taken to the nearest 10, with 6 counting as 10 and 5 as zero. The opponent then subtracts the total from 250 to determine his score.

Game. The first player to reach a total of 1000 points wins a game, provided that his opponent does not reach 1000 in the same deal. If the latter event, play continues for a goal of 1250, and if both again reach that total, for 1500, and so on. To avoid such prolongation, it is usual to agree to *declaring out*. A player who believes that he has reached 1000, in melds and cards won up to that juncture, may claim the game. Play stops at once and the cards are counted. If the claim is correct, it stands; if it is incorrect, the claimant loses the game.

An alternative, favored by some stake players, is to treat each deal as a separate game, settling after each according to the difference of scores or counting each game won as a unit regardless of the margin by which it is won.

STRATEGY OF TWO-HAND PINOCHLE

Melds. As a matter of course, save high trumps and aces so long as there is any hope of making a flush or 100 aces. There is more reason for this rule than the high count of the melds. These cards should be saved, if feasible, to build up the strongest possible hand for the last twelve tricks.

Letting go a high trump or an ace in the early play, even from duplicates, has at the very minimum the disadvantage that it informs the opponent he cannot make a flush or 100 aces. It is therefore the last resort of desperation when entry is needed to make some valuable meld, 80 kings or 60 queens. It may also be proper when the opponent has already melded a flush or 100 aces, or otherwise scuttled one's own prospects of making the same.

Having a dix, you clearly should hasten to take the trump card with it. This exchange has first priority. By taking the high trump you increase your own chances of making a flush and also decrease your opponent's chances.

The most economical meld is pinochle. With only two cards, you score 40. It is therefore good policy to save a queen of spades or a jack of diamonds so long as a chance of making pinochle exists.

As a rule, don't strain to save cards for simple marriages and 40 jacks. Meld these combinations if you draw them and can gain the lead easily. But be ready to abandon them in preference to giving up an ace or trump to gain the lead, or to discarding a card needed for a more valuable meld. There are only twelve chances to meld, to be divided between two players. You must be somewhat conservative about giving up entry cards (usually, tens) for low melds. Given a cheap opportunity to meld, however, do so. Once you have tabled, say, a simple marriage, these cards are available for play (unless you are saving for 80 kings or 60 queens). Every card that has already scored, and that is not wanted in a possible second meld, is a card that can be ditched to make space for another in the hand.

Early Play. The ranks that can never be melded are tens and plain nines. Nines of course are regularly ditched, whenever the hand does not care about capturing or holding the lead. Tens are the natural cards of entry, and are second only to aces in intrinsic value. Thought should be given to timing the play of tens. At the very beginning of play, they are naturally conserved toward future entry; as the play progresses, the urgency becomes more acute to save tens for the points, even when the hand has nothing to meld.

It is of course harder to hold the lead than to win it from your opponent. If you wish to hold the lead to make a meld, and your opponent knows it, the best course is usually to lead a ten. Then he can capture the lead only by giving up an ace or a trump—possibly ruining his chances for a big meld. Conversely, when your opponent leads a ten, do not be too reluctant to take it. The cash points gained (a difference of 20), plus the possibility that your opponent may have to hurt his hand to get later re-entry for his meld, go far to offset what chance you give up of a flush or 100 aces.

At the outset of play, it is well to be wary of leading new suits. If you have started, say, clubs, and your opponent has discarded a diamond, continue clubs if you can afford to do so. The idea is that he may want cheap entry, and he has already shown that he cannot gain it in clubs. Later, breaking a new suit without forethought may give him a welcome chance to save a ten.

Toward the end of the early play, it is sometimes evident that your opponent has or can have a flush or 100 aces. Drastic defensive measures are called for—lead and continue to lead cards that he cannot win without breaking up his meld. For example, against a flush, lead trumps. He cannot win and hold his meld unless he chances to have duplicates. Against 100 aces, lead tens, or kings if the tens are gone, etc. Here he might get in with a trump—but at least he will then go into the final play with one trump less.

To become expert, you should learn to remember every card played. But don't try to do that all at once: take it in easy stages. At the outset, aim to keep track of (a) any aces and trumps played, (b) all tens, (c) melds that have become impossible by the play of both duplicates of a component card. Presently you will find it fairly easy to know what your opponent holds after the stock is exhausted.

Later Play. The drawing and discarding produces one of two situations as the final play begins: (a) the trumps are fairly well divided, or (b) one player has a great preponderance of trump length in strength. In the first case, the proper play by each player is likely to be to lead his longest side suit at every opportunity, forcing his opponent to trump. Trumps are not led until the leader has nothing else. In the second case, the strong trump hand may find it best to lead trumps and exhaust his opponent, so that he may then cash his plain aces and tens without molestation.

The exact holdings may, however, indicate as best some deviation from the usual plan. For example, a powerful trump hand may still find it best to lead and continue a worthless side suit, letting the weaker hand gather a few points in kings and queens.

The final play revolves about two efforts: to capture all possible aces and tens, and to win *stich,* the last trick. Stich usually goes to the longer trump hand regardless of other considerations, but incorrect play of the trump suit may lose stich needlessly. For example, suppose that with two cards left the leader has A-10 and his opponent A-K. The leader lays down the ace, with some vague notion of saving his ten (perhaps he has miscounted the trumps). He thereby loses stich. By leading the ten first, he forces out the ace and wins stich.

Myriads of end-situations may arise; we cannot cover them in a word. But if you will deal the twelve trumps at random, six and six, and then play them out, you will discover some propositions of general utility. Until there are only three cards left, the leader can rarely do better than lead his lowest card. Thereafter, the correct plays depend on the distribution of the aces and tens. Stich can always be won by the hand with stronger tops, as double-ace or ace and double-ten. With precisely equal holdings, the leader at this juncture can always win stich.

AUCTION PINOCHLE

The card table of the eighteenth century was triangular; the card table of today is square. Nothing could mark more clearly the trend of the centuries. The three-hand games of yore have mostly been usurped by modern four-hand games. However, Auction Pinochle is one excellent three-hand game that has returned to popularity. It is a natural three-hand game, and consequently a better game for three players than three-hand adaptations of games planned for two or four players.

How to Play Auction Pinochle

The Deck. Use the regular Pinochle deck of 48 cards. This deck comprises two duplicates of each rank in each of four suits. The cards in each suit rank: A (high), 10, K, Q, J, 9. When duplicate cards are played to the same trick, the the first-played ranks higher. The suits have no relative rank, but Spades usually have a special scoring value.

The Deal. The game is often played by four or five players in rotation, only three being active in each deal. In such case, the dealer is always inactive.

Decide the precedence by drawing cards from the deck, spread face down. Lowest card decides the first dealer; next-lowest sits at his left, and so on. The position of dealer rotates clockwise, as usual.

To the three active players, the dealer gives fifteen cards each. The cards are dealt in batches, either three per batch throughout the deal, or three batches of four each and a final round of three. After the first round of the deal, three cards are dealt face down in the center of the table to form the *widow*.

The Bidding. Each player in turn, beginning with the one at the left of the dealer, must make a *bid* or *pass*. Bidding is by points only (without reference to suits), and always in multiples of 10. There is always a minimum permissible bid; the usual minimum is 300, but some players agree on 250 or 200. Local practices differ also as to whether the player at the left of the dealer may pass. Most prevalent is the rule that a pass by this first hand is equivalent to a bid of 300, which he is stuck with if the other two players pass. The first voluntary bid must thus be 310 or more.

Once having passed, a player may not enter the bidding. But a player who has bid may in turn continue to bid in order to overcall any competing bids. After two players have passed, the third (who has made the highest bid) becomes the *Bidder* (a term corresponding to *Declarer* in Bridge and *Player* in Skat).

The Widow; Concessions. If stuck with a bid of 300 (or whatever is the agreed minimum), the Bidder may refuse to play the hand and instead pay a forfeit. Or, before making a decision, he may turn the three widow cards face up on the table. He has no option but to turn up the widow on any higher bid. Having seen the widow, he may concede defeat and incur *single bete*. He retains the right to concede up to the moment he makes any opening lead (he may try out various melds and name a trump suit, before deciding).

If the Bidder elects to play the hand, and then fails to make his bid, he incurs *double bete*. The significance of going bete is explained under *Scoring*.

When the Bidder decides to play, he puts the widow cards in his hand. Then he makes what *melds* he can and will. Next he *buries* (discards) three cards from his hand face down on the table, reducing his hand once more to fifteen cards. He must be careful not to bury a card he has melded (the usual penalty for this error is double bete). The buried cards count for the Bidder and are therefore added to the tricks he wins in play.

The Bidder finally names the trump suit. This ceremony is often omitted because the intended trump is obvious—as it must be when a flush is melded. To prepare for play, the Bidder picks up all his melds and restores them to his hand.

Melding. Only the Bidder may meld. To meld is to place face up on the table any of the following combinations, which score as shown:

SEQUENCES

A-K-Q-J-10 of trumps, called *flush*	150
K-Q of trumps, called *royal marriage*	40
K-Q of a plain suit, called *marriage*	20

GROUPS

Four aces, one of each suit, called *100 aces* . . .	100
Four kings, one of each suit, called *80 kings* . . .	80
Four queens, one of each suit, called *60 queens* . .	60
Four jacks, one of each suit, called *40 jacks* . . .	40

SPECIAL

♠ Q and ♦ J, called *pinochle*	40
9 of trumps, called *dix* (pronounced deece) . . .	10

The same card may be used in two or three melds, provided that they are of different classes. For example, the ♠ Q can be used simultaneously in a marriage, 60 queens, and pinochle. When a flush is melded, the royal marriage it contains does not score separately. Two melds of the same kind or class may be counted, provided that separate cards are used to make each. For example, two heart marriages may be scored with two kings and two queens of hearts, but not with two kings and one queen, or two queens and one king.

The Play. The Bidder makes the opening lead. He may lead any card. A lead calls upon each other player to follow suit if able; if unable to follow suit the hand must play a trump if able to a plain-suit lead. When unable to meet any of these requirements, the hand may play any card. On a trump lead, each other hand in turn must if able *go over* —that is, play a trump higher than any previously played to the trick. (But the third player need not *go over* when he is void of a plain suit that the second player has already trumped.)

A trick is won by the highest trump, or, if the trick contains no trump, by the highest card of the suit led. The winner of a trick leads to the next.

The two opponents combine in temporary partnership against the Bidder, and one of them gathers all the tricks taken by his side.

Point Values. The object of play is to win points, as follows:

Each ace	11
Each ten	10
Each king	4
Each queen	3
Each jack	2
Last trick	10

Ninespots have no scoring value. The total of points to be won in play, including 10 for *stich* (last trick), is 250.

The Bidder makes his contract if the points he wins in tricks, plus the value of his melds, is at least equal to his bid. If he falls short, he is *bete*.

Scoring. The scores may be recorded on paper and settled when a session ends, but simpler is to use Poker chips and settle after every deal.

The basis of settlement is an agreed scale of basic values for bids. Local practices differ widely as to this scale; the following is typical but not universal:

Bid	Base value
300 to 340	3
350 to 390	5
400 to 440	10
450 to 490	15
500 to 540	20
etc.	etc.

A common pool called the *kitty* is formed by equal contributions from all players at the outset. If the kitty nears exhaustion, it is replenished by equal contributions. When a session ends, the chips in the kitty are divided equally among the players.

The kitty is treated as an extra player who shares in most of the winnings and losses. Here again local practices differ, but the following plan is largely prevalent:

If the bid is 300 (or other minimum), and the Bidder concedes without looking at the widow, he pays 3 chips to the kitty only.

In all other circumstances, when the bid is less than 350, the kitty is ignored in settlement. The Bidder pays the base value of his bid to each other player, if he incurs *single bete* by conceding before making a lead; or twice the base value, if he incurs *double bete* by playing the hand and failing to make contract. If he plays and makes his bid, the Bidder collects its base value from each other player.

The same method of settlement applies to bids of 350 or more, except that the kitty shares in all winnings and losses.

"Double in spades" is an optional but widely prevalent rule—when spades are named for trump, all payments are doubled.

Strategy of Three-hand Pinochle

Hand Valuation. In the question of whether or what to bid, the first factor is the intrinsic value of the hand, apart from any prospects of improvement by the widow.

First total all the melds. For example:

♠ A A 10 K Q J 9	160	flush and dix
♥ A K Q	20	marriage
♦ A K J 9	40	pinochle
♣ K	80	kings
	300	

Next estimate what the hand can make in play. This is of course the crux of hand valuation. A hand strong enough to be bid at all can usually be valued by counting the maximum of points that *might be* piled into the tricks that the hand must lose. The count of the above hand proceeds thus:

SPADES: If the five outstanding spades are split 3-2, there are no losers, as the three top cards will drop them all.

HEARTS: Two tricks must be lost, on which the opponents might gather A, 10, 10, K, K, Q, a total of 42.

DIAMONDS: With a long (four or more cards) weak suit, it is simpler to count *winners* than *losers*. The only sure trick is the ace, which may catch no more than a jack, for a total of 13. The rest of the suit, 47 points, is written off as lost.

CLUBS: The one loser can cost no more than 26 points (for A, A, K).

The maximum loss expected by this count is 115 points, leaving 135 points to the Bidder.

Add the probable playing value of the hand to the melds. In this example, 135 plus 300 gives 435. The margin is ample to justify a bid of 400. The hand might be bid to 420 if necessary, but any higher bid is hazardous.

A rough-and-ready valuation method used by many players is to count each losing trick worth 15 to the opponents. Of course this scale is often wide of the mark.

It must be recognized, however, that even a precise reckoning of the specific cards that the opponents stand to win is not infallible. The method makes certain assumptions; you should be alert to discount these assumptions when danger signals show. To wit:

(a) The subtraction of the points credited to the opponents from 250 assumes that the Bidder will win stich. This usually happens when the Bidder has a good majority of the trumps, or short strong trumps backed by enough side aces. On some biddable hands, the Bidder can see that he will probably lose stich.

(b) It is assumed that whenever the Bidder becomes void of a plain suit he will win all remaining points in that suit. Of course this is not true if his trumps cannot stand all the forces the opponents can give him.

(c) Normal splits are assumed. An odd number of cards in a suit is assumed to split as evenly as possible, as 3-2 or 4-3. An even number is assumed to split evenly or next-to-evenly, as 3-3 or 4-2. An abnormal split, as 4-1, 5-2, may cost 20 or 30 more points than expected.

(d) It is assumed that the opponents will save no aces or tens by *smearing*—discarding on each other's tricks. The chief objective in the play is to prevent smears. But sometimes (especially when the opponents hold top trumps) it is forseeable that smears will occur, and unexpected bad splits always enhance the danger.

Despite the foregoing hazards, a hand (if pushed) may be bid within 20 or even less points of its expected maximum value—because there is a cushion of compensating values:

(a) The opponents win their counted maximum in a suit only through favorable high-card splits plus 100% accurate play.

(b) Taking the widow gives the Bidder opportunity to lay away cash points otherwise hard to save (as tens not accompanied by aces), and to improve the pattern of his hand.

Chances of Improvement. The foregoing expresses *all* of what help you should expect from the widow. To repeat: the opportunity to bury three cards gives you a chance to save some cash points, as unguarded tens, and to improve the pattern of your hand. Don't expect the widow also to provide you with additional melds! This is too much of a load! The abstract probabilities, plus all experience, go to show that you are rarely dealt a hand with enough "places open" to warrant bidding on the melds in the widow.

What to Bid. For scoring purposes, a bid of 420 is equivalent to a bid of 400. The normal course is to bid the even multiple of 50 next below the calculated value of your hand. However, be sure to allow a sufficient margin —especially if you are not skillful in the play. If your hand counts 410, bid 350 and be satisfied. Especially when the count is nebulous—as when you have a broken trump suit —don't stretch to reach the next-higher 50.

Among experienced players there is some "jockeying for position" in the choice of bids between the 50's. For example, if a player is prepared to go to 430, and his bid of 400 is overcalled by 410, he will usually jump to 430 at once; to bid 420 might let the opposing bidder in at 430. Little can be said of these niceties in general; learn them by experience and base them on your particular opponents.

Burying. What to bury is often a simple question. After you have melded what you must, you discard from one or two short plain suits, keeping your longest plain suit intact. The reason for this policy is obvious. If you name spades, and then discard three small hearts to void yourself of the suit, you stand to win all 60 points in hearts instead of losing 50 to 60. There is no such proportionate gain in discarding from a long suit. A holding of A-K-Q stands to lose just about as much as A-K-Q-J-J-9. On the other hand, a long side suit is a great help in weakening the adverse trumps.

Sometimes, to meld marriages or groups, you have to leave yourself with losers in short suits. Then weigh the value of the meld against the playing value of a void. On occasion, it pays to abandon a low-scoring meld.

A plain ten, not accompanied by at least an ace, is usually hard to save in play. The normal procedure is to bury all such unguarded tens. But give a thought to saving *stoppers* in all suits when your trumps are short (six or five) and not very strong at top. Give a thought also to whether you want to risk playing the hand at all!

Just to clear up a point on which many Pinochle players are foggy—if you bury a trump, you do not have to announce the fact. Of course, you can play Pinochle all your life without seeing a valid occasion to bury a trump. It arises only when you have melded so much that you have nothing left to discard.

Bidder's Play. Having any blank ace, with no other cards of the suit, the Bidder should cash it at once. This ceremony is essential to save the ace from falling to an opponent's lead of the duplicate ace.

The normal general plan of play is to open the longest plain suit, and to continue it so long as the opponents can win tricks in it. The idea is that, if one opponent becomes void while the other still holds winners in the suit, he is estopped from smearing by the rule that he must trump. The Bridge player's instinct—to take out adverse trumps —is diametrically wrong most of the time in Pinochle. A few trumps in the hand of an opponent operate to the opponents' detriment more often than to their advantage, by estopping smears.

Opponents' Play. The chief points to be remembered in defending a hand are:

(a) Be sure of your maximum in suits of which the Bidder is short, by fattening the tricks your side wins.

(b) Leading trumps through the Bidder, from a holding of one or two small, often strengthens your partner's trumps and paves the way to smears.

(c) Look for opportunities to short-suit yourself by discards on trump leads, to pave the way for smears.

The integration of defensive principles in a particular plan depends largely on inferences from the bid, the melds, the Bidder's play—and on the ability of your partner to co-operate. Most of the time, you should know just about what the Bidder holds, from his melds and from what else he needs to have a play for his contract. His opening lead, nine times out of ten, spots his long side suit (if any). When in doubt what to do, plug away at your own long suit, forcing the Bidder's trumps. Many a bete is gained by this routine process.

SKAT

One of the best of three-handed games, Skat unfortunately repels many card players by the intricacy of its rules. However, considerable simplification has been achieved in the variant Räuber Skat, here described.

How to Play Skat

The Deck. Use a deck of 32 cards, made by discarding from a regular deck all the sixes, fives, fours, threes, and twos.

When there is no trump, the cards of each suit rank: A (high), K, Q, J, 10, 9, 8, 7. When there is a trump, the four jacks are the highest trumps, ranking: ♣ J (high), ♠ J, ♥ J, ♦ J. The rest of the trump suit, as well as each plain suit, ranks: A (high), 10, K, Q, 9, 8, 7.

The Deal. The dealer gives ten cards to each player, in batches of three and four at a time. Custom allows him choice of dealing in rounds of 3-4-3 or 3-3-4. After the first round, he deals two cards face down in the center of the table for a *widow* (or *skat*).

The Bidding. In order to left of the dealer, the three players are called *forehand, middlehand, endhand.* With only three persons at the table, endhand is the dealer. The game is often played, however, by four or five in rotation, and in such cases the dealer is not an active player.

Forehand has the vested right to name *the game*—the trump suit, no trump, etc. The others may bid against him in turn, to purchase this right. The bidding is begun by middlehand, who must either pass or make a bid. Forehand can keep his right by expressing willingness to bid the same amount; if he thus *stays,* middlehand may increase the bid, again and again, until one of the two players drops out. The survivor then settles in the same way with endhand, who must pass or bid. Endhand can buy the right only by making a higher bid than the other is willing to meet.

The high bidder becomes the *Player* (this term has the same meaning as *Declarer* in Bridge).

If both other players pass without a bid, forehand is the Player.

A bid is made in terms of points alone; the bidder does not specify his intended *game*. On becoming the Player, he must of course name a game whose value (intrinsic or potential) is at least as great as his bid. For example, having bid 24, he might name any suit as trump, because any might count 24 or more; he would not be permitted, how-ever, to name *simple nullo,* because this game has the invariant value 23.

The lowest possible competitive bid is 18. Every bid must be for a number that is the possible value of some game. At the lower end of the scale, the bids that answer this rule are 18, 20, 22, 23, 24, 27, 30, etc. The maximum possible value is 204.

The Games. The most complex part of Skat is determining the value of a *game,* for purposes of bidding and scoring. Let us take up this matter in easy stages.

There are nine possible games, with *base values* as follows:

	Game	Base value
Trump	Diamonds	9
	Hearts	10
	Spades	11
	Clubs	12
	Jacks (*grand*)	20
	Jacks (*reject*)	10
No trump	Nullo, simple	23
	Nullo, open	46
	Nullo, open handplay	59

When a suit is declared trump, or *grand* is named (when the only trumps are the four jacks), the Player's objective is to win as many points as he can in play. The ultimate value of his game is the product of its *base value* and another integer, never less than 2, that is the sum of all applicable *multipliers.* We will defer to the next section the question of what these multipliers are.

Each *nullo* game is an undertaking by the Player to win no tricks at all. There are no trumps. The values 23, 46, 59 are invariant, being neither increased nor decreased by any factors. In a *simple nullo,* the widow is set aside. In either *open nullo,* the Player puts his whole hand face up on the table before the opening lead, defying the opponents to force him to win a trick even with full knowledge of his cards. The Player has choice of using the widow or not. In the former case, he takes the widow into his hand, discards two cards face down, then exposes his hand. If he chooses not to use the widow, called *handplay,* he pushes the widow aside without looking at it and exposes his hand at once.

Reject is not a competitive bid. This game may be declared only by forehand, in the event that both other players pass without any bid. Jacks are trumps. The widow is set aside but goes eventually to the winner of the last trick. Each plays for himself, the objective being to win in tricks as few points as possible. Reject is a refuge provided for forehand in case he is compelled to name the game but holds cards that do not warrant a positive declaration. It is scored in a special way, described later.

Multipliers. The ultimate value of a trump game (not *reject*) is its base value times another integer, which is the sum of all applicable *multipliers*.

For example, if diamonds are trumps and the sum of the multipliers is 3, the game counts $3 \times 9 = 27$.

Here is the list of all possible multipliers:

Matadors (*with* or *without*)	from 1 to 11
Game	1
Handplay	1
Little slam	1
Big slam	1
Little slam, announced	1
Big slam, announced	1

MATADORS. At any trump game, the four highest trumps are the jacks. If the Player holds the ♣ J (in hand or widow), he is said to be *with* as many *matadors* as he holds trumps in unbroken sequence with the ♣ J. For example, if his trumps are topped by ♣ J, ♠ J, ♦ J, he is *with two;* if by ♣ J, ♥ J, ♦ J, he is *with one*. If the Player lacks the ♣ J, he is said to be *without* as many matadors as there are trumps higher than his highest. For example, if his highest trump is the ♦ J, he is *without three*.

The multiplier for matadors is the number that the Player is either *with* or *without*. Note that bidding *with* is safer than bidding *without*. If the widow (which belongs to the Player, whether he uses it or not) contains a high trump, it can but increase the number of matadors *with* or decrease the number *without*.

GAME. The multiplier for "game" is an arbitrary point always added to the matadors. It is not a reward to the Player for making his bid, for it is counted in even when he fails. Since there must be at least 1 point for matadors, the minimum sum of multipliers is 2.

HANDPLAY. This multiplier is earned by electing to play without using the widow.

SLAMS. The meaning of *little slam* and *big slam* will be explained later. The multipliers for slams are cumulative; when any one applies, all preceding items of the four also apply. A simpler way to reckon is to pick out the one appropriate item from the following schedule:

Little slam is made, not announced 1
Big slam is made, not announced 2
Little slam is announced by Player and made . . 3
Big slam is announced by Player and made . . 4

The 1 or 2 for unannounced slam applies regardless of whether the slam is made by the Player or the Opponents. But a slam may be *announced* only by the Player. The *announcement* consists in stating, before the first lead, that he will undertake to win little or big slam. Such announcement is permitted only in *handplay*, so that the extra multiplier for handplay is necessarily added into the total. The largest possible game would be an announced big slam at clubs with all eleven trumps, counting 17 (all possible multipliers) times 12 (club base value), or 204.

The Play. The bidding finished, the Player may elect handplay or may pick up the widow. In the latter case, he may defer naming the game until he has examined the widow. He must then discard two cards face down. In any event (except in *reject*), his discards or the untouched widow belong to him after the play is finished, and are counted with points won in play.

The opening lead is invariably made by forehand, regardless of who is the Player. This fact should be duly taken into account in bidding. The leader to any trick may choose any card. The other two players must follow suit to the lead if able; if unable to follow, a player may play any card, discarding or trumping as he pleases. A trick is won by the highest trump, or, if it contains no trump, by the highest card of the suit led. The winner of a trick leads to the next.

Except in *reject,* the Opponents combine against the Player in the effort to defeat him, and it is usual for one Opponent alone to gather all the tricks won by both.

Point Values. The high cards have *point values* as follows:

Each ace	11
Each ten	10
Each king	4
Each queen	3
Each jack	2
(No count for 9, 8, 7)	

Each suit contains 30 points; the whole deck, 120. In any positive trump game, the Player is committed to gather at least 61 points in tricks (and widow). If he fails, he *goes bete.* If he wins 91 or more, he scores *little slam;* if the Opponents win 90 or more, little slam is scored against the Player. A side winning all the tricks—not merely all the points—scores *big slam.* If the Opponents win all the tricks, the rule that the widow belongs to the player does not deprive them of big slam.

Reject. When *reject* is declared, jacks are trumps, the widow is set aside and later added to the last trick. Each plays for himself, with the object of taking as few points as possible. If one player takes no tricks at all, he scores 20 and the others score nothing. If one player takes all the tricks, he loses 30 and the others score nothing. If each player takes 40 points, forehand is deemed the winner and scores 10. If two players tie for low score, the one who did not take the last trick as between the two is deemed the winner and scores 10. In all other cases, the lowest number of points gathered scores 10 and the others score nothing.

Scoring. In any game but reject, the Player is the only one that scores. He receives, as a plus quantity, the value of his game if (a) he fulfills his undertaking in the play (simple game of 61 or more, 91 for announced little slam, or all the tricks for announced big slam); and if (b) the value of his game is at least equal to his bid.

If he fails in either respect, the value of his game is deducted from his score if he elected handplay, and twice the value if he picked up the widow. It is permissible for the Player, on seeing the widow, to concede *bete* without play, in order to save possible loss of slam. In this event he must name some game, so that the amount of his loss can be determined.

The Player has *overbid* when he fails in respect (b). In this event, the value of his game is fixed at the multiple of the base value next higher than his bid. For example, suppose that he has bid 40 and named spades, at handplay. His hand is *without two,* so that he expects to have at least 4 in multipliers. He wins more than 60 but less than 91 in play. The widow is found to contain the ♠ J. He is now *without one,* and the value of his game is only $3 \times 11 = 33$. He has overbid. His loss is fixed at 44, the next multiple of 11 higher than his bid of 40. (Had he picked up the widow, he might have elected to play in the effort to make little slam, but if he failed he would lose 88.)

The score is usually recorded on paper, with one column for each player.

Settlement. There is no prefixed goal of points. Each deal is in effect a separate game. Settlement of monetary stakes can be made after each deal or deferred until the end of a session. Each player pays or collects according to the difference between his final total and the average of all the totals. For example, suppose that at the end of a session the scores are:

A	279
B	106
C	58

$$3 \overline{)\ 443} \quad (148$$

The total of the scores being 443, the average is 148 approximately. Player B pays 42, Player C pays 90, and Player A collects 132.

STRATEGY OF SKAT

Suit Bids. A rule-of-thumb for suit bids is: Count each trump as 1, each side ace or ten as 1; a total of 7 makes the hand a minimum suit bid. For example, here are (rock bottom!) minimum club bids:

(1) ♠ J ♦ J ♣ A Q 9 ♠ 7 ♥ A 7 ♦ 10 8

Being *without one,* the hand may be bid up to 24.

(2) ♣ J ♠ J ♣ 10 Q 8 7 ♠ A 8 ♥ 9 ♦ Q

Being *with two,* the hand may be bid up to 36.

Like all rules-of-thumb, this one must be applied with discretion. The minimum trump length normally necessary to assure the Player a sufficient command of trumps is five. If the hand has only four trumps, the count should be 8 or 9. Even with five or six trumps, the hand should have some "plus" values over the 7. The following is too weak for a bid of 36, intending clubs:

(3) ♥ J ♣ A K 8 ♠ A 8 ♥ 10 7 ♦ 10 7

Better, though still borderline, would be:

(4) ♥ J ♦ J ♣ A 8 ♠ A 8 ♥ A 7 ♦ 10 K

The "plus" values not counted directly by the above method—but often decisive—are: protection of a side ten by possession of the ace; strengthening kings and queens under tens and aces; position of forehand, with its right to make the opening lead.

Grands. A rule-of-thumb for grands is: Count each jack as 1, each ace as 1, position of forehand as 1; a minimum bid requires 5 of the 9 points. Examples of minimum bids:

(5) ♠ J ♦ J ♣ A 8 7 ♥ A K ♦ Q 7 ♣ A

Being *without one,* the hand may be bid to 40.

(6) ♣ J   ♠ J   ♦ J   ♣ K Q 9   ♥ 7   ♦ A   ♣ A 7

Being *with two,* the hand may be bid to 60. The trump holding makes this hand much stronger than No. 5.

The Widow. Don't make a sub-minimum bid in the hope of finding the right ace or ten in the widow. In average probability, the widow is simply a "plus" value, and it has already been taken into account in fixing the normal minimums.

The choice of discard, after taking the widow, is usually made (a) to void the hand of a suit, or (b) to save a ten that might otherwise fall to the Opponents. For example, you pick up the widow, name clubs, and hold:

(7) ♣ J   ♠ J   ♣ 10 Q 8 7   ♥ Q 9   ♠ A 8   ♦ K Q

Discard the ♦ K Q. By voiding yourself of one red suit, you assure that all its 28 points will go to you (because of your adequate trump length). Choose diamonds instead of hearts so as to lose the lesser number of points.

(8) ♠ J   ♥ J   ♣ A K 8   ♠ A 8 7   ♥ 10 7   ♦ 10 7

Discard ♥ 10, ♦ 10. It is not easy for the Player to win a trick with a ten when he lacks the ace; two such tens are too much of a load. But bury the 20 points, and the hand becomes simple to play—you need but concentrate on catching one of the black tens.

A third principle sometimes supervenes—(c) to save all possible stoppers against the running of a side suit against you, when your trumps are short. For example, you have named grand, holding (with the widow):

(9) ♠ J   ♦ J   ♠ A 8 7   ♥ A K   ♦ 10 Q 7   ♣ A 8

Discard two of your three low black cards. Don't lay away the ♦ 10; it is better saved as a stopper.

Handplay. To forego use of the widow, you should normally have about an ace more than the minimum to bid.

But better than any rule-of-thumb is to count directly what points you stand to lose. If a hand is not solid enough for facile counting, it is not strong enough for handplay!

Suppose that you are dealt:

(10) ♣ J ♦ J ♣ A 10 9 7 ♠ — ♥ A Q 7 ♦ Q

If you win the bid and name clubs, you expect to lose at most two trump tricks (with a 3-2 split of the five outstanding trumps), two heart tricks, and one diamond trick. If these tricks are as "fat" as they can be for the Opponents, they will count: trumps, 11; hearts, 17; diamonds, 24; total 52. As Player, you should make over 60 easily. Therefore the hand is worth handplay and should be bid to 36 if necessary.

Nullo. To lose *all* the tricks you need a practically iron-clad hand. The chances of a nullo candidate can be reckoned directly. For example:

(11) ♣ K J 9 7 ♠ Q 9 7 ♥ Q 10 8 ♦ K J 8

The club holding is impregnable against adverse leads, even if all the clubs are in one hand. The spade holding is so close to impregnable that you don't give it a second thought. The heart holding is fairly safe against average breaks, and certainly should not deter you from a nullo bid. The diamond holding is less safe, but still worth a gamble.

The Play. At a trump make, the Player should usually open trumps at his earliest opportunity. In doing so, he drops two adverse trumps for one of his own, and so decreases the chance that his own side winners will be trumped. Also (often more important) he explores the trump split, to decide how to manage the trumps so as to avoid a fatal *smear*.

A *smear* (or *schmeer*) is the throwing of a high card by an Opponent on a trick won by the other. Suppose that you have named clubs on a hand previously cited:

(12) ♣ J ♦ J ♣ A 10 9 7 ♠ — ♥ A Q 7 ♦ Q

We have pointed out that this hand rates to lose a maximum of 52 points. This count assumes that you will gather all

28 points in spades. But if one Opponent wins a trump trick on which the other can smear the ♠ A or ♠ 10, you may go bete. The antidote is to give away sure trump losers early rather than late. The Opponents hold five trumps, of which the most favorable split for you is 3-2. Reserve the ♣ J, if necessary, to win the vital third round of trumps. Start with the ♦ J or ♣ 7.

With a minimum hand, the Player's campaign is perforce usually based on trying to catch one or two tens from the Opponents. He must refrain from taking cheap tricks, holding up his aces and trumps for bigger game.

Opponent's Play. Advice to the Opponents is cheap, but not easy to heed. Obviously the Opponent at right of the Player should win leads when possible, and the other should stay out when possible, so that adverse leads will go through the player rather than up to him. Both Opponents should watch for chances to smear, and try to steer the play toward a smear. Putting these precepts into practice is a matter of the specific situation, the specific inferences that can be drawn as to what the Player holds, what he has laid away. One word of caution: if you are experienced in either Pinochle or Bridge, don't try to play Skat the same way. In Pinochle, for example, you can always force the Bidder to trump by leading a suit of which he is void. In Skat, the Player does not have to trump, and such policy may let him discard to his advantage. In Bridge, one trick counts as much as another. In Skat, the objective is to win "fat" tricks. The majority of points often goes to the side having won the minority of tricks.

EUCHRE

Those who like a partnership game of bidding and play, but who shrink from the intricacies of Bridge, will find Euchre ideal. Euchre is a "short" game—less than the full deck is dealt out. The uncertainty as to just what cards are in play limits both the opportunity and necessity for skill. The few principles of strategy are mostly of the order "play 'em as you see 'em." At the same time, the partnership feature gives you leeway to be bold—you can always hope that your partner will turn up with the "funds" to cover your speculations.

The basic Euchre game is for four players, in two partnerships. It can also be played by three, each for himself.

How to Play Euchre

The Deck. From a regular deck, discard all sixes, fives, fours, threes, and twos. That leaves eight cards in each suit, which rank, when the suit is *plain* (non-trump), as follows: A (high), K, Q, J, 10, 9, 8, 7.

In the trump suit—and there always is a trump—the highest card is the jack, called the *right bower*. The second-highest, the *left bower,* is the other jack of same color as the trump suit. For example, when spades are trumps, the ♣ J is the left bower. After the bowers, the remaining cards of the trump suit rank as usual. Thus, if hearts are trumps, the nine trumps rank: ♥ J (high), ♦ J, ♥ A, K, Q, 10, 9, 8, 7.

For convenience of reference, the other suit of same color as the trump is called *next,* while either suit of opposite color as the trump is called *cross.* Note that the trump suit always comprises nine cards, the next suit seven, and the cross suits eight cards each.

It is usual to use two decks alternately, one being shuffled while the other is dealt.

The Deal. Decide who is to deal first by drawing cards from the deck, spread face down. Highest card deals. For the draw alone, an ace ranks low, below the seven. A jack ranks between queen and ten. There is no ranking of suits, so that players drawing equal high cards must draw again. You may let the same draw decide the partnerships: the two highest are partners against the two lowest. Partners sit opposite each other at the table.

After the first deal, the deal rotates as usual to the left, clockwise.

The dealer gives five cards to each player. He deals in batches—a batch of three to each hand, then a batch of two to each. He may reverse the order—a round of two, then a round of three—but whichever way he starts he must complete.

The rest of the deck is placed face down on the table, and the top card is turned face up. This card is the *turn-up*.

Making. The first part of the game is concerned with *making the trump*, i.e., deciding what the trump suit is to be. The turn-up is a proposed trump. Beginning with the opponent at the dealer's left, each player in turn has a chance to accept or reject the proposal, provided, of course, that the turn reaches him because all ahead of him have rejected it. If any accepts the turn-up, the trump is made.

To reject the turn-up, a player says "Pass" or "No." To accept it, an opponent of the dealer says "I order it up," but dealer's partner says "I assist." The dealer can show acceptance by discarding, without speaking.

If the turn-up is accepted by any player, the card itself belongs to the dealer. By custom, he does not take it into his hand, but leaves it on the deck until he chooses to play it to a trick. But on any acceptance, he must immediately discard one card from his hand, face down. The discard is by custom put crosswise under the deck.

If all four players reject the turn-up, the dealer moves the card below the deck, leaving it crosswise still face up.

This act is called *turning it down*. The opponent at left of the dealer may then name the trump suit or pass; if he passes, the option rotates clockwise until some player in turn has *made it*. If all four players again pass, the cards are tossed in (*bunched*) and reshuffled, and the next dealer deals.

The suit of the turn-up, after it has been turned down, may not be named for trump. The choice may fall on *next* or on one of the two *cross* suits.

Playing Alone. Whoever decides the trump suit, by ordering up, assisting, accepting, or by naming a suit in the second round, is the *maker*. The maker has the right, if he wishes, to *play alone*. If he announces, after making the trump, "I play alone," his partner's hand is placed face down on the table and the other three hands fight out the battle. The partner of the lone player shares equally, however, in the winnings or losses of the maker. The object in playing alone is to increase the winnings.

The Play. If the maker plays alone, the opening lead is made by the opponent at his left. In any other case, the opening lead is made by the player at the left of the dealer, regardless of who is the maker.

The leader to a trick may choose any card. Each other hand must follow suit if able; if unable to follow suit, the hand may play any card. A trick is won by the highest trump in it, or, if it contains no trump, by the highest card of the suit led. The winner of a trick leads to the next.

The primary object of play is to win at least three tricks: the secondary object is to win all five. If the maker's side wins less than three, it is *euchred*. Winning all five tricks is a *march*.

Scoring. If two partners of the making side together win three or four tricks, they score 1 point; for all five tricks, they score 2. If the maker playing alone wins three or four tricks, his side scores 1 point; for all five tricks, 4. If the maker, alone or with partner, is euchred, the opponents score 2.

The side first reaching a total of 5 points win a game.

Sometimes the game is increased by agreement to 7 or 10 points.

With such small numbers involved, it is not necessary to score on paper. The 5-point game is customarily scored with low cards taken from the discarded part of the deck, as shown in the diagram.

FIG. 3—Euchre scoring with two low cards. The number of exposed pips shows the current total, 1, 2, 3, or 4.

Rubbers. The side that first wins two games wins a *rubber,* and wins therefor a *rubber bonus* of 2 points. In addition it scores the difference between its total and the opponents' total of *rubber points.* These rubber points are awarded to the winner of each game, separately from the game points, as follows: for a game in which the losers had 0, 3 rubber points; for a game in which the losers had 1 or 2, 2 rubber points; for a game in which the losers had 3 or 4, 1 rubber point. Obviously, if a side loses two games out of two, it has no rubber points at all to deduct from the winners' total.

STRATEGY OF EUCHRE

Hand Valuation. You can make only the roughest sort of estimate of how many tricks your hand can be expected to win. Any system of hand valuation must be based on average expectation, but with so few cards in play this expectation is bound to be upset many times. The following rules of thumb are suggested—but don't expect them to be infallible.

Average expectation is that there will be six trumps in play; that three or four tricks will be won by trumps, leaving two or one to be won by plain cards. If the turn-up is accepted by anyone, dealer has at least one trump, and the expectation is that he was dealt at least another.

A holding of three trumps is a relatively long suit. Count it worth a sure trick for mere length, plus whatever it can win in tops. Likewise, any two trumps give fair assurance of one trick; count it sure if you have two trumps topped by the king or better.

Count a plain ace a sure trick if your side is the maker; a probable or merely possible trick if the opponents have made it. The difference is that the making side has better chances to trump the first round of a plain suit than the opponents, having (presumably) more of the trumps. On the offense, count more than one possible plain suit winner only to the extent that you have trumps strong enough to lead.

Requirements. The normal requirement to make the trump is two fairly sure tricks. Don't wait for three tricks in sight—the opponents will steal your shirt. You are entitled to expect to find one trick in your partner's hand, and you should include this in your decision. In Euchre, unlike Bridge, your partner has no way of telling you whether he has tricks or not, so you have to bid his "average expectation" for him.

But whether you *should* make the trump depends on other factors also. One of them is your position with respect to the dealer. Another is the state of the score.

Eldest Hand. The player at the left of the dealer, *eldest hand,* has least to gain of all the players by ordering it up. If the turn-up is turned down, he will have first chance to make it. If he has a good make in some other suit, he should (usually) pass. If he has one or two probable tricks at the turn-up suit, he should (usually) pass and hope that dealer's side will accept and be euchred. If he has three fairly sure tricks at the turn-up suit, he should (usually) order it up. The doubtful hands are (usually) those where it is hard to fix a solid valuation, as between two tricks and three tricks. For example, with the ♠ 7 turned up:

(1) ♠ J ♠ K ♠ 8 ♥ A ♣ 7   Eldest hand should order it up.

(2) ♠ A ♠ K ♥ A ♦ 7 ♣ Q   Eldest hand should pass.

(3) ♠ 9 ♠ 8 ♥ Q ♦ 7 ♣ J   *You* guess what to do! Will the hand take two tricks or three?

Now to explain the string of "usuallys" above. Suppose that eldest hand's side is *at the bridge,* i.e., has a score of 4 in the 5-point game. Suppose that the dealer's side has a score of 1 or 2. If this side makes it, plays alone, and makes march, it will win the game. Eldest hand is willing to donate 2 points in euchre to avert this catastrophe—next deal will be his and he will be in the driver's seat. In this scoring situation, eldest hand should not pass if he lacks a sure trick at the turn-up suit. Unless he can stop march, he should take his chances on euchre.

Take another score situation: dealer's side 3, opponents anything. This is the point at which a euchre gained by dealer's side will put it out, whereas an ordinary make will only put it at the bridge. Eldest hand should be most conservative; he should not order it up without solid values.

In short, the only time for untrammelled speculation, by way of ordering up as an *offensive* proposition, is when the dealer's side has no more than 2.

Dealer's Partner. Knowing that dealer will have one trump, his partner can afford to assist on the normal minimum—two fairly sure tricks. Here it is better to be aggressive than conservative, for if dealer has a dubious hand and passes, eldest hand will have first make. But if the turn-up is a bower, don't be over-anxious to assist. The dealer can probably afford to take it anyhow, and he may be strong enough to play alone. Don't get in his way.

Here are some examples. The ♠ 7 is turned.

(4) ♠ 10 ♠ 9 ♠ 8 ♥ 7 ♣ 7   Partner should assist.

(5) ♠ 8 ♥ Q ♦ K ♦ 7 ♣ 7   Partner should assist.

Now suppose the ♠ J is turned.

(6) ♠ Q ♠ 9 ♥ A ♦ 7 ♣ 7

Partner should usually pass, to give dealer a chance to play alone. But he should assist if the score is: dealer's side, 0 or 3 or 4; opponents, 3. Here the dealer might pass with a middling hand, lest he give the opponents the game by a euchre; also, nothing would be gained should he be strong enough to play alone.

Partner of Eldest Hand. The man in the third seat has heard his partner and one opponent pass. The partner's pass is usually forced without a solid hand, but does not deny having fair values. The opponent's pass is usually the most marked confession of weakness possible. Hence the player in this position can speculate on ordering it up, with the normal minimum—always provided that he takes account of the trump he donates the dealer. However, the character of his tricks is vital. If one of them is a plain ace, it has better chances of taking a trick if eldest hand has named the trump. If the hand has cards in all suits, and thus some kind of support for all, the player should incline to pass. The hand on which to order up is one that is largely worthless if some other suit is trump.

For example, with the ♠ 7 turned up:

(7) ♠ Q ♠ 10 ♠ 9 ♥ Q ♥ 7   Third man should order
it up.

(8) ♠ K ♥ A ♦ K ♦ 7 ♣ J   Third man should pass.

The speculative make in this position is fortified by the fact that the partner (eldest hand) has the opening lead—the most favorable playing situation for the making side. It is usually advantageous and often decisive for the partner of the maker to be able to show at once whether he holds any high plain cards.

The Dealer. Much the same considerations govern the dealer's decision as affect the third man's, including the score. He may speculate on a weak acceptance when the opponents have 2 or less; should not risk euchre when they have 3; and should accept almost automatically when they have 4. The reason for the last is that eldest hand will have first make if dealer passes. Hence dealer might make exception if he has a hand strong in two or three other suits, so that a pass might trap the opponents into a euchre.

The dealer's position is different from all the others, however, in that he can take the turn-up and make a discard. This opportunity to reshape the hand is often decisive, impelling an otherwise dubious acceptance.

The Discard. The natural choice of discard by dealer is a small card from his shortest suit, preferably a singleton. This leaves him able to trump the first round of the suit. While a void does not in itself add any positive tricks to the hand, it does increase the chance that the player will get in the lead quickly and take command. It also increases the chance of making a small trump, in a situation where the opponents, did they but know their own strength, could lead trumps and extract it.

Second Round. If the turn-up is turned down, the question of whether to make is much the same for all players—name a trump with two fairly sure tricks, thus counting on partner for a probable trick. The rejected suit may be a factor in a choice. Thus, it is an old rule of thumb for eldest hand to name *next,* and for dealer's partner to *cross.* Rejection of a suit by dealer's side is some indication that it does not hold the left bower, whereas the opponents might have it and reject the turn-up for other considerations. However, this old rule is of more interest to people who like to bid because it is their turn than to people who bid on values in sight.

Playing Alone. Apart from the possession of three or more sure tricks, the warrant for playing alone is the state of the score. All that is to be gained is 4 points for march instead of 2. Of course when his hand is ironclad for three tricks, the player should call alone. But he cannot always wait for this insurance. If the opponents are at the bridge, and his side has 1 or 2, he must play alone if he makes at all, else his side's chance of winning the game is microscopic. Contrariwise, a side with 3 or 4 should never call alone.

The Play. A player with three trumps plus any plain card he hopes to win should normally lead a trump, to lessen the chances that the plain card will be trumped. He may not be able to afford this luxury if he has to use a trump to gain the lead, or if he is an opponent of the dealer (who thus has one trump and may have two or more). The partner of the maker, with one small trump and no void suit, may well lead it for the same general purpose.

Other than this occasional opportunity to lead trumps, the play is mostly a matter of putting up the highest card on every lead and leading the highest plain card after winning a trick. The chance for partners to "show each other" what they have is fleeting. If there is any dependable rule, it is: Lead a plain ace or king at once when you get in, lest your partner never discover it.

CRIBBAGE

Cribbage is essentially a two-hand game, but its devotees have adapted it to play by three and by four players—also, by one player, for there are several Cribbage Solitaires! We describe the standard two-hand game.

In Cribbage the primary objective is to form the hand into certain scoring combinations. Unlike other games of "structure," Cribbage combines this feature with play of the cards, from which additional scoring arises. The method and objective of the play is unique among all card games.

How to Play Cribbage

The Cribbage Board. The scoring is by small increments, accruing rapidly, so that keeping track with pencil and paper is fussy business. Practically indispensable is a *cribbage board*. This scoring device is a good investment, for it can be utilized in many different games.

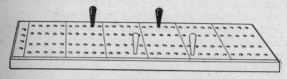

Fig. 4—Cribbage board.

The board is an oblong wooden or plastic panel, having 120 holes arranged in four rows of 30 each. There may be two or four extra holes, called *game holes,* at one end. With the board are supplied two *pegs* of one color and two pegs of another color. Each player keeps his own score by advancing the two pegs of his allotted color along the two rows of holes on his side of the board. The customary route is away from the game hole, on the outside row, then back toward the game hole on the inside row.

For his first score, the player puts one peg the appropriate distance along the outside row, each hole representing one point. For the second score, the second peg is put the appropriate distance ahead of the first. Thereafter, the rear peg is jumped ahead of the forward peg, the distance between the two always showing the amount of the last score earned, and the forward peg always showing the player's total score.

Before commencing a game of Cribbage, settle with your opponent whether the *game* shall be 121 points or 61 points. "Twice around" (121) is a fairer test, but some players prefer the "murder or sudden death" of "once around."

Scoring, particularly during the play, is called *pegging*.

The Deal. Use a regular deck of 52 cards. As the dealer has an advantage, you should cut cards for the right to deal first. The lower card wins. The ace ranks lowest, king highest.

Deal cards one at a time, until each player has six cards. After these hands are played out, gather all the cards, shuffle, and deal again. The right to deal alternates.

Laying Away. After looking at his cards, each player *lays away* two cards face down. The remaining four are his *hand*. The four cards laid away form the *crib*, which is a second hand belonging to the dealer.

Next, the non-dealer cuts the stock and the dealer turns up the top card of the bottom packet. (This card is customarily placed on top of the stock after the cut is closed.) This card is the *starter*. If the starter is a jack, the dealer pegs 2, for *his heels*, as the saying goes.

Combinations. The object in laying away is primarily to retain the four cards that will give the highest count of scoring combinations. The starter is construed as being a part of both hands and of the crib, so that it may add further combinations. Scoring is as follows:

FIFTEENS. Each combination of two or more cards that totals 15 scores 2 points. The king, queen, jack, and ten have the numerical value of 10 each (therefore being called *tenth cards*); ace is 1; each other card counts its pip value. Thus any tenth card and a fivespot make a *fifteen;* so do an ace, a six, and an eight; etc.

Throughout the scoring, "combination" is used in its precise sense. For example, suppose your hand to contain ♠ K, ♥ 5, ♦ 5. You may peg 2 for the fifteen given by ♠ K-♥ 5; you may also peg 2 for the ♠ K-♦ 5. Although you have used the ♠ K in both combinations, you may score separately for each grouping of the cards that differs by one or more individual cards from any other grouping. Take another example; suppose your hand is ♥ 8, ♣ 8, ♥ 7, ♣ 7. Each eightspot can be combined with either of two sevens, making four combinations, each of which is a *fifteen;* you therefore peg $4 \times 2 = 8$. In each case you will score, in addition for *pair*, as explained below.

When you first learn Cribbage, you may find difficulty in determining how many scoring combinations you hold. But • with a little practice you learn certain common patterns and their (minimum) value. Some of the patterns are given later in this article.

RUNS. Each combination of three or more cards in sequence scores one point for each card in the sequence. For example, 3-4-5 (the cards being of any suits) scores 3 points; Q-J-10-9 scores four points. Here again each *combination* scores separately. Thus, 9-9-8-7 scores 6 points for two runs, since either ninespot may be used at the head of the sequence. Observe, however, that you are not permitted to construe a run of four (Q-J-10-9) as two runs of three (Q-J-10 and J-10-9). You must include all possible cards in a single sequence.

PAIRS. Each combination of two cards of the same rank scores 2 points. Three-of-a-kind (*pair royal,* sometimes condensed to *proil*) scores 6, since it contains three combinations of two. Four-of-a-kind (*double pair royal*) scores 12.

FLUSH. Four cards of the same suit in the hand score 4 points for *flush*. A flush in the crib scores nothing unless the starter is also of the same suit, when it scores 5.

HIS NOBS. If the jack of the same suit as the starter is in either hand or in the crib, the owner pegs one point for *his nobs,* as the saying goes.

The hand having the highest possible score is J-5-5-5, when the starter is the 5 of the same suit as the jack. It counts 8 for fifteens made with the jack, plus 8 for fifteens made with fives alone, plus 12 for double pair royal, plus 1 for his nobs: a total of 29.

Hands can occur that total anything between zero and 29, except 19, 25, 26, and 27. A traditional way of saying "I have no score" is to say "I have nineteen."

Besides the specific cards that make fifteens, the following are desirable patterns:

DOUBLE RUN, a run of three with one card duplicated, as 10-9-9-8. It scores 8 for runs and pair.

TRIPLE RUN, a run of three with one card triplicated, as 10-9-9-9-8. It scores 15 for runs and pair royal.

QUADRUPLE RUN, a run of three with two different cards duplicated, as 10-10-9-9-8. It scores 16 for runs and pairs.

The Play. The starter being turned, the play begins. The non-dealer begins by laying a card face up on the table, announcing its numerical value. The dealer then faces any card, announcing the total of the two cards. For example, the non-dealer may begin with the ♠ 4, saying "Four." The dealer show the ♥ Q, saying "Fourteen."

Cards are thus laid down alternately, each player stating the cumulative total and keeping possession of his own cards. The total may not exceed 31. If a player is unable to play in turn without exceeding 31, he must say "Go," whereupon his opponent pegs one point. If a player makes exactly 31, it is an automatic *go* and he pegs 2.

After a player has said "Go," his opponent must continue play if possible, stopping only when he is unable to lay down any more cards.

After a player has scored for a *go*, his opponent must play first for the next series of plays, starting again from zero. Sometimes all the eight cards are exhausted by the first series of plays; sometimes there are three series.

The dealer is bound to score at least one go, since non-dealer must play the first card. Playing the last card of the eight always scores a go, even though the same hand may have played twice in succession, the opponent having no cards left. For example, suppose that the dealer has four jacks and the non-dealer has four aces. The play proceeds: A, J, A, J, A, "Go" by dealer, whereupon non-dealer must play his last card (making 24) ; dealer then plays J, J, and scores for last card. Similarly, suppose that all the cards in play total less than 32; they are all played out in one series, and dealer scores 1 for last (or 2, if it makes 31).

Pegging. During the play, the following points additional to *go* may be pegged:

FIFTEEN. Peg 2 for making the cumulative total 15.

PAIRS. Peg 2 for playing a card of same rank as the last previously played (either by opponent or self). Peg 6 for playing the third successive card of same rank, or 12 for the fourth of the same rank.

RUNS. Peg one for each card in the run for adding the third, fourth, or later card, whenever three or more cards played in succession make a run. This score counts regardless of whether the cards are played in strict sequence, so long as taken together they constitute a run. For example, if the successive plays are 9-7-8, the player of the eightspot pegs 3 just as though the order were 9-8-7. The players may score alternately for the same sequence by extending it. For example: 4-6-5 (peg 3 for run plus 2 for fifteen) -3 (peg 4 for run) -7 (peg 5 for run). As with pairs, a player may score for run with extra cards he plays after his opponent has called "Go."

Showing. After the hands are played out, the scoring combinations they contain are counted and scored. The non-dealer *shows* (counts his hand) first. This point is important, because if he reaches 121 or 61 by virtue of his first turn, he wins the game forthwith; it does not matter that the dealer might reach a greater total if allowed to count his hand and crib.

The customary method of counting is to reckon in order: fifteens, runs, pairs, flush, his nobs. The total in each category is announced, and finally the grand total. An optional feature is *muggins*—if a player counts less than his due, his opponent may call "Muggins!" and peg the missed score for himself. You had better discuss muggins with your opponent before beginning a game, and agree on it, else there may be hard feelings. You ought to waive muggins when your opponent is inexperienced; help him to learn how to score his hands.

After the non-dealer has shown, dealer shows (counts) his hand, and finally turns the crib face up and shows it.

Settlement. The player who first reaches game (121 or 61) wins forthwith, and any settlement of stakes is based upon his opponent's score at that moment. Thus a player may "peg out" during the play of a hand, whereupon all the scoring combinations in the two hands and the crib go for naught.

The loser of a game is *lurched* if he has not passed the halfway mark, i.e. if he has not reached 31 when the game is "once around" or 61 when it is "twice around." For lurch, the winner collects double the basic stake.

STRATEGY OF CRIBBAGE

Laying Away. The dealer, in laying away, should naturally strive to retain the maximum count in his hand and crib after the separation. For example:

(1) Hand Q-J-9-7-7-4. Lay away Q-J.

(2) Hand Q-10-8-7-5-3. Lay away 8-7.

(3) Hand 8-6-6-4-3-2. Lay away 6-6.

(4) Hand K-9-6-6-5-4. Lay away K-9.

(5) Hand J-7-4-4-4-A. Lay away J-A.

The combination having the greatest chance of being improved by the starter is the run. Scarcely a hand can be concocted where it would be good policy to break up a run. In Example 3, the 6-6-3 combination could be preserved only by splitting the 4-3-2; as between a fifteen and a run, the experienced player splits the fifteen automatically. With a poor hand, when nothing better offers, keep *near* cards that could be promoted to a run by the starter. Thus:

(6) Hand K-9-7-6-3-A. Lay away K-3. Keep the 9-6 for the count, and the 7 because of the run possibility. The A is the best choice for the fourth card, as it will give an extra fifteen if the desired 8 turns up.

When feasible, keep one or two low cards, since they have better chance than high cards of scoring for go. An ace is of course best of all; this is an added reason for the choice in Example 6.

(7) Hand K-J-9-7-4-3. Lay away K-J. With this score-
less hand, keep all the lower cards as the best
chance of pegging in play.

The non-dealer, in laying away, should naturally strive
to keep maximum count if he has a good hand. But an
additional factor must be weighed. Since his cards go to his
opponent, he should try to *balk* the chance formation of
scoring combinations in the crib, so far as he can. This
factor is of minor importance if he has such a hand as
Example 4 or Example 5, but affects all the other examples,
and all middling or poor hands generally.

The non-dealer should never give a fivespot—such a card
has maximum potential value, since the starter is more
likely to be a tenth card than any other. To a much less
degree, a jack is better kept, as it may score for his nobs.
In Example 1, the non-dealer should lay away Q-9. To give
Q-J would be wrong in two ways—it might give dealer a
sequence; it might give his nobs. These considerations
outweigh the chance for a killing that is given up by letting
go the 9 (turn of an 8 would make double run if 9-7-7 were
kept).

It is obvious that *wide* cards (separated in rank by three
or more) are better *balking cards* than *near cards*. In Example 7, the non-dealer would take double risk if he gave
the K-J. Preferable is to lay away the king and either the 9
or the 7.

Close questions arise with hands that have large chances
for improvement. In Example 3, non-dealer certainly should
not give the 6-6. Safest, perhaps, would be to give the 8-2,
also keeping 4 points intact. But best is to give 8-6, even
though they are near cards, in order to keep 5 points including the run.

(8) Hand J-J-8-7-7-6. Either player should lay away J-J.
The value of the double run (8, plus 4 for
fifteens) is enough to justify non-dealer's risk in
giving the jacks—2 cash points plus chances of
his nobs and of fifteens. As starter, only a jack

> or a five will improve the jacks, while any card
> but a 4 or a tenth card will improve the double
> run.

For various reasons, the non-dealer is likely to give the
crib a tenth card, wherefore the dealer should, if feasible,
lay away a fivespot rather than keep it in his hand.

> (9) Hand Q-9-7-5-4-2. Dealer should lay away the Q-5.
> He cannot keep both fifteens (Q-5 and 9-4-2)
> otherwise; this factor plus the potential value of
> the 5 to the crib warrants giving up the potential
> run (5-4).

The Play. The paramount problem of the play is whether
to play *on* or *off*. To play *on* is to give your opponent a
likely chance to score, as by making a fifteen or a run. To
play *off* is to head away from such chances. For example,
if the leader starts with a 6 and you play an 8, you are
playing *on*, because he could peg 3 for run with a 7. You
would give him this chance with such a hand as Q-J-8-5,
for if he pegged 3 you would play the 5 and peg 4. But if
your hand were Q-J-8-4, play of the 8 would be a mistake;
you should play *off* with a tenth card, preventing both
fifteen and a run.

Whether to play on or off depends on the situation—the
count, the cards you hold, what inferences you can draw
about your opponent's cards. In general, the hands that
invite playing on hold several near or sequential inter-
mediates (8, 7, 6). For example, the non-dealer with 8-7
may well start with one of them (although such inter-
mediates are usually treasured) because if the dealer makes
a fifteen, the non-dealer can play the other and score for
pair. Better still is to lead an 8 from 8-8-7 or 7 from 8-7-7,
because then if dealer makes a pair the leader can retort
with pair royal.

Obviously the most undesirable opening lead is a fivespot,
for it gives the dealer maximum chance to make fifteen.
Proverbially the best opening lead is a four, since the dealer
can neither make fifteen nor pass fifteen. A lower card

would have the same effect, but such lower cards are best treasured to eke out a go when the count is high. Next to a fourspot, a tenth card is best, if only to get rid of it. But, as shown by the above examples, a particular hand may suggest playing *on* at the opening lead, with some intermediate rank.

Except to make a scoring combination, a very low card should not be played until it is forced out. Some players make a fetish of never laying away an ace, so likely is this card to eke out a go. If no other consideration supervenes, play your highest card at each turn.

CASINO

This game is a hardy perennial among juveniles. We tend to look down our nose at Casino as a trivial pastime; yet it is in fact a game of greater skill and imagination than many of the superficially complex games played so solemnly by adults.

The variant here described is Royal Casino, not the austere parent game in which face cards can be won only by pairing. It is best for two players, though it can easily be adapted for three or four.

How to Play Casino

The Deal. Use a regular deck of 52 cards. The deck is brought into play by stages, through successive deals of four cards at a time to each hand. One player deals until the deck is exhausted; then the cards are gathered, shuffled, and the other player deals until the deck is again exhausted.

Custom is to deal cards in batches of two at a time. For the first deal with the newly-shuffled deck, the dealer gives two cards to his opponent, then two face up on the table, then two to himself, then repeats this round so that each player has four cards and there are four face up on the table. For the remaining deals of the series, each player again receives four cards but no additional cards are dealt to the table. The dealer traditionally gives warning when he reaches the end of the deck, by saying "Last deal."

The Play. Beginning with non-dealer, each player alternately plays one card from his hand, until the two hands are exhausted. The played card may be used to *take in* cards, or to *build,* or to *trail.*

To *trail* is to lay the card face up on the table, separate from the rest. It is a negative act that says, in effect, "I cannot or will not make positive use of the card at this time."

To *take in* is to gather cards from the table with the card from the hand. Each player keeps the cards he gathers in, face down in one pile. The object of the play is to take in as many cards as possible, and also to win certain specific cards.

Building will be explained later.

Scoring Points. The points to be scored by cards taken in are as follows:

Cards, a majority of the 52 cards	3
Spades, a majority of the 13 spades	1
Big Casino, the ♦10	2
Little Casino, the ♠ 2	1
Aces, each ace counting	1
Sweeps, each counting	1

A *sweep* is scored when a player takes in all cards remaining on the table, leaving it bare. To mark the sweep, he turns one card face up in his pile of cards taken in.

After the last deal is played out, any cards remaining on the table belong to the player who was last to *take in,* but gathering these cards by default, as it were, does not score a sweep.

Pairing. The simplest way of taking in cards is by *pairing.* A card on the table may be taken by another of the same rank, from the hand. Furthermore, several of the same rank may be taken by one card. For example, suppose that there are two jacks on the table. You can take them both with a jack from your hand. Or suppose you have two sixes and there is also a six on the table. In one turn you may place a six from your hand on top of that on the table, leaving the pile to be gathered by your remaining six at your next turn. You must give due notice by saying "Building sixes."

Building. Cards may also be taken in by building. For this purpose, every card has a numerical value, as follows:

Ace, at option of player . . 1 or 14
King 13
Queen 12
Jack 11
Each other card, its nominal value

Two or more cards may be taken in at one turn, with a card equal to their numerical total. For example, you may take a five and a two with a seven, or a five, a four, and a three with a queen. Furthermore, such builds may be duplicated and paired as many times as the available cards permit. For example, you may gather a king, a seven, and a six with another king, or ten, four, eight, six, with an ace.

The high card necessary to take in a build must come from your hand, never from the table. For example, if you find a seven and a four on the table, you may not play a three and then gather the three cards.

A card from the hand may be added to one or more on the table, making a build that can be taken next turn. For example, you may put a seven from your hand on a four on the table, if you have a jack in your hand. On making any such build, you must announce what you are building, as "Eleven." While the cards in this case make your intention obvious, in other cases the cards may be ambiguous. For example, when you build a six on a six, you might intend to take the pile with a third six or with a queen; you must specify.

When a build is left on the table (not taken at once), the cards are put in one pile. The pile may not be broken up, to use the separate cards in a different way, but may be captured as a whole by the opponent of the builder. For example, suppose you have built thirteen and your opponent has a king; he may take your build.

Under certain circumstances, a build may be *increased*. Suppose that your opponent has built seven. You hold a four and a jack. You may add the four to his build, calling "Eleven," and next turn take the pile with your jack. In the meantime he might of course take it with a jack, or even increase it again with two or ace to make thirteen or twelve.

To increase a build, you must add a card from your hand, never from the table. For example, if your opponent has built seven and there is a fourspot on the table, you may not add it to the build and gather all with a jack. This rule, plus the rule that to make a build you must have a card in your hand that can take in the build, rarely allows you to increase your own build, although it is theoretically possible to do so. For example, suppose your cards are 2-4-J-K. There is a seven on the table. You put your four on it, calling "Eleven." Next turn you add the two, calling "Thirteen."

A build that is duplicated in any way may not be increased. For example, your opponent has built a four, five, and nine, calling "Nines." It would not be permissible for you to add, say, a three, and call "Twelve."

A player who has left a build on the table must, at his next turn, take in something or else add to his existing build —he may not *trail*. For example, suppose that you have built ten, having in your hand a tenspot and a three. Your opponent trails with a seven. You may play the three on the seven and add the two cards to your existing build. Or suppose he trails with a three. You may take it by pairing, reserving your ten in the hope of catching something more next turn. But suppose he plays a queen, and you find nothing on the table to take in but your build. You must take it; you may not trail.

Scoring. After the last deal is played out (residual cards on the table going to the player last to take in), the points taken in by each player are counted. The custom is for the player with the fewer cards to run through them and count; the opponent's score is then determined by the fact that the points to be won, exclusive of sweeps, total 11.

A game is won by the first to reach 21 points. Many players allow *counting out*. If, during the play, a player claims correctly that he has won enough points to bring his total to 21, he wins forthwith, even though his opponent might reach an equal or greater total were the deal played out. If the claim is incorrect, the claimant loses the game forthwith.

If *counting out* is not allowed, the final deal is played out. If the points are so split that both players could reach 21, the points are counted in order: cards, spades, Big Casino, Little Casino, ♠ A, ♣ A, ♥ A, ♦ A, sweeps. The first to reach 21 on this count wins the game.

STRATEGY OF CASINO

The non-dealer has an advantage, most of the time, in his opportunity to play first after each deal. He should capitalize it in every way. One way is to gather as many low cards as he can on his first turn, so reducing the chances for the dealer to make builds. Another way is to save a low card for a final trail in one deal, so as to use it (probably) in his first turn of the next. This tactic gives non-dealer a better chance than dealer to save the "cash points" dealt to him—aces and little casino. Of course, these low cards should be saved by pairing and building, when possible, and the right to make an ace 14 should be worked for all it is worth. But sometimes no opportunity presents itself; non-dealer can often pick up his cash point on the ensuing deal by saving it for his last trail. The dealer at that time has only one card left, and so can take in only by finding the right numbers on the table.

The dealer must offset his disadvantage, so far as he can, by pressing his chance to play last in a deal. He should reserve a high card, usually, to pick up low cards by building in his last turn. If the residual cards on the table will decide who wins the big 3 points for *cards,* dealer should plan his whole play so as to be sure of *taking in* last.

Keep track of all the cards you can without undue fatigue. With a little practice you will find that you can keep track of a good deal. Start by remembering merely the cash points—aces and the casinos. Bear in mind how many are yet to be dealt. Next count the spades won by each side. Watch the piles of cards taken in, and learn to estimate when a pile has reached 26 cards or more. Presently you will find that you can also keep track of kings, queens, and jacks. The question of how many of the high cards are still in play has important bearing on the safety of your builds.

Offensive tactics are fairly obvious. Try for *cards* so long as there is a chance; therefore take in two or three cards at a time in preference to one. Take a spade in preference to another card of the same rank. Grab a cash point when you can, and if dealt a cash card concentrate on saving it.

Defensive tactics are not so obvious. If forced to trail, try to avoid leaving a combination on the table that totals ten or fourteen—so long as Big Casino or any ace is yet to come. If there is only one card on the table, trail with a card that carries the total over fourteen—so as to avert a sweep. If dealt four low cards, with prospect of having to trail at every turn, try to minimize the extent to which you "feed" your opponent. For example, if he takes in some cards with a jack, trail thereafter when you can so as to make a combination of eleven on the table, rather than twelve, thirteen, etc., on the assumption that he does not have a second jack. Avoid trailing with a card that would allow the board to be swept. For example, with queen and eight only on the board, don't trail with a four—pick a five or three. If nothing better offers, trail with your four cards from highest down—the lowest card is most likely to be useful to him, and the longer you hold it the more likely he is to have lost the opportunity to use it.

HEARTS

You can be just as studious or just as carefree as you wish in playing Hearts—either way it's a good game. You have no partner to placate. Four or five may join in; six or more, if you shuffle two decks together. Hearts is a good party game, for the rules can be learned in two minutes, and the play lends itself to boisterousness. At the same time, the serious-minded find no less opportunity for skill than exists in, say, Contract Bridge.

The best game for serious play is four-handed, each person playing for himself.

How to Play Hearts

The Deal. Use a regular deck of 52 cards. The dealer distributes the whole deck, one card at a time, beginning with the player at his left. With four players, each receives thirteen cards. (With five players, discard the two of clubs and two of diamonds, and deal ten to each.)

The Pass. After looking at his hand, each player passes any three cards face down to the player at his left. He must not look at the cards he receives from his right until he has passed to his left.

Some players follow the plan of passing to left and then to right in alternate deals. This is a good plan when there are five or more players, for it savors of equalization. But passing to the right compounds the chances of being ruined by the pass, whereas passing to the left offsets the potential damage. (In the latter case, the recipient plays *after* the donor, in the clockwise rotation of play.) This difference is perhaps palatable in a large game, where the player has relatively little control of his destiny anyhow, but it rather spoils the four-hand game.

The Play. The opening lead is made by the player at the left of the dealer. He may lead any card. Each other hand must follow suit to a lead if able; if unable, the hand may play any card. A trick is won by the highest card of the suit led. The winner of a trick leads to the next. Each player gathers his own tricks in one pile. In some circles it is the custom to turn the *counters* (cards of scoring value) face up, as they are won.

Object of Play. Each heart taken in tricks counts 1 point against the player. The queen of spades (known as *Black Lady, Black Maria, Calamity Jane,* etc.) counts 13 against the winner.

The ten of diamonds counts 10 plus to the winner. If one player gathers all the counters—the thirteen hearts, the queen of spades, and the ten of diamonds—he earns 26 plus for *take-all,* the other players scoring nothing.

The object of play is simply to avoid winning minus cards and to win the diamond ten or make a take-all.

Scoring. After each deal, each player runs through his tricks and reports his net of minus or plus points. The running total for each player is recorded on paper, one column for each player.

The game ends when some player reaches or exceeds a total score of minus 100. The winner is the one who has the best score at that time. If there are monetary stakes, each player settles with every other according to the difference of their scores. Another plan is to treat each deal as a separate game, settle at once, and terminate the session at some prefixed time.

STRATEGY OF HEARTS

Collusion. Though each plays for himself, Hearts is perforce a game of tacit collusion. For example, suppose that the scores are: A, -21; B, -42; C, -59; D, -86. Player A wants to put D down to -100, for then he himself will win the game. Players B and C have every interest in saving D from this fate, until such time as they can reduce A's commanding lead. Consequently, there is a conspiracy among the other three players against A.

Conspiracies frequently arise during the play of a deal. For example: A and B both lead spades when they can. C has the ace and king insufficiently guarded, and D—who does not know this fact—feels himself in trouble because he has the queen insufficiently guarded. C and D naturally combine to help D get rid of Black Maria by discard. D leads a singleton club, and C captures the first lead he can in order to lead a second round of clubs.

The make-up of these collusive combinations shifts from time to time, perhaps from trick to trick, in accordance with circumstances. Now, the cardinal rule of serious Hearts is that players must not "talk across the table." Collusion must proceed by tacit recognition of common advantage, not by exhortation and not by verbal revelation of facts that properly a player is entitled to know only by inference. One of the commonest and most grievous sins is to ask a fellow-player, "Have you won any hearts?" The purpose is to ascertain whether a third player can possibly make a *take-all*. The inquiry unfairly draws attention to the possible necessity of defending against a take-all attempt.

The Four Campaigns. According to his hand, a player may essay any of four general plans:

(a) *Take-none:* win only non-dangerous tricks, avoid minus cards;

(b) *Catch-the-ten:* accept a few hearts, if necessary, to catch the ♦ 10;

(c) *Save-the-ten:* win a trick with the ♦ 10, at minimum cost in hearts;

(d) *Take-all:* win all the counters.

Easily ninety percent of the hands you are dealt will allow only (a) or (b); a goodly number of them will leave you choice between the two, according to what you receive and how the play goes. In any case, you rarely have to choose before the pass. But if you decide on (c) or (d), you must make the pass with your objective clearly in mind.

The Pass. The primary function of the pass is to give you opportunity to mitigate dangerous holdings.

In spades, the queen accompanied by two or less other spades is very dangerous: pass the queen. Even three other spades may be hazardous, but if one of them is high—ace, king, or even jack—don't pass the queen. Similarly, the ace and/or king of spades with only two lower cards is dangerous: you must usually pass the tops. But with three or more lower cards, usually keep the tops. You may also speculate on keeping A x x or K x x if you are the dealer. (The player at your left may open spades.)

As a matter of course, never pass spades below the rank of queen. These cards are guards against the receipt of top spades from your neighbor.

In all other suits, an intrinsically dangerous holding is three or more cards lacking any low cards, such as J 9 8, K 10 8 7. The danger is in being forced to win two or three leads of the suit, on one of which Black Maria is discarded. The relative danger of the suits may be broadly estimated as: clubs, most dangerous; diamonds, middling; hearts, least dangerous. This estimate is based on the observed frequency with which the pass establishes a void. Any short club holding is usually passed by a hand that has "spade trouble." Diamonds are passed for the same reason, but top honors tend to be saved to catch the ten. Low hearts are rarely passed; they are saved as protection against the receipt of high hearts.

For take-none, pass two or three cards from a danger suit, if you have no more pressing trouble (spades). Pass all of a short high holding in hearts, if you can. Pass the ten of diamonds—it is better out of your hand than in unless you have the rare save-the-ten type of hand. Usually save low hearts and top diamonds.

Here are some examples of passing for take-none.

(1) ♠ A 7 5   ♥ J 8 4 3   ♦ Q 9   ♣ K Q 9 8

Pass ♠ A, ♣ Q, ♣ 9, mitigating the worst dangers.

(2) ♠ A Q 9 7   ♥ K J   ♦ K 8 5 3 2   ♣ 7

Pass ♥ K, ♥ J, ♣ 7. The spade holding is fairly safe. Reduce the danger of gathering a flock of hearts, and establish a club void for possible discard of the ♠ Q.

(3) ♠ Q 4   ♥ A J 5 3   ♦ J 10 9 8   ♣ Q 9 2

Pass ♠ Q, ♦ 10, ♣ 9. Against the receipt of high spades you are helpless. But by giving a diamond and a club with the ♠ Q, you are sure of being able to play a high card safely on the first round of each suit.

A *catch-the-ten* campaign is suggested by a hand with some well-guarded high cards. The ideal course of play for this hand is to have the ♠ Q forced out early, whereupon all high cards are saved in the effort to win the last several tricks, catching the ♦ 10 by default. (Catching the ten on straight diamond leads is very rare.) The typical catch-the-ten suits are: clubs, some high and some very low cards; diamonds, few low cards or none; hearts, same as clubs; spades, a safe holding from which spades can be led repeatedly to force out the queen.

Here are some examples of passing with catch-the-ten in view.

(4) ♠ 10 8 6 3   ♥ 4   ♦ K 7 3   ♣ A Q J 3 2

Pass ♦ 7, ♦ 3, ♣ J. Any top hearts, or ♠ A, ♠ K, received in the pass will help, for then this hand should gain entry several times to lead spades and still be left with some top cards.

(5) ♠ A Q 7 6 4 2   ♥ J   ♦ A 10 7 4   ♣ K Q 7

Pass ♥ J, ♦ 10, ♦ 7. The hope is to get rid of the ♠ Q early, on the ♠ K or on a heart trick. Receipt of low diamonds would spoil the fun; top hearts would cost some minus points; but nothing, probably, can seriously endanger this hand even if the ♦ 10 goes glimmering, while some high cards would promote it to a take-all prospect.

A *take-all* sometimes results, without premeditation, from the receipt of specific high cards or from the vagaries of play. As is shown by Example 5, a catch-the-ten pass may turn into a take-all hand. But in the majority of cases, a take-all is planned before the pass. For this purpose, the most dangerous cards are: the ♦ 10, fatal; low hearts, unless accompanied by several tops, fatal; low diamonds, dangerous; a long club suit without the ace, dubious.

Here are some examples of passing for a take-all.

(6) ♠ K Q 5   ♥ A Q 7   ♦ K 10 6   ♣ A K 10 5

Pass ♥ 7, ♦ 10, ♦ 6. As with most prospects, this hand stands to be ruined by receipt of small hearts or diamonds.

(7) ♠ 7   ♥ K Q J 9 8 3   ♦ 6 4 2   ♣ A J 5

Pass ♦ 6, ♦ 4, ♦ 2. This pass is a two-way proposition. The spade situation is desperate. The best defense when dealt only one or two small spades is to void your hand of clubs or diamonds. Choose the diamonds so that if you miraculously receive the ♥ A you have take-all prospects.

The campaign hardest to plan with any likelihood of success is *save-the-ten*. Here is an "angle" that sometimes occurs; you are dealer, and your hand is

(8) ♠ A K 7 4   ♥ 3   ♦ A J 10 9 4   ♣ 8 7 3

Pass ♠ A, ♠ K, ♦ 9. That may give your left neighbor "spade trouble," so that he will not open the suit. If he has shortened himself in diamonds, he may then open the ♦ 9, hoping to get rid of top spades on diamond leads. Maybe both the ♦ K and ♦ Q will be withheld. All this may be a pipe dream—but so is any *save-the-ten* plan!

The Play. Where no player has special ambitions (save-the-ten or take-all), the normal course of play is that spades are led at every opportunity by hands that do not have "spade trouble." The best insurance against gathering Black Maria as a discard is to force her out on straight leads. Failure of eldest hand to open spades carries the inference: spade trouble or special interests.

Most of the time, you can infer very early who has Black Maria. Use this knowledge to stay out of trouble—by getting rid of dangerous high cards on tricks to which he has already played. Note what he leads and whether you have a dangerous holding in that suit. He will probably lead his shortest suit—perhaps cashing some top cards first, to avoid being thrown back—and if you have no special interests to serve, continue that suit when you can from a safe holding.

In a thorough-going take-none campaign, put up your top cards from short holdings on the first round rather than later. For example, from ♣ K 2, play or lead the king first (unless Black Maria has already been shed on the lead!) But there is no percentage in ditching well-guarded top cards. With ♣ A Q 7 4 2, you can scarcely be forced to win a dangerous trick; save the ace on the general principle that sometime you might *want* to win a trick to take advantage of a special situation that has arisen.

When you intend to *exit* (get out of the lead), decide what you want to do—do you want to get out merely at this moment, or do you want to stay out so long as possible? Mediocre players make ludicrous mistakes in exiting; the commonest is to lead one precious low card prematurely, leaving the hand replete with forced entries. Give a thought to the possible necessity of cashing singleton or doubleton high cards, before exiting. In the extreme you may have to execute "the grand exit," gathering some hearts to avoid a worse fate. For example, you hold

(9) ♠ A Q 7 6 5   ♥ K J   ♦ A 7 3   ♣ K 8 4

With visions of take-all, you pass ♦ 7, ♦ 3, ♣ 8. But you receive the ♦ 10, which ruins the hope, plus ♣ J, ♣ 9. The play goes badly for you, too. Spades are led twice through you, leaving only the ♠ 3 and ♠ 2 at large. Then clubs are plugged, and you are eventually forced in, either through a club or a heart.

You cannot take all; you cannot save the ten; all you can do is to avoid gathering your own ♠ Q besides a due flock of hearts. The only sure exit is (say) the ♦ 10. Get rid first of the cards that might stick you back in the lead. Clean out the low spades by cashing the ace. Cash the hearts. Lead any club you have left. (Incidentally, this showing of take-all stuff may induce someone to capture one of your heart leads, thus reducing your eventual loss.) Only after you are void of hearts and clubs, cash the ♦ A and then lead the ♦ 10.

Generalizations about the play are largely futile—so much depends on specific inferences. To improve your game, keep track of all the cards played, and be alert to the many inferences available about the distribution of the remaining cards.

EIGHTS

This game is sometimes called Swedish Rummy, though it is neither Swedish nor Rummy. It is a member of the Stops family (another Stops game is Michigan), and is the only really good two-hand variant of that group. It may also be played by three or more, up to about seven.

How to Play Eights

The Deal. Use a regular deck of 52 cards. With two players, deal seven cards to each. With more than two, each hand is five cards. Large games—say six or seven players—may well use two regular decks shuffled together.

After the hands are dealt, the rest of the deck is placed face down in the center of the table to form the *stock*. The top card is turned face up beside it, to form the *starter*.

The Play. The hand at the left of the dealer plays first. He must lay on the starter a card from his hand that matches it, either in suit or in rank. For example, if the starter is the six of clubs, he must play a club or a six. If unable to play, he must draw cards one by one from the top of the stock until he can.

The turn rotates clockwise, and each player in turn must

play a card on the face-up pile that matches the last played. When unable to play from his hand, the player must draw from the stock.

The eights are *wild* cards. An eight is always playable, regardless of what card lies at that moment on the discard pile. On playing an eight, the owner must specify a suit, and the next hand must follow with that suit. (The eight may never be named to call a rank.)

After the stock is exhausted, a hand that cannot play says "Pass" and the turn goes to the next player. It is illegal to pass when holding an eight.

The player who first gets rid of all his cards wins the deal.

Scoring. The winner of a deal scores all the points remaining in the other hands. Face cards count 10 each, aces 1, eights 50, and other cards their index value. The player who first reaches a total of 100 points wins a game. An alternative method (usual with three or more players) is to use Poker chips; all players contribute equal antes to a pool, and the winner of the deal takes the pool.

STRATEGY OF EIGHTS

There is more to this simple game than meets the eye. It is rare for a deal to be won by a hand that has never drawn from the stock. In two-hand play especially, thought must be given to the possible advantage of holding up an eight, even at the cost of drawing from the stock. Many times, a player who has more cards in his hand than his opponent is able to go out first. He runs the opponent out of one suit (often aided by his monopoly of this suit), and reserves his eights to call for this suit. Sometimes he thus compels the opponent to draw the rest of the stock—from which the named suit is exhausted. At other times, he may get rid of most of his hand before the opponent again has opportunity to play.

If you are dealt an eight, commence with the idea of holding it for your next-to-last play. If you get rid of all but two cards without drawing, you then play the eight and call for the suit of your last card.

If you have to draw, and you get an eight before you get a natural card, dig a little deeper—it is worth a few extra cards to be able to save the eight.

Keeping track of the number of cards of each suit played is a great help in deciding questions of tactics. When you can so remember the cards, you will often find opportunity to turn imminent defeat into victory. You "dig" to get an eight or save an eight, and then block your opponent in the end-play after the stock is exhausted.

If you are the victim of a "penultimate eight" or any such maneuver, weigh your immediate loss against the potential gain if you fight back. Accept the loss of a few points, let your opponent win the deal, rather than embark on a desperate counterattack in which your chances are incalculable. Don't "dig" for an eight with which to cross up the "penultimate eight" when you have only a few cards left anyhow. The time to draw voluntarily is when you know that you can eventually force your opponent to collect even more cards in his hand.

OH HELL

In certain family journals you are likely to find this game bowdlerized to "Oh Pshaw" or "Blackout." The genesis of the name "Oh Hell" will be obvious to you when you play it—your best-laid schemes gang aft agley. The game is among the simplest of all card games to learn, and can be pursued in a spirit of hilarity by any number from three to about seven. At the same time, it happens to offer opportunity for skill second only to a few other games, especially when played four-handed. Whatever the number, each plays for himself.

How to Play Oh Hell

The Deal. Use a regular deck of 52 cards. A game comprises a series of deals; in the first deal, each player receives one card; in the second deal, two cards; and so on. With three players, the game is fifteen deals; with four players, thirteen; with five, ten deals; with six, eight deals; with seven, seven deals.

The dealer distributes cards one at a time, beginning with the player at his left, until each has as many cards as the ordinal number of the deal. The rest of the deck is laid aside, but the top card is turned up to fix the trump suit. In four-hand, the whole deck is dealt out for the thirteenth deal and there is no trump suit.

The Bidding. After the deal, each player in turn to left of the dealer makes one bid. A scorekeeper must be appointed to record all the bids on paper. The player bids the number of tricks he will undertake to win—the exact number, not a minimum. He may bid zero if he wishes (in some circles, indicated by "Pass"). On the first deal, the only choice is between "One" and "Zero." As the number of cards per hand increases, the range of bidding increases. In the thirteenth deal, a player may bid zero or any number up to thirteen.

The Play. All players having bid, the player at left of the dealer makes the opening lead. He may lead any card. A lead calls upon each other player to follow suit if able; if unable, the hand may play any card. A trick is won by the highest trump, or, if it contains no trump, by the highest card of the suit led. The winner of a trick leads to the next.

Scoring. A player makes his bid if he takes exactly that number of tricks; he "busts" if he takes either more or less. Every player who makes his bid scores 10 points plus the bid. For example, if he makes a bid of three, he scores 13. Every player who busts scores nothing for that deal.

(This primitive scoring system does not take account of the ease of making zero bids with few cards, and the difficulty with many cards. It will doubtless be improved in time. The best proposal we have seen is to give 5 points plus the number of tricks in the deal, for a zero bid. Thus in the first deal, zero scores only 6 while a bid of one scores 11. The score for zero increases until at the sixth deal it is equal to a bid of one. Thereafter it is greater than a one-bid, until on the thirteenth deal it is equal to a bid of eight. This sliding scale is much more in accordance with the realities than the primitive system above.)

The player having the highest total score after the last deal wins the game. Settlement of monetary stakes is made between each pair of players on the difference of their scores; the winner of the game should receive an agreed bonus, say 10 points.

STRATEGY OF OH HELL

In the early deals, with few tricks in play, bidding is largely guesswork. Yet there are principles that will win on balance in the long run. In the first or second deal, possibly the third, a player should bid one on any trump if all ahead of him have passed. In the first deal (not more than four players) the leader should bid one on any card as high as a jack (possibly ten or nine); if he busts because another holds a higher card of the suit or a low trump, he will probably bust this player too by inducing him to bid zero.

After the third deal, follow a consistent policy of under-bidding rather than overbidding—it is easier to get rid of potential winners than to make them stand up by force. For example, suppose that spades are trumps and you hold ♠ A Q 3, ♥ 7. Bid two, not three. The chances are that at least one other trump has been dealt, and that you can get rid of the ♠ 3 by leading it. Another example: four-hand game; clubs are trumps and you hold ♠ 5 ♥ A 4 3 ♦ K J ♣ 9 6. The natural bid is two. The high diamonds might force you to win two tricks in the suit; on the other hand, you might take none. To bid three would be unwise; to count two diamonds, plus a heart, plus a possible trump, and to bid four, would be folly. In hearts you can probably take a trick or not as you please; a trump trick is a "maybe." Treat these holdings as a reserve on which you can fall back if you take only one diamond or none.

A primary principle of play is to lead first from an inflexible suit, rather than a flexible suit. A suit is inflexible when you have little or no control over whether you win or lose tricks in it. The typical holding is from one to three cards, none low, as J alone or 10 8 or Q 8 7. The trick-winning prospects of such suits depend on the number of cards in play, but in any case there is slight chance of *avoiding* capture of one or two tricks if the other players conspire. A single low card may make a suit flexible; two low cards almost always insure it. For example, A 2 or K J 3, have fair prospect of winning no trick in a deal not later than about the sixth, and at the same time have good prospect of winning a trick by force. A holding of A J 5 2 is practically sure-fire to win one or none as you choose.

The object in opening an inflexible suit first is of course to find out how many tricks it takes, before deciding what to do with your flexible suits.

Keep track of the bids and of the tricks at all times. The question of who will do what depends in part on who wants some more tricks and who wants none. Another factor is the total of the bids. If this total is equal to the number of tricks, the deal is *even* and all will conspire pleasantly to help each other make—to help themselves. (In some circles, the dealer is prohibited from making the deal *even*. This makes a rugged game, especially in the early deals.) In the plurality of instances, good bidding all around will make the deal *under* by one trick, so that all players will try to stick some other with an extra trick. When the deal is *under*, don't be in a hurry to grab the tricks you have bid; look rather for chances to escape the lead until such time as you can get out and stay out after making your bid.

Keep alert to read the probable cards on which the bids were based. For example, suppose that your neighbor has bid one, and in the early play he gets rid of high and intermediate cards at every opportunity—the deal being underbid. With only two cards left, he has not taken a trick. Neither have you, and you want one. Shall you trump the next-to-last trick, and risk that you will take the last also, with, say, a long club? Well, give a thought to what your neighbor should have. His play suggests that he has bid on one high trump. Better grab this trick; if you don't, your trump may fall under his.

SOLITAIRES

In this section are described some of the most popular Solitaire or Patience games. Certain features are common to all Solitaires, and a traditional terminology peculiar to them has grown up. Though such terms as we use in the individual Solitaire games below are defined in every case by the context, by way of introduction we summarize here the principal terms and their meaning. As the name implies, Solitaires are games to be played by one person.

The assemblage of all cards dealt to commence a game is called the *layout*. In directions for dealing, a *row* of cards extends from left to right, parallel to the edge of the table at which the player is seated. A *column* extends at right angles to that edge, and is usually dealt from its farthest point away (the top in a diagram) toward the player. A *pile* is a batch of cards squared up. A pile may be *spread* downward to form cards *overlapping in column,* or spread to the right to form cards *overlapping in row*.

The layout may comprise one or more of these components: *foundations, tableau, reserve*.

Foundations are all the cards of a specified rank, such as aces, where the object of play is to *build* the whole pack on the foundations. The usual rank of the cards is from ace (low) up to king (high), but where some rank other than aces may be foundations (as in Canfield) the ace and king are in sequence, since the foundation rank is invariably the lowest.

A *tableau* is an array of cards that provides "feeders" for the foundations. Usually, *building* is allowed in the tableau, in reverse direction and sometimes with greater latitude than the building on foundations. Such building allows more than the original quota of cards to be kept in active play. The tableau usually comprises a fixed number of cards or piles, and when a pile is cleared away a *space* is created that aids in building.

A *reserve* is a pile or batch of cards, of fixed number, that may be brought into play only one by one, the removal of one card releasing the next. There is never any building on a reserve.

The balance of the pack (if any) remaining after the layout is the *stock*. If the stock is turned up one card at a time, the momentarily-unplayable cards are laid face up in a *waste-pile*.

A card is *available* if under the rules it may be picked up and moved elsewhere. In most cases, the following are available: one card at a time from the reserve, any tableau card not covered by another, the top card of the waste-pile, and a card newly-turned from the stock.

Building is the act of placing one card on another, where it is restricted by rules of relationship between the cards so combined. It is almost always optional whether to make a possible build, and tableau builds can always be "unbuilt." But cards built on the *foundations* may not be retracted, except in certain special cases (as in Spider).

KLONDIKE

Many people know this popular Solitaire as Canfield, although its correct name is Klondike. The name Canfield actually belongs to another Solitaire, which we describe after this game.

A standard 52-card deck is used in Klondike.

Deal a row of seven cards, one face up at the left and the rest face down. Deal six cards in a row overlapping the six at the right of the first row. Turn the first card of this new row face up, the rest face down. Continue in the same way, with successive rows of five, four, three, two, and one. The first card of each row is face up, the rest face down. The cards may be overlapped or pushed together to make seven separate piles. The twenty-eight cards thus dealt form the *tableau*.

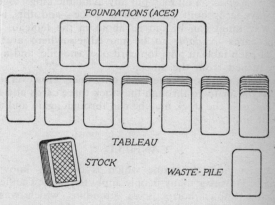

FIG. 5—Klondike layout. In each tableau pile, all cards below the top are face down.

The rest of the deck forms the *stock*. Bring these cards into play by turning them up one at a time. Any that cannot be put elsewhere are laid in one *waste-pile*, face up.

Whenever an ace becomes available, put it in a *foundation* row above the tableau. The object of play is to build each suit up on its ace, from two to king. Once you have built any card on a foundation pile, it must stay there—you may not take it back to help the building on the tableau.

On the tableau, you may build on the face-up cards in

downward sequence and alternating color. Example: the
♥ 8 may be laid on the ♠ 9 or ♣ 9. You may move either
one card at a time from the top of a pile, or all the face-up
cards together as a unit. Example: the face-up cards being
♠ 9, ♥ 8, ♣ 7, you may move the ♣ 7 (on the ♦ 8 elsewhere or on the ♣ 6 in the foundation row) or move the
three cards together (on the ♥ 10 or ♦ 10). When the
face-up cards are all cleared off a pile, turn up the top
face-down card; this card now becomes available for
building. When you clear away any tableau pile entire,
you have a *space*. You may put any available king (together
with any cards built on it) in a space—and this is the
only way kings can be moved about in the tableau.

The cards *available* to be moved elsewhere are: top
card of each tableau pile, top card of waste-pile, and a card
newly-turned from the stock.

You may go through the stock only once. However, some
persons prefer to go through the stock three cards at a time,
in which case the stock may be run through again and again
without limit.

CANFIELD

We give here the game which is correctly known as
Canfield. However many people apply the name Canfield to
the game known correctly as Klondike, which was described just before this.

From a standard 52-card deck, count off thirteen cards
face down. This is the *reserve*. In removing cards one at a
time from the top of the reserve, be careful not to expose
any of the lower cards.

To the right of the reserve, deal a row of four cards
face up, forming the *tableau*. Deal one more card above
the tableau; this is the first *foundation*. The other three
cards of the same rank are also foundations; when any
becomes available, put it in a row with the first. The object
of play is to build each suit up on the foundation. Example:
if the first foundation is the ♥ 5, the other foundations are

the ♣ 5, ♠ 5, and ♦ 5. On each you must build the suit in order: 6, 7, 8, 9, 10, J, Q, K, A, 2, 3, 4.

The undealt remainder of the deck is the *stock*. Bring these cards into play by going through the stock in batches

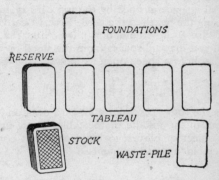

FIG. 6—Canfield layout. The reserve pile must be kept squared up so that only the top card is exposed.

of three at a time (there may be a short batch of two or one at the end). Turn each batch face up on one *waste-pile;* the top card of this pile is available to be played off, thus releasing lower cards of the batch. After you have exhausted the stock, turn over the waste-pile to form a new stock, without shuffling or disarranging the order of the cards. You may thus run through the stock without limit, until you have won the game or it ends in a block.

On the tableau you may build cards from tableau or stock, in downward sequence and alternating color. Example: the ♥ Q may be built on the ♠ K or ♣ K. Remember that kings may be built on aces, if your first foundation is not a king or ace. Foundation cards must be moved up to the foundation row as soon as they become available, where they are built upward in suit. From a tableau pile, the top card or the whole pile may be moved as a unit.

Example: if the pile comprise ♦ 2, ♠ A, ♥ K, you may move the ♥ K (to the ♣ A elsewhere or on the ♥ Q in a foundation row) or the three cards together (on the ♣ 3 or ♠ 3).

On clearing away any of the four tableau piles, you have a *space*. Fill a space at once by the top card of the reserve, thus releasing the next reserve card. Reserve cards may also be moved directly to foundation piles. After the reserve is exhausted, you may fill spaces from the stock or waste-pile, but you may hold a space open as long as you wish.

BELEAGUERED CASTLE

Remove the four aces from a 52-card deck and put them in a column in the middle of the table. These are *foundations;* the object of play is to build each suit complete on its own ace, in upward sequence.

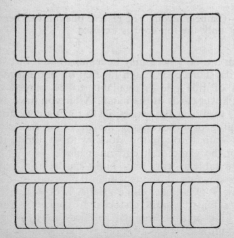

Fig. 7—Beleaguered Castle layout. The center column consists of aces.

Deal the rest of the deck face up in eight rows of six cards each, four rows on each side of the aces. Overlap the cards in each row to save space. You may deal a whole row at a time, if you wish, but it helps to shuffle the cards if you deal by columns; one card at a time to each of the eight rows.

The uncovered card at the right end of each row is *available*. Of course removal of this card releases the next below it. The available cards may be built on each other in sequence, either up or down, and without regard to suit or color. Example: the ♠ 5 may be built on any 6 or any 4; on the ♦ 9 may be laid any 10 or any 8.

When you clear off any entire row, you have a space. You may move any available card into a space. Since the foundation aces break the sequence, a king is immovable except into a space or on its foundation pile.

PYRAMID

Deal 28 cards from a 52-card deck face up in a pyramid shown by the accompanying illustration. Note that except in the bottom row every card is covered by two others at its lower corners. All cards of the bottom row are initially *available;* each other card becomes available as both covering cards are played off it.

The rest of the deck forms the *stock*. Bring these cards into play by turning them up one at a time from the top. Any that you cannot match up at once are laid face up in one *waste-pile*. Spread the waste-pile in any overlapping row, so that you can inspect all the cards.

The object of play is to *discard* all the cards in pairs that total 13, kings being discarded singly. Jacks count 11, queens 12, kings 13, other cards their pip value. Available for matching are: all uncovered cards of the pyramid, the top card of the waste-pile, and a card newly turned from the stock. Don't overlook that there are several ways of matching cards—a stock card with one in the pyramid, or two available pyramid cards, or the waste-pile card with a newly

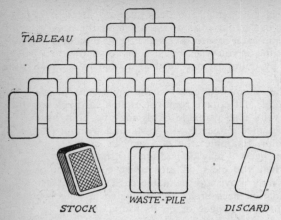

FIG. 8—Pyramid layout. A tableau card is available if wholly uncovered.

released card of the pyramid or with a newly turned card from the stock. Toss out kings singly. Put all *discards* in a pile separate from the waste-pile. You may consider it half a victory to clear away the entire pyramid; for full victory, you must have no stock or waste-pile left.

SPIDER

Shuffle two 52-card decks together. Deal ten piles by rows, six cards in each of the first four piles and five cards in each of the other six piles. Turn the top card of each pile face up, keeping the rest face down.

FIG. 9—Spider layout. In each pile, all cards below the top are face down.

The face up cards are available to be built on each other, in downward sequence regardless of suit or color. Example: the ♣ 10 may be built on any jack. When choice offers, it is usually preferable to make *natural* builds, that is in the same suit. On uncovering any face-down card, turn it up; it then becomes available. If you clear away any of the ten piles entirely, you have a *space*. You may put any available card in a space.

One card at a time may always be moved from the top of a pile. But if the pile is topped by a build of two or more cards wholly *in suit,* any or all may be moved as a unit. Example: ♥ 3 lies on ♦ 4, only the ♥ 3 may be moved first; ♥ 3 lies on ♥ 4, both may be moved together (on a 5).

Whenever play comes to a standstill, deal an additional row of ten cards face up, one card on each pile. Prior to the deal, every space must be filled. After the last deal, exhausting the deck, you are beaten if play again comes to a standstill before the game is won.

To win the game you must assemble thirteen cards of each suit in turn, built in upward sequence from ace to king. Whenever such a build of thirteen lies on top of a pile, you may lift it off and discard it from the game. (But you can keep it in play as long as you wish, to help in other building.) Since the sequence of rank is broken by the ace and king, you may not build any card on an ace, and a king may not be moved except to a space or to the discard.

FORTY THIEVES

Shuffle two 52-card decks together. Deal four rows of ten cards each, all face up, overlapping the cards in columns. These forty cards form the *tableau.* The uncovered card at the bottom of each column is *available* to be moved elsewhere. Of course playing off a card releases the one it covered.

FIG. 10—Forty Thieves layout. The waste-pile (not shown) is kept spread so that all cards are readable.

On the tableau, you may build downward in suit. Example: the ♦ Q may be built only on the ♦ K. Only one card at a time may be moved for building.

The undealt remainder of the deck is the *stock*. Bring the cards into play by turning them one at a time from the top of the stock. Put cards not immediately playable face up in a single wastepile.

Each ace, as it becomes available, must be put in a row above the tableau. The aces are *foundations*. The object of play is to build cards in suit and upward sequence on each ace, from two to king, until all eight suits are complete.

Available for building are: uncovered cards of the tableau, the top of the waste-pile, and a card newly-turned from the stock. When any column of the tableau is removed entire, the *space* may be filled by any available card.

You may run through the stock only once.

RUSSIAN BANK

Russian Bank is a double solitaire, a game for two persons based on a layout, foundations, and other constituents of patience play. It is distinguished from other double solitaires by the rule that the opponents play alternately, not simultaneously. The order of play is prescribed by rigid rules; a move out of order loses the player his turn. The "skill" of the game is thorough knowledge of the rules and ability to give unflagging attention to every move.

The Decks. Each player is provided with a regular deck of fifty-two cards. The two decks should have different backs. Each player shuffles his opponent's deck, then the decks are exchanged and the layout is dealt.

The Layout. Each player first deals a pile of twelve cards face down at his right; this is his *reserve*. Next he deals a column of four cards above his reserve, extending to his opponent's side of the table. The columns so dealt by the two players form the *tableau*. Space is left between the columns for two additional columns of *foundations,* to be put in place as the cards become available. The foundations collectively are called the *center*. Finally, each player leaves the undealt remainder of his deck, called his *stock,* face down at his left.

FIG. 11—Russian Bank layout. The two players are imagined to be sitting at the sides of the diagram, facing each other across a table.

The Center. All aces are *foundations,* and must be moved to the center as they become available. Cards of the same suit are built up on each ace, from deuce to king. The first rule of procedure is:

> *Moves to the center take precedence over all other moves.*

If able to put an ace in place, build a two on an ace, etc., the player must do so before making any other move, with one exception: at his second and all later turns, the player is entitled to see the top card of his reserve, and may therefore turn it face up before making any play.

When several cards can be moved to the center:

> *The precedence in play to the center is: (1) the exposed reserve card; (2) the exposed stock cards; (3) uncovered tableau cards.*

Where there is choice among tableau cards, they may be played up in any order the player pleases.

The Tableau. On the tableau, cards may be built in downward sequence and alternating color. For example, the ♠ 6 may be placed on the ♥ 7 or ♦ 7. Only one card at a time may be lifted off a tableau pile to be moved elsewhere, but the removal of the top card of course releases the one below. Available for tableau building, subject to the rules of order, are the top cards of the player's reserve and stock, as well as the top cards of other tableau piles.

> *All tableau building is optional.*

The player may release what cards he pleases and keep covered what he pleases. It is not a violation of rule to fail to release a card playable to the center, when it can be released; the first rule above means simply that a card, *if available,* must at once be moved to the center.

When any of the eight tableau piles is cleared away, a *space* exists. Into this space may be put any available card from tableau, reserve, or stock. As a matter of strategy, spaces are used for two consecutive purposes: (1) to consolidate tableau piles and so make more spaces; (2) to move cards off the reserve pile. To serve purpose (1), the player may keep a space open as long as he pleases, but:

> *All spaces must be filled before a card is turned from the stock.*

Furthermore, as a matter of sound strategy as well as rule:

No card from the stock may be put in a space unless the player's reserve is exhausted.

The Play. First turn to play may be decided by tossing a coin. The first player must begin by moving any aces from tableau to center, also any cards that can be built on them. Having satisfied the center, he may turn up the top card of his reserve. (At all later turns he is entitled to see his reserve card before making any play.)

He may continue by manipulating the tableau to create spaces, and may use the spaces to play cards off his reserve. As soon as one card is removed from this pile, the next is turned up. Since tableau building is optional, he need not build his reserve card on a tableau pile, if he wishes to hold this play in abeyance. Likewise, he need not load his opponent (see below), from his own reserve or elsewhere, unless he wishes. But he must fill all spaces in the tableau before turning up his stock card.

If the stock card proves unplayable, it must be laid face up between the player's stock and reserve, starting his *discard pile.* All unplayable cards from the stock are laid in this one pile. After the stock is exhausted, the discard pile is turned over to form a new stock.

The act of laying the stock card on the discard pile ends the player's turn, even though this card was in fact playable.

The player may continue playing so long as he finds place in the tableau or center for each successive stock card. Having played such a card, he may return to his reserve, or to the tableau, to make any additional plays thereby opened.

The second player, at his first turn, likewise must commence by satisfying the center (in the event that he has stopped his opponent for failure to do so). Only afterward may he turn up his top reserve card. At all later turns he may see his top reserve card before making any move.

Loading. There is one other recourse to make spaces, play off reserve cards, etc. A player may *load* his opponent's reserve and discard pile. That is, he may build available cards on them, in suit and sequence, either up or down. For example, the ♥ Q might be moved from the tableau and placed on the ♥ K or ♥ J, should either card lie on the opponent's reserve or discard pile. The direction of sequence in loading may be changed as often as the player pleases, For example, he might load the ♥ Q on the ♥ K, then the other ♥ K on the ♥ Q.

There is no point in loading the adverse reserve from tableau alone, unless some essential change is made in the tableau that prevents the opponent in his turn from building all the cards back again. But builds on the discard pile are non-retractable, under the rule:

> *The cards of the discard pile are never available.*

Cards may not be lifted off the discard pile to be built in center or tableau. These cards can return to play only when the discard pile is turned over to make a new stock.

Stops. If a player violates any of the foregoing rules of procedure, his opponent may call "Stop!" The error being proved or agreed, the turn passes to the other. The erroneous play must be retracted on demand.

To decide the justice of stops, precise rules are necessary as to what constitutes a play or move. The strictest rule is that a player errs if he touches a card (except for stated purpose of arranging) when another card *must* be moved first. A mistake in building, as putting the ♦ 8 on the ♣ 10, must be retracted on demand, but is not usually construed as allowing a stop.

Scoring. Play continues by alternate turns until one player wins, by getting rid of all cards from his reserve and stock, building them in the center and tableau. The winner scores 30 points for a game, plus 1 point for each card left in his opponent's stock and discard pile, plus 2 points for each left in the adverse reserve.

PART TWO

Board and Piece Games

CHESS

Chess is a game for two, played with pieces upon a checkered board. It is the foremost game of intellectual skill and it gains in fascination with increasing understanding and mastery.

You can enjoy Chess both as a player and as a spectator. Many people find it exceedingly interesting to follow the records and reports of tournament games which appear in magazines and newspapers, and to replay these games, observing the "brilliancies" of master players.

We give here first the directions and rules of the game and then take up the fundamentals of Chess strategy, providing basic information for the beginner and also useful pointers for those already familiar with the game.

How to Play Chess

The Board. The familiar 8×8 board of checkered squares is so placed that each player finds a white square in the corner at his right (see Fig. 12). A row of squares parallel to the player (horizontal in the diagram) is a *rank*. A row of squares extending from the White side of the board to the Black is a *file*. Also used is the self-explanatory term *diagonal*.

BLACK

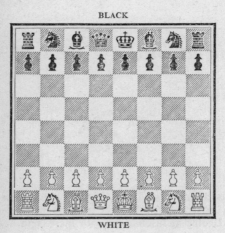

WHITE

FIG. 12—Initial position of Chess.

The Pieces. Each player commences with sixteen pieces, set up on the two ranks nearest himself. In Fig. 12 the pieces on the bottom rank are, left to right: *rook, knight, bishop, queen, king, bishop, knight, rook*. On the rank just above are eight *pawns*. Observe that each queen "goes on her own color"—the White queen on the white central square, and the Black queen on the black central square.

Chessmen vary in design, but the following characteristics are usually preserved: the king is always the tallest piece and wears a central spike or cross on its crown; the queen is second-tallest, and has a crenellated crown; the bishop has a cleft head suggesting a miter; the knight has a horse's head; the rook looks like a cylindrical or conical tower, and has a flat top; the pawn is the smallest piece, and has a simple knob at top. The individual pieces as conventionally represented are shown in the initial array in Fig. 1.

The King. The object of play is to capture the enemy king. It is never actually removed from the board. If it is attacked and cannot escape capture, it is said to be *checkmated* or *mated*, and the game ends forthwith. On making a move that attacks the enemy king, a player by custom (not legal compulsion) says "Check!" His opponent must avert the *check* or lose the game.

The king moves in any direction, on rank, file, or diagonal, one square at a time. (But see *Castling*, below.)

The Queen. The most powerful piece is the queen. It moves in any direction, on rank, file, or diagonal, any distance so far as the line is unobstructed.

The Rook. The rook (sometimes called *castle*) moves along rank or file, any distance so long as the line is unobstructed.

The Bishop. The bishop moves on any diagonal, any distance so far as the line is unobstructed. Note that each player commences with a "white" bishop (on a white square) and a "black" bishop. Neither bishop can ever change the color of the squares on which it moves.

The Knight. When not hemmed in by the edge of the board, a knight can move to any of eight squares, as shown in Fig. 13. One description of the peculiar knight move is "to the nearest square of opposite color that is not adjacent." This is not a line move in the sense that it can be obstructed by intervening pieces, but a move from point to point.

The Pawn. From its home square on the second rank, a pawn has option of moving one or two squares forward on the file. Having once moved, it may thereafter move only one square at a time, always forward on the file except when capturing (*post*). A pawn that reaches the eighth rank, farthest from the player, *promotes* or *queens*. That is, the pawn is at once removed from the board and replaced by a queen, rook, bishop, or knight, as the owner pleases. The usual choice is of course a queen, the most powerful piece. Through pawn promotion a player may have more than one queen on the board. (A chess set does not include extra queens. When a player has two queens, one is represented by an inverted rook, or by a pawn on which a finger ring has been placed.)

BLACK

WHITE

Fig. 13—Knight move. The White knight can move to any of the eight squares indicated by Black pawns.

Capture. Any piece, other than a pawn, may capture an enemy piece standing on square to which it can legally move. Capture is *not* effected by jumping, as in Checkers. The captured piece is removed from the board, and the captor is placed on the square so vacated.

The pawn has two peculiarities of capture. First, its line of capture is different from its ordinary move. It may take an enemy that stands adjacent, diagonally forward (see Fig. 14). Second, it may capture an enemy pawn *in passing* (or *en passant*). The situation in which this is legal is: a pawn stands on the fifth rank (counting from the owner's side of the board); an enemy pawn has just advanced by a double-jump from its home square so as to stand adjacent on the rank; the first-mentioned pawn may capture this enemy *in passing* by moving to the square that the enemy has jumped over (see Fig. 14). The reason for the rule is to prevent a pawn from using the double-

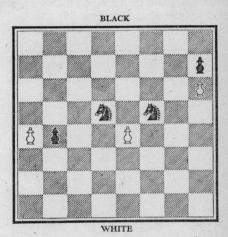

BLACK

WHITE

FIG. 14—Pawn capture. In the center of the board, the White pawn can capture either Black knight. At the upper right corner, the Black and White pawns stop but do not attack each other. At the left, if the White pawn has just advanced by a double-jump from the second rank, the Black pawn can capture it "in passing" by moving to the third-rank square it jumped over.

jump to escape entirely the attack by an adverse pawn on a neighboring file. The capture *in passing* must be made immediately after the double-jump, if at all; it may not be made at any later turn.

Castling. The move *castling* is a compound move by the king and one rook. A player may *castle* only once in a game, and then only under the following conditions: (a) Both the king and the rook stand on their original squares and neither has ever moved; (b) the squares on the rank between king and rook are vacant, and neither of the two nearest the king is under attack by an enemy piece; (c) the king is not in check.

Castling is executed by moving the king two squares toward either rook, and then placing the rook on the square jumped over by the king (see Fig. 15).

BLACK

WHITE

Fig. 15—Castling. The White king can castle with the queen's rook (left), but not with the king's rook (right), for in the latter case the king would have to pass over a square guarded by the Black bishop. The Black pieces at the top show the position of king and rook after castling respectively on queen's side and king's side.

Checks and Pins. A check must be met in one of three ways: (a) By capturing the piece that attacks the king; (b) by moving the king; (c) by *interposing* a piece on a line of check from an enemy queen, rook, or bishop.

Interposition cannot meet a check by a knight, whose move is not a line move; nor is interposition available when a pawn gives check, because then the pawn stands adjacent to the king.

A *discovered check* is given by moving a piece off a line, so as to unmask attack by a queen, rook, or bishop. A *double check* is (usually) a discovered check in which the piece vacating the line goes to a post from which it also attacks the enemy king. Manifestly, the only possible answer to a double check is to move the king.

BLACK

WHITE

FIG. 16—Checks and pins. In the upper left corner, the White queen checks the Black king. To avert the check, Black may move his king, interpose his knight, or capture the queen with his rook. In the upper right corner, any move of the bishop checks the Black king by discovery. At lower right, the White king is mated: the pawn cannot capture the Black rook because it is pinned by the bishop. At lower left, Black can checkmate by moving his rook to the first rank. This is a double-check, from rook and queen, and although both these checking pieces are attacked by White pieces, White loses because he cannot capture both at once.

When a piece stands on an open line between its own king and an enemy queen, rook, or bishop, it is said to be *pinned*. It may not legally move off the line, for any move exposing one's own king to check is illegal. (For this reason, the two kings can never stand adjacent.) The term *pin* is also applied where a line-vacating move, though legal, would expose a superior piece to capture by an inferior. Thus, a bishop frequently pins a knight when the queen or a rook stand shielded by the knight.

Drawn Game. A game may end as a draw in any of the following ways:

(a) If a player in his turn can make no legal move, but his king is not in check, he is *stalemated* and the game must be abandoned.

(b) If a player demonstrates that he can give *perpetual check*, unceasing checks from which the enemy king cannot escape, he may claim a draw.

(c) If the same position recurs three times in a game, with the same player to move each time, that player may claim a draw.

(d) If the pieces remaining on the board are inadequate (as known from analysis) to force checkmate, the game must be abandoned.

(e) At any time, a player may invoke the *fifty-move rule*: if during the next fifty moves no non-retractable change has occurred in the position, he may claim a draw. Non-retractable changes are produced by captures and pawn moves. Exception is made to this rule if the opponent can demonstrate that he has a theoretical win requiring more than fifty moves (analysis has found a few such endings).

Notation. The *descriptive notation* for recording games is illustrated by the following:

	White	Black
1	P-K4	P-K4
2	N-KB3	N-QB3
3	B-N5	P-QR3

4	BxN		QPxB
5	P-Q4		PxP

The initial of the name of the piece moved is written first: P for pawn, B for bishop, R for rook, Q for queen, K for king; Kt was formerly used for knight but is giving way to N, and in problem books S is usual (German *Springer*).

BLACK

QR1 / QR8	QKt1 / QKt8	QB1 / QB8	Q1 / Q8	K1 / K8	KB1 / KB8	KKt1 / KKt8	KR1 / KR8
QR2 / QR7	QKt2 / QKt7	QB2 / QB7	Q2 / Q7	K2 / K7	KB2 / KB7	KKt2 / KKt7	KR2 / KR7
QR3 / QR6	QKt3 / QKt6	QB3 / QB6	Q3 / Q6	K3 / K6	KB3 / KB6	KKt3 / KKt6	KR3 / KR6
QR4 / QR5	QKt4 / QKt5	QB4 / QB5	Q4 / Q5	K4 / K5	KB4 / KB5	KKt4 / KKt5	KR4 / KR5
QR5 / QR4	QKt5 / QKt4	QB5 / QB4	Q5 / Q4	K5 / K4	KB5 / KB4	KKt5 / KKt4	KR5 / KR4
QR6 / QR3	QKt6 / QKt3	QB6 / QB3	Q6 / Q3	K6 / K3	KB6 / KB3	KKt6 / KKt3	KR6 / KR3
QR7 / QR2	QKt7 / QKt2	QB7 / QB2	Q7 / Q2	K7 / K2	KB7 / KB2	KKt7 / KKt2	KR7 / KR2
QR8 / QR1	QKt8 / QKt1	QB8 / QB1	Q8 / Q1	K8 / K1	KB8 / KB1	KKt8 / KKt1	KR8 / KR1

WHITE

FIG. 17—Notation of the squares. The letters designating the files are the same for both players, but the ranks are numbered by each player away from his own side of the board.

The hyphen, as in P-K4, indicates a non-capturing move, while "x" (read "takes") indicates a capture. Following the symbol comes the square moved to, or the initial of the piece captured.

Squares are indicated by letters for the files and numbers

for the ranks. A file is designated by the initial of the first-rank piece posted there at the start of the game; for example, -K, indicating the file on which the kings originally stand. Where necessary to avoid ambiguity, Q or K may be prefixed to indicate the R, N, or B file on the queen's side or the king's side of the board. Thus N-KB3 is written where N-QB3 would also be possible in the position, so that N-B3 would be ambiguous. The ranks are counted from each player, away from himself, from 1 to 8. Thus each rank has a dual notation, according as the piece moving is White or Black. The White rank 1 is the Black rank 8, and so on.

Symbols in common use are:

0-0	Castles king-side
0-0-0	Castles queen-side
e.p.	Captures *en passant*
?	Marks a bad or dubious move
!	Marks a good move

STRATEGY OF CHESS

Several thousand books have been written about Chess, and for at least two hundred years the game has been carefully studied and analyzed by experts who have developed many basic principles of procedure. We devote ourselves here to the most important points and to the chief aspects of Chess strategy.

Phases of a Game. It is convenient to recognize three phases in a game, more or less distinct: (a) the opening, (b) the mid-game, (c) the end-game. As these terms are commonly used, the opening is conceived to end after each *minor* piece (bishops and knights) is moved off the first rank, also the queen, and the rooks are "connected" by castling or moving the king off the rank. The end-game is conceived to begin whenever the queens are removed by capture—though "queen endings" also exist. These phases are not mutually exclusive; they often merge insensibly. Yet the distinction is often useful, because it is grounded on certain differences of objective.

If the objective of each phase were to be summed up in a single word, these words would be: in the opening, *development;* in the mid-game, *co-ordination* in the end-game, *accuracy.*

We will discuss these phases in the reverse of chronological order, because the principles of opening and mid-game play depend on the merits of positions that may arise in later phases.

Minimum Mating Force. The beginner should first learn what is the minimum of additional pieces that must be placed on the board, besides the two kings, so that one player can checkmate the other.

KING AND ROOK VS. KING. Checkmate can be forced, and the method is shown below. This ending exemplifies in simplest form the principles underlying all lone-king mates.

BLACK

WHITE

FIG. 18—Forcing checkmate with a rook.

The play from Fig. 18 might proceed as follows:

White	*Black*
1 R-R5	

The Black king is first confined to a rectangle bounded by the fifth rank and three sides of the board.

| 1 — | K-B5 |
| 2 K-N2 | K-N5 |

Attacking the rook. To move the rook along the file would enlarge the prison, hence—

3 R-KR5	K-B5
4 K-B3	K-Q5
5 K-B4	

The White king now co-operates with the rook to decrease the rectangle of imprisonment. The Black king must be driven to the edge of the board, and usually to a corner.

| 5 — | K-B5 |
| 6 K-K4 | K-B6 |

The king moves off the fourth rank to escape being driven to the QR file in two more moves.

| 7 R-QB5 ch | |

In this ending, checks should usually be avoided, but here the Black king cannot escape to any larger area than his present prison.

7 —	K-N5
8 K-Q4	K-N6
9 R-N5 ch	K-B7

Trying to get around the White king. White cannot improve the position of his pieces until Black gives way in some direction, and therefore makes a pure waiting move.

| 10 R-N8 | K-Q7 |
| 11 R-N2 ch | K-B8 |

12	R-K2	K-Q8
13	K-Q3	K-B8
14	R-Q2	K-N8
15	R-QB2	K-R8
16	K-B3	K-N8
17	K-N3	K-R8
18	R-B1 mate	

KING AND QUEEN VS. KING. Evidently, the stronger party can give mate by using his queen as a rook. But the queen's added powers shorten the process, since the king can never attack the queen. The king must be forced to the edge of the board, not necessarily to a corner. Care must be taken to avoid stalemate. For example: Black king on KR1, White queen on KN6. If it is Black's turn to move, the game is drawn by stalemate.

KING AND BISHOP OR KNIGHT VS. KING. No mate position can be set up when the stronger party has only a bishop or knight. Hence these pieces are called *minor;* the queen and rook, either of which can give mate, are *major* pieces.

KING AND TWO KNIGHTS VS. KING. A mate position can be set up in the corner, but cannot be reached by force, because the lone king would have to be held in stalemate for one move while the mating knight gets to a square of correct color. Hence there are many positions in which the king is undone if he also has a pawn, since the ability of this pawn to move averts the stalemate. (If the pawn is on the rook file, blocking his own king in the corner, mate can be delivered by a single bishop or knight.)

KING AND TWO BISHOPS VS. KING. Mate can be forced. The two bishops standing side by side make a diagonal line across the board that the long king cannot cross. The king is therefore confined to a triangular prison, which can be reduced until the king is forced in a corner.

KING, BISHOP, AND KNIGHT VS. KING. Mate can be forced. This is the most difficult of the endings, and its method will not be detailed here.

OTHER PAWNLESS ENDINGS. King and queen can win

against king and rook. It is fairly easy to force the king to the edge of the board, then to a corner. The rook can never stray far from the king, else it can be won by a *fork* (a simultaneous attack on two pieces). In the final stages, there are some stalemate traps to be avoided.

King and queen vs. king, rook, and a minor piece, or king and two bishops, is usually a draw. But bishop and knight, or two knights, usually lose against a queen.

King and rook vs. king and a minor piece is usually a draw. Similarly, king, rook, and bishop against king and rook is usually a draw. But in both cases the weaker party must play accurately to avoid all of the positions that have been shown to be wins for the stronger party.

Pawn Endings. A single pawn cannot, of course give mate. But it is a potential queen, and the merits of king and pawn vs. king depends on whether the pawn can be forced to the eighth rank.

The pawn will of course queen if the lone king is too

BLACK

WHITE

FIG. 19—Queening a pawn.

far away to catch it. A convenient way of calculating this matter is as follows: imagine a large square defined by two corners—the square on which the pawn stands and the square on which it will queen. For example, White pawn on its K5; the large square has corners at K5, K8, QN5, QN8. The *rule of the square* is that the adverse king can catch the pawn if it can move inside the square. To continue the example, the enemy king on QR5 can move to QN4 and catch the pawn, but on QR6 cannot catch it.

If the pawn is guarded by its king, the outcome depends on whether the lone king can get in front of the pawn and stay there. Fundamental is the position shown in Fig. 19. Incorrect is the following play.

	White	*Black*
1	P-K4	K-K2
2	K-K2	K-K3
3	K-K3	K-K4
4	K-B3	K-K3
5	K-B4	K-B3
6	P-K5 ch	K-K3
7	K-K4	K-K2
8	K-B5	K-B2
9	P-K6 ch	K-K2
10	K-K5	K-K1 !

Any other move by Black loses.

11	K-B6	K-B1
12	P-K7 ch	K-K1

Now if White moves K-K6, the position is a draw by stalemate. If he makes any other move, Black captures the pawn.

The correct play by which White wins from the position of Fig. 19 is as follows:

	White	*Black*
1	K-Q2	K-K2
2	K-K3	K-K3
3	K-K4	K-Q3

White takes the *opposition* against the enemy king, in front of his pawn. The *opposition* is discussed below. The point of moving the king in front of the pawn is to reserve a pawn move to change the *opposition*, if necessary.

4   K-B5

This move is the crux of the *opposition*. It is a "passing move," i.e., the player forces his king upon a rank previously barred by the enemy king, thus advancing his own king nearer the vital square of queening from which the defender must be excluded.

4 —   K-K2

If Black maintains the diagonal opposition by K-Q2, White simply plays K-B6, and then Black's K-Q3 is answered by P-K4, and Black cannot reach the pawn.

5   K-K5

Again taking the opposition.

5 —   K-K1

If K-Q2, then White plays K-B6, repeating the previous maneuver.

6   K-K6   K-Q1
7   K-B7   K-Q2
8   P-K4

The pawn is free to advance at any time that the enemy cannot seize the opposition.

8 —   K-Q3
9   K-B6

Necessary to save the pawn. But nothing is lost, as White still can exclude the enemy king from the vital square K8.

9 —   K-Q2
10   P-K5

A point to remember that simplifies these endings: the

present configuration is a win for the stronger party *whichever side has the move.*

    10 —   K-K1
    11 K-K6

Taking the opposition in front of his pawn for the last time. In explanation of the foregoing observation, suppose 10 — K-Q1. Then 11 K-B7, and no matter how many more rows lie ahead of the kings, to the Black edge of the board, the White king is in position to seize the frontal opposition if the Black king moves upon the K-file.

    11 —   K-Q1
    12 K-B7

Now the pawn marches straight down to queen, as the White king has excluded the Black king from the file.

A lone pawn on a rook-file cannot be queened if the enemy king can once get in front of it (at any distance). Suppose a White KRP, with the White king nearby. If the Black king can reach KB1, the game is a draw. Once in the corner, the king shuttles between KN1 and KR1 and cannot be driven out. If the White king stands on KR7 or KR8 and thereby excludes the Black king from the corner, Black shuttles between B1 and B2; the advancing KRP is blocked by its own king, but if the White king vacates, the Black king will enter the corner.

When two pawns are pitted against one, three against two, etc., the stronger party can in general force a win. According to the position, one of the following methods may be applied:

(a) Pawn exchanges are forced until the stronger party has a *passed* pawn that cannot be stopped. Example: White K on K3, P on Q2, P on QB2; Black K on Q4, P on QB5. White moves 1 P-Q4. If Black does not capture, the pawn is *passed,* and to stop it Black will have to relinquish guard of his own pawn. White will emerge two pawns ahead. But if 1 — PxP e.p. (en passant), then 2 KxP, and White has the opposition ahead of his pawn.

(b) With separated pawns, the extra pawn on one side compels the adverse king to remain in its vicinity, so that his own pawns on the other side are left unguarded. Example: White K on K1, P on KR2, P on QR2; Black K on K1, P on KR2. White advances his king toward the Black pawn. The Black king cannot continue to guard it, but must go to the queen-side when White advances his QRP. White will capture the Black pawn, timing his moves so that the Black king cannot get back to the king-side in time to stop the White KRP.

(c) The stronger party forces his king toward the base of the enemy pawn chain and increases his material superiority. For illustration, see the next section. This process, depending primarily on *superior king position* and the *opposition,* may produce a win even when the forces are initially equal.

The Opposition. In Fig. 20, it is easy to see that if White is to move he can make no headway—literally. Wherever he moves along the fourth rank, the Black king can oppose

BLACK

WHITE

FIG. 20—The opposition.

him on the same file, and so prevent his reaching the fifth rank. But Black to move finds the *opposition* against him and cannot prevent the advance of the enemy. Owing to the initially superior position of the White king—abreast of his own pawn, while the Black king is one rank behind his pawn—the White king can capture the Black pawn. Thus:

1	—	K-Q3
2	K-B5	K-Q2
3	K-K5	K-B3
4	K-K6	K-B2
5	K-Q5	K-N3
6	K-Q6	

Now the Black king has to relinquish guard, and his pawn falls. In the given position, gain of the pawn does not allow White to win, for

| 6 | — | K-N2! |
| 7 | KxP | K-B2 |

and Black has the opposition. (6 —K-B2 would lose.) But with additional pawns anywhere on the board, the gain of the pawn would almost surely allow White to win.

The meaning of *opposition* is easy to see when the kings face each other, across one square, on the same file or rank. But there are many complex situations of *distant opposition,* and opposition where the kings stand on squares of opposite color, through peculiarity of the pawn configuration.

With queens off the board—and sometimes with queens on—the kings may engage fairly freely in offensive action. The weaker and fewer the remaining pieces, the more important it becomes to hurl the king as an offensive unit against the enemy forces. Many an end game, between initially equal arrays of pawns, is decided in favor of the king that can occupy the more centralized position, or find a path to reach and besiege an enemy weak point, e.g., the base of a pawn chain.

Pawn Configurations. The most static element of a position is the configuration of the pawns. One of the long-range objectives in every Chess game is to maintain a pawn-skeleton free of organic weaknesses. In Fig. 21, White's QRP is *isolated,* since it has no ally on an adjacent file. It can be protected only by a piece; if all pieces be-

BLACK

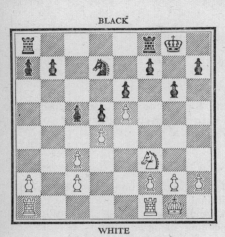

WHITE

FIG. 21—Pawn formations.

come "swapped off," the White king will have to be ready at all times to fly to the defense of this pawn if the Black king goes to the queen-side.

The White pawns on the QB file are *doubled.* They are an end-game liability because of their vulnerability to attack on the file. The Black KN pawn has advanced, leaving *holes* at KB3 and KR3. These third-rank holes are likely to be a mid-game weakness, for if White pieces occupy them the pieces cannot be expelled by pawn attack. For defensive purpose, the pawns in front of the castled king are strongest when unmoved, like White's. The *hole* may turn into an end-game weakness (though they disappear when the KBP and KRP are moved ahead) through providing an avenue for incursion of the White king. By contrast, the unmoved White king-side pawns can be reached only from the central route, White's Q3 and K2.

The strongest offensive position of pawns is the *phalanx* —abreast on a row—as the Black QBP and QP in Fig. 21. Together the two pawns attack four squares on the rank ahead. The strongest defensive position is the *chain*, illustrated by Black's QP, KP, KBP, and White's KP, QP, QBP. Each pawn defends the one ahead, leaving only the *base* to be protected by pieces.

Organic weaknesses such as isolated, doubled, and backward pawns can often be borne because a decision is expected in mid-game—there may be no end-game. Still, the weakness may make itself felt in early play. Consequently, moves by the lowly pawns must usually be weighed with much more attention to the long-range effects than are moves of pieces.

Mid-game Objectives. A pioneer analyst has described the winning process as "the accumulation of small advantages." The tyro, intent only upon attacking the enemy king, is continually surprised at the "trifling" objectives of the master player—to post a piece here, to advance a pawn there. In master games, long campaigns may be waged over these small matters that seem very remote from the business of checkmate.

The answer is of course that the expert has learned, from his own experience and from book analysis, how a small initial advantage may be pressed to make additional gains and eventually reach a decisive superiority.

Throughout the game, the advantages sought are of two kinds—*material* and *positional*. The first is relatively easy to understand. A player is superior materially if he has more pieces left than his opponent—or, more accurately, if the total *power* of his army is greater than the power of the other. This matter is discussed in the next section. The question of what is *positional* superiority is the crux of

Chess; he who can answer it fully has learned all there is to know.

Value of the Pieces. In the sections on end-play, we have seen that a player having one more pawn than his opponent —pieces being equal—usually can win. We have also seen that the process need not necessarily be to swap off pieces so as to leave king and pawn vs. king. The slight superiority of *fighting force* will usually enable the stronger party to make additional material gains.

This being so, it is incumbent on a player to try to maintain at least strict equality of force with his opponent. He can afford to accept *material inferiority* only for *positional advantage* of sufficient magnitude. In this discussion of the value of the pieces, then, there is a constant proviso "if positional considerations do not supervene."

The two armies are initially equal in numbers and kind. They are changed only by capture (and promotion). If all captures were "swaps" of like pieces, the material equality would not change. But many times there are captures and counter-captures of unlike pieces. How are we to compare force among the remaining unlike pieces?

One basis for comparison is this approximate scale of the relative powers of the pieces:

Pawn	1
Knight	3
Bishop	3
Rook	5
Queen	9

On the same scale, the fighting power of the king is about 5, but of course the king cannot enter into a "swap" of pieces.

From a mid-game position, i.e., where there is scope for gaining additional material advantage, it is usually decisive to capture a knight or bishop for one or two pawns, a rook for a knight or bishop, a queen for a rook or a rook and one minor piece. Advantageous but not so surely decisive is to gain two minor pieces for a rook, a rook and two minor pieces for a queen. The relative fighting power of unlike pieces depends very much on the position, and this is most likely to fix the merits of three pawns vs. a minor piece, a queen vs. two rooks. For example, in mid-game a knight or bishop is likely to be worth more than three pawns, since it can be used for direct attack on the enemy king, while in end-game the pawns may be superior.

The knight and bishop are approximately equal, but positional considerations usually ·favor the bishop. It is a long-range piece, capable of pressing on the enemy from a distance. The knight has to find an advanced post in enemy territory to attack with like force. In an end-game with pawns on both wings of the board, the bishop may restrain pawns on both wings at once; the short-stepping knight cannot. Conversely, in a blocked position with no open diagonals, the knight may maneuver better than the bishop. Yet, the basis for victory in many a master game has been the possession of two bishops against a bishop and knight, or even more advantageous, against two knights.

Avenues of Infiltration. Many of the *positional* objectives are concerned with opening avenues through which one's pieces may advance into enemy territory or press upon the enemy from a distance.

A knight on the third rank (as, on KB3 or QB3) attacks only the most advanced rank of enemy territory (his fourth rank). In the beginning of a game, the knight often serves well by pressing upon enemy pawns that advance to this rank. In the mid-game, the knight usually seeks to advance to the fourth, fifth, or even sixth rank, in order to come to closer grips with the enemy. Whether it can do so depends first of all upon the enemy pawn skeleton. The knight is peculiarly vulnerable to attack by a pawn, since it does not counterattack the pawn. The natural advanced post for a knight is therefore a *hole* in the enemy pawn position, or a point that the enemy cannot advantageously attack by a pawn.

Refer to Fig. 21 on page 164. Black has left a hole at his KB3. Such a hole, it has been well said, always "beckons" to a knight. If the White knight reaches it, a fatal constriction will be exerted on the Black king-side. The knight will not only attack Black's KN1 and KR2, but will also block advance of the KBP, which advance would allow a rook or queen on the second rank to guard KR2 and KN2. The *outpost knight* is especially strong when guarded by a pawn, so that if the outpost is assailed and captured a pawn replaces it. In Fig. 10, the Black knight may wait at Q2 until the White knight settles on KB3, then capture it. But after the recapture by White's KP, Black's KBP is still blocked and his KN2 is assailed. With the skeletonized force of Fig. 21, this would not be dangerous (in fact, the advanced White pawn would be a liability because hard to defend with the remaining pieces). But with queens still on the board, it would be a terrible menace, because White would threaten to bring his queen to the hole at KR6 and then mate at KN7.

It is rare that a knight can be permanently posted so far forward. But it often can reach the fifth rank and be maintained there. Squares often invaded are K5 and Q5. A knight is sometimes sent to KB5 or KN5, not because it can be maintained there, but because to repel it the enemy has to advance a pawn in front of his castled king, and thereby weaken its defense.

The bishop can press on the enemy from afar. It needs only an open diagonal to assail enemy forces, and can serve as a powerful backer for a pawn attacking an enemy pawn. From a central square it can press on both wings of the adverse position. In opening as well as mid-game play, a constant objective is to bring bishops to their most effective posts, or to create effective posts by opening diagonals through pawn advances. The commonest opening moves, 1 P-Q4 and 1 P-K4, have a twofold immediate purpose: (a) to seize some command of the center; (b) to open a lane of development for a bishop. According to the further progress of the opening, the bishop may then find its best preliminary post at Q2 or K2, K3 or Q3, B4, or N5. But there is a marked tendency in modern play to *fianchetto* bishops, i.e., post the bishop at N2 after advancing P-N3. From this post the bishop rakes the central squares while well-sheltered from attack.

The rook, until the forces are considerably depleted, cannot well be advanced toward the center or into enemy territory. Avenues of advance are lacking, and when assailed by any lesser piece (pawn, knight, or bishop) the rook must beat an ignominious retreat. In early midgame, the rook is likely to function (if at all) from the first rank. But here it may guard an advanced pawn, back up a pawn advance, and above all be ready to seize an *open file*. A file from which all pawns have been cleared "beckons" a rook as a hole beckons a knight. Likewise, a *half-open file* (from which one's own pawn has been removed) gives the rook opportunity to exert frontal pressure on the enemy pawn, or to defend an own outpost piece. Many mid-games revolve around the effort to open a file by enforcing pawn exchanges, to seize and hold an open file, to *double* the rooks on an open file.

The queen in early play, like the rook, is likely to have to stay behind its own front lines, guarding and backing up the pawns and minor pieces. Yet the queen has peculiar offensive powers that must be reckoned with from the first move. Radiating attack on all lines, the queen is powerful in ability to *fork*—attack two enemy pieces or points simultaneously. A sudden sally of the enemy queen may bring retribution for the thoughtless advance of pieces to posts where they are unguarded.

Direct Attack. It is a basic tenet of modern play that no direct attack upon the enemy king can succeed (against competent defense) if not based on definite and sufficient strategical advantages, previously acquired. The attempt to attack "with insufficient means" is time-wasting, and may in turn yield the enemy lasting strategical advantages. For example:

1	P-K4	P-K4
2	B-B4	N-QB3
3	Q-R5?	

This is an effort to enforce what is known as the *Scholar's Mate*, e.g., 3 — N-KB3?? 4 QxBP mate. But Black can defend simply by 3 — Q-K2 or Q-B3, and the "lighthorse attack" is over. The White queen will presently have to retreat, and its sally has simply yielded up the advantage of first move.

On the other hand, a serious *tactical* error may lay a player open to a direct attack as fatally as positional inferiority. For example:

| 1 | P-K4 | P-K4 |
| 2 | N-KB3 | P-KB3? |

This way of defending the KP is positionally dubious, since it deprives the KN of its best square of development. Still, the move is playable in some openings, the KN being developed on K2, and Black might well hope to steer into a typical position of such an opening. But at this early stage the move has a fatal tactical flaw. Thus:

| 3 | NxKP! | PxN |
| 4 | Q-R5 ch | |

Now if 4 — P-N3, then 5 QxKP ch forks the king and rook, winning more than the knight sacrificed. But if 4 —K-K2, 5 QxKP ch, K-B2, the king quickly succumbs to a direct attack (6 B-B4 ch, etc.).

Direct attacks, especially on the castled king, tend to fall into patterns. We will show some of the common patterns later in a series of illustrative games.

Constriction. In the initial position, all the pieces except the knights are hemmed in by pawns. To gain freedom for maneuver, the player must advance at least two pawns, usually three or four. A battle ensues for *command* of terrain—not only over particular squares for the posting of pieces, lines for infiltration into enemy territory, but for *space as a whole*. It has been abundantly demonstrated that a player who commands notably less space than his opponent must eventually die of strangulation. His own pieces and pawns obstruct his inner lines of communication, necessary to swing his pieces to the defense of one assailed wing or the other. The player at all times has to think, not only of defending his king from direct attack, but also of gaining and holding sufficient "elbow room." Therefore a frequent short-range objective, especially in mid-game, is to *constrict* the range of enemy pieces, hold back his pawns, otherwise *blockade* him.

Objectives of the Opening. Opening maneuvers have the over-all purpose of:

(a) Establishing actual or potential command of some of the central squares, K4, K5, Q4, Q5.

(b) Posting each minor piece on its initially most effective square.

(c) Placing the king in a position of safety, usually by castling.

(d) Clearing other pieces off the first rank so as to give the rooks access to the central files.

The importance of the center is that pieces posted there exert their maximum power. Superior command of the center may split the enemy forces into two wings, assailed simultaneously from the center or impeded in intercommunication. Early play tends to focus on the struggle for command of the central squares—but command does not necessarily mean immediate occupation. For example, after 1 P-K4, P-K3, the best move is 2 P-Q4. It may be said that both central pawns should be advanced to the fourth rank when no disadvantage is thereby incurred. But after 1 P-K4, P-K4, the move 2 P-Q4 is inferior. Black can "dissolve" the center by 2 — PxP, and after 3 QxP, N-QB3, Black gains a *tempo* because the queen has to move a second time. The clue to opening maneuvers is that at the outset the objective is simply *to exclude enemy pieces from the center.*

In developing the minor pieces, it is important to avoid wasting time, as by moving the same piece twice unnecessarily. For example: 1 P-K4, P-K4; 2 P-KB4, PxP; 3 N-B3. Many a tyro has now played 4 —B-B4. Then 5 P-Q4! develops with gain of a tempo by the attack on the bishop, which has to retreat. An old, but still useful, rule-of-thumb was "Move each piece once."

The best initial post for the KN is almost invariably KB3. The QN may emerge at QB3 or Q2, according to the kind of opening. The KB is usually brought out fairly early, to prepare for king-side castling. It may go to N5, B4, Q3, K2, according to circumstance. The QB has similar choice of post, and the decision is often deferred until after castling. Mid-game maneuver, actually, often begins before the *development* is technically complete (rooks connected), and the most frequent stay-at-home in such cases is the QB.

The queen's initial post is most frequently Q2 or K2, after the bishop has been brought out. But many other moves are found in regular openings.

Of castling, it has been said "Castle if you must, or if you will, but not because you can." The tyro perhaps tends to exaggerate the importance of tucking the king in a corner quickly. An experienced player often defers castling, or forgoes it entirely, to launch at once into favorable mid-game maneuvers. But in the majority of games each player *must* castle quickly, to get his king away from open central lines. For example: 1 P-K4, P-K3; 2 P-Q4, P-Q4; 3 PxP, PxP. With the K-file opened, each player must hasten to castle, before an adverse rook brought to the file causes embarrassment.

The King-side Openings. A great many variations of opening play have been recorded and analyzed. The "regular" openings fall broadly into two categories: king-side and queen-side, according to which central pawn is moved to the fourth rank first. At the simplest, the difference is between 1 P-K4 and 1 P-Q4. But well-known positions are often reached by transposition of moves, commencing with 1 N-KB3, 1 P-QB4, etc.

After 1 P-K4, Black's chief options are the "regular" defense, 1 —P-K4; the French Defense, 1 —P-K3; the Sicilian Defense, 1—PQB4; Alekhine's Defense, 1 — N-KB3.

The idea of the French Defense, 1 —P-K3, is to follow up with 2 —P-Q4. If White later plays PxP (the Exchange Variation), the center is stabilized and equal; Black has easy equality. Having established Q4 solidly, Black will soon continue with P-QB4, attacking the White QP. When White avoids KPxQP, the game usually develops into a king-side attack by White and a queen-side attack by Black. The principal hazard of the opening for Black is that if he is ever compelled to play QPxKP he leaves White with a superior command of the center, often decisive.

The idea of the Sicilian Defense, 1 —P-QB4, is to secure command of Q5, or else compel White to swap his QP for a wing pawn. The latter is the better course; the usual continuation is 2 N-KB3, N-QB3 (or P-Q3), 3 P-Q4, PxP. As the game progresses, Black often utilizes the half-open QB file for a queen-side attack and White counters by a king-side attack (often prepared by P-KB4).

The idea of Alekhine's Defense 1 — N-KB3, is to compel an immediate decision about the defense of the White KP. Its feasability rests on the discovery that after 2 P-K5, N-Q4; 3 P-QB4, N-N3; 4 P-Q4, Black's losses of tempos by the repeated moves of the knight are not fatal. The imposing White center is in fact precarious, and Black proceeds to assail it with his center pawns and minor pieces.

In the regular line 1 P-K4, P-K4, the strongest continuation is 2 N-KB3, but there are such options as 2 P-KB4 (King's Gambit), 2 B-B4 (King's Bishop Opening), 2 N-QB3 (Vienna Game).

The idea of the King's Gambit, 2 P-KB4, (a *gambit* is an offer of material, usually a pawn, which the player expects to regain sooner or later if the gambit is accepted) is to open the KB file, in order later to assail the enemy's weakest point, his KB2. Then 2—PxP can lead to any of a myriad variations, much-analyzed in the last century. The gambit can be declined by 2 —B-B4, for the Black KP is at the moment immune. (3 PxP?? Q-R5 ch and wins.) The purpose of this move is to get the bishop out before

playing P-Q3 to protect the KP. The strongest answer to
the King's Gambit is considered to be 2 —P-Q4, the
Falkbeer counter-gambit. The main idea is to answer 3
KPxQP with 3 — P-K5, temporarily sacrificing a pawn
to avert the opening of a file and at the same time cramp
the White development. The King's Gambit has largely
disappeared from master play because the Falkbeer has
pulled its sting.

The idea of the King's Bishop Opening, 2 B-B4, is to
reserve the possibility of P-KB4 while preventing the
counter-thrust P-Q4. For example, if 2 —N-KB3, 3
P-Q3, N-QB3, White can continue 4 P-KB4, leading to
play like that of the King's Gambit.

The idea of the Vienna Game, 2 N-QB3, is likewise to
reserve the option of P-KB4, according to circumstance.

The best reply to 2 N-KB3 is 2 —N-QB3. Options are
2 —P-Q3 (Philidor's Defense) and 2 —N-KB3 (Petroff
Defense). The idea of Philidor's Defense is to maintain a
pawn at K4 even after White's 3 P-Q4. Locking in the
KB imposes on Black a cramped game, which Black seeks
to relieve by bringing the bishop to KN2 or KB3, the
queen to QB2 after P-QB3, and eventually P-Q4. The idea
of the Petroff Defense is to swap off the KP's, e.g., 3 NxP,
P-Q3; (not good is 3—NxP; 4 Q-K2, N-B3??; 5 N-B6
ch, winning the queen) 4 N-KB3; NxP; 5 P-Q4, P-Q4.
The question is then whether Black can maintain his
knight at K5, for to retreat it will hand White several
tempos.

In the regular line 1 P-K4, P-K4; 2 N-KB3, N-QB3,
the strongest continuation is considered to be 3 B-N5
(Ruy Lopez). Other options are 3 B-B4, 3 N-QB3, 3
P-Q4 (Scotch Game). Either of the first two may lead
to the typical position of the Giuoco Piano ("quiet
game"), e.g., 3 B-B4, N-KB3, 4 N-QB3, B-B4, 5 P-Q3,
P-Q3. The tyro should begin the study of openings with
this symmetrical position. The play leading to it typifies
the classical ideals of straightforward development. The
continuation must reckon first of all with the possible

consequences of QB-N5, pinning the adverse KN; if this move can be followed up by N-Q5 the "bind" is very powerful (in some known positions, it is decisive).

From the line 3 B-B4 stem 3 —B-B4 (Giuoco Piano) and 3 —N-KB3 (Two Knights Defense). After the latter move may follow 4 N-N5, the Prussian Attack. This looks "lighthorse," but it carries a sting, and the best defense is still in question. Compulsory at the moment is 4—P-Q4, 5 PxP. Now not 5—NxP?? which is fatal, but the classical 5—N-QR4 or the Ulvestad Variation 5—P-QN4!?

The move 3 N-QB3 may develop into the Giuoco Piano, or into the Double Ruy Lopez by 3 —N-KB3, 4 B-N5, B-N5.

Returning now to the Ruy Lopez, we will discuss the principal defenses to this most-played of king-side openings.

After 1 P-K4, P-K4; 2 N-KB3, N-QB3; 3 B-N5, best is considered to be the Morphy Defense, 3 — P-QR3. The attack on the knight is a threat against the Black KP which it defends, but at the moment the threat cannot be executed to advantage. That is, 4 BxN, QPxB, 5 NxP is met by 4—Q-Q5, forking the knight and KP. Black thus regains his pawn and White has nothing to show for his opening advantage. The usual lines are: 4 BxN, QPxB; 5 P-Q4, PxP; 6 QxP, QxQ; 7 NxQ. Or, 4 B-R4, N-B3; 5 O-O, B-K2; 6 R-K1, P-QN4 (thus realizing the idea of the defense, which is to drive the bishop back); 7 B-N3, P-Q3.

Less good is considered to be the Steinitz Defense 3 — P-Q3 and 4—B-Q2. The same idea is sometimes carried out with interpolation of 3 —P-QR3, 4 B-R4.

A "fighting" but difficult line is the Berlin defense, 3 —N-B3; 4 O-O, NxP. Many continuations have been analyzed, e.g., 4 P-Q4, N-Q3; 5 BxN, NPxB; 6 PxP, N-N2.

The Queen-side Openings. Many theorists consider that the Queen's Gambit offers the best way for White to prolong his initial advantage of the opening move. The characteristic formation of the Queen's Gambit can be reached at once by 1 P-Q4, P-Q4; 2 P-QB4. But any or all of these moves may be deferred, in favor of extensive preparations, without altering the essential character of the game. The queen-side openings all tend to be *close,* i.e., the center remains flexible, not stabilized by pawn exchanges. The same eventual positions can be reached by transpositions of moves, with more freedom in close game than in open games.

The underlying idea of the Queen's Gambit is to exchange a wing pawn for a center pawn, thus keeping two pawns in the center against the opponent's one. But additional and often more important strategical objectives develop. Chief of these is the constriction of the Black army. The White pawn phalanx on the fourth rank makes it difficult for Black to enforce P-K4 or P-QB4, yet without one of these advances his QB especially suffers from lack of scope.

After 1 P-Q4, P-Q4; 2 P-QB4, Black may accept the gambit by 2 —PxP. White can immediately regain the pawn by 3 Q-R4 ch and 4 QxP, but this puerile course is inferior. Better is to develop naturally, as by 3 N-KB3 (preventing a counter-gambit by 3 —P-K4), N-KB3; 4 P-K3, P-K3; 5 BxP. Any effort by Black to save his advanced pawn would be useless, and would incur decisive positional disadvantage, e.g., 3 N-KB3, P-QN4? 4 P-QR4, P-QB3 (not P-QR3, 5 PxP, PxP?? 6 RxR); 5 Q-B3, B-N2 or B-Q2?? 6 PxP! and Black cannot recapture.

Better for Black is to defer acceptance of the gambit until he is better developed. For example, the main line of the Slav Defense is 2 —P-QB3, 3 N-KB3, N-B3; 4 N-B3, PxP. One continuation is 5 P-K3, P-QN4. This move is now playable because the move P-QB3 has already been made. If 6 P-QR4, Black can move 6 —P-N5; White will regain his pawn but Black has imposed a ragged queen-side on him. To avoid dislodgment of the knight, White may continue 5 P-QR4 (instead of P-K3), preventing P-QN4; this still cedes Black some queen-side prospects.

Nevertheless, any time that Black plays PxP, he cedes White two pawns to one in the center, and facilitates the White advance P-K4, establishing a formidable phalanx. Hence the most-played Black defenses try to maintain the pawn at Q4 at least until Black is ready to challenge the center with P-K4 or P-QB4. The classical line of the Queen's Gambit Declined continues: 2—P-K3; 3 N-QB3, N-KB3; 4 B-N5, QN-Q2; 5 P-K3, B-K2; 6 N-B3, O-O. This still leaves Black the problem of what to do about his QB. The Orthodox Defense (now out of favor) tried to solve this problem by fianchettoing the bishop, by P-QN3 and B-N2. The danger is in allowing the dreaded Pillsbury Attack: White himself plays BPxQP and after Black's KPxQP (BxP or NxP would let White get in P-K4 soon), he advances his KN to K5, moves P-KB4, and gets a direct attack. Black has three pawns to two on the queen-side in consequence of the pawn exchange, but his queen-side attack comes too late to save the day. The superior Capablanca Defense is to play QPxQBP, then move N-Q4. The idea is that if White then plays BxB, Black can recapture with the queen, and after due preparation (retreat of the knight from Q4 is necessary) move P-K4.

The Cambridge Springs Defense is an effort to compel White to play PxP or otherwise release the tension in the center, by attacking at once the weakness of the White queen-side. After 1 P-Q4, P-Q4; 2 P-QB4, P-K3; 3 N-QB3, N-KB3; 4 B-N5, QN-Q2; 5 P-K3, it proceeds with 5 — P-B3; 6 N-B3, Q-R4 with intention of moving 7 —B-N5. This is a lively game full of plausible traps for both sides.

The modern tendency is to defer the advance of center pawns in the effort to make the opponent commit himself first to his pawn configuration. This is exemplified in the *Nimzoindian Defense* (a compound of the Nimzovich and Indian Defenses). After 1 P-Q4, Black plays N-KB3, merely holding back the White KP. Then 2 P-QB4, P-K3, merely preventing P-Q5. The basic idea is to meet 3 N-QB3 with B-N5, or 3N-KB3 with P-QN2. In either case Black reserves the option of how to place his center pawns.

In the first event, he follows soon with P-Q4; in the second case he moves P-Q3 and follows soon with P-K4.

The Queen's Pawn Opening, 1 P-Q4, is distinguished from the Queen's Gambit in that White does not follow it up soon with P-QB4. He thereby usually allows Black to make this move, and the game may develop into a Queen's Gambit Declined, with colors reversed. White's move ahead still gives him a grip that may take many moves to overcome. A typical variation is the Colle System: 1 P-Q4, P-Q4; 2 N-KB3, N-KB3; 3 P-K3, P-B4; 4 P-B3. White voluntarily locks in his own QB, while Black's is free to emerge; yet the close character of the game prolongs the advantage of the move and many victories for White have been scored.

Among irregular defenses to 1 P-Q4, the chief is the Dutch Defense, 1—P-KB4. Whether it is sound is moot. Black strives to create an outpost station for his KN at his K5, as a basis for a direct attack. The strategical counter for White is to enforce P-K4 after due preparation (repelling the outpost knight by P-KB3).

EXAMPLE GAMES

The following example games, played between first-rank masters, are selected to illustrate some of the broad strategical ideas discussed above. Some of the tactical reasons why some moves are playable and others are not are explained in notes.

Game 1. Lead in Development

White	*Black*
Anderssen	Kieseritzki
1 P-K4	P-K4
2 P-KB4	PxP
3 B-B4	P-QN4
4 BxNP	Q-R5 ch

5	K-B1	N-KB3
6	N-KB3	Q-R3
7	P-Q3	N-R4
8	N-R4	P-QB3
9	N-B5	Q-N4
10	P-KN4	N-B3
11	R-N1	PxB
12	P-KR4	Q-N3
13	P-R5	Q-N4
14	Q-B3	N-N1
15	BxP	Q-B3
16	N-B3 (a)	B-B4 (b)
17	N-Q5	QxP
18	B-Q6 (c)	BxR
19	P-K5 (d)	QxR ch
20	K-K2	N-QR3 (e)
21	NxP ch	K-Q1
22	Q-B6 ch!	NxQ
23	B-K7 mate (f)	

NOTES

(a) We make no comment on the early part of this game, which was played in the days when it was the fashion to try to attack from the opening move. But survey the situation at this juncture. The only Black piece that is moved from its initial square is the queen—and this is worse off than at home because it is threatened with attack by N-Q5. White, on the other hand, has managed to develop four pieces, all of which now press upon the uncastled king. Such a huge lead in development is a decisive advantage. It breeds "brilliant" attack in which pieces can be sacrificed—especially if they are the stay-at-homes not essential to the mating net!

In later days, when the urgency of developing before attacking was fully recognized, many games demonstrated that a considerably less overwhelming lead in development can be made the basis of a winning attack.

(b) Black is ludicrously helpless. If he tries to keep the knight out by 16 —B-N2, then 17 N-Q5, BxN; 18 PxB and the file opened on his king will be murderous. The next move is made, not so much to assail the rook, which White can spare, but to give his king a little elbow room.

(c) White can grandly offer both rooks, e.g., 18 —QxR ch; 19 K-K2, QxR? 20 NxP ch, K-Q1; 21 B-B7 mate.

(d) Shutting off the queen's guard of KN2, and so threatening the mate noted above.

(e) Guarding his QB2. But White demonstrates that "there is more than one way to skin a cat."

(f) Three active White pieces triumph over seven misplaced Black pieces! Admiring contemporaries dubbed this the "Immortal Game."

Game 2. The Compromised King-side

White	*Black*
Mackenzie	Mason

	White	Black
1	P-K4	P-K3
2	P-Q4	P-Q4
3	N-QB3	N-KB3
4	PxP	PxP
5	N-B3	B-Q3
6	B-Q3	0-0
7	0-0	N-B3 (a)
8	B-KN5	N-K2 (b)
9	BxN	PxB
10	N-KR4 (c)	K-N2
11	Q-R5	R-R1
12	P-KB4 (d)	P-B3 (e)
13	R-B3	N-N3
14	QR-KB1 (f)	Q-B2 (g)
15	N-K2	B-Q2
16	N-N3 (h)	QR-KN1 (i)
17	Q-R6 ch!	KxQ
18	N(R4)-B5 ch	BxN
19	NxB ch	K-R4
20	P-N4 ch	KxP
21	R-N3 ch	K-R4
22	B-K2 mate	

NOTES

(a) This variation is apt to lead to symmetrical positions, where White's advantage is minimal. Black might have avoided the symmetry by 7—B-KN5, planning to follow with P-QB3, QN-Q2, Q-B2, etc. But he was evidently intent on trying out another plan.

(*b*) "Putting the question" to the White QB. The idea is to lift the pin of the Black KN by playing N-N3, then P-KR3 (so that if B-R4, then NxB). The move gives White the opportunity to double the Black KBP. The question in all such positions is: will Black's disadvantage in having his king-side pawns compromised be outweighed by his advantage in gaining an open file through which to attack the White king-side? The present game, played in 1878, is of course not the final word, but it drastically refuted Black's eighth move.

(*c*) The key to the attack is to move Q-R5, attacking KR7 and also supporting the effort to post a minor piece on KB5. Black's method of defending his KR2 is here shown to be insufficient. The only alternative is 10—N-N3; 11 Q-R5, P-KB4. But then 12 NxKBP wins a pawn, at least.

(*d*) In order to bring his KR to N3.

(*e*) In order to relieve the knight of the duty of guarding the QP. (Note that White did not actually threaten the QP prior to P-KB4, e.g., 12 NxP? NxN; 13 QxN, BxP ch followed by QxQ.)

(*f*) Guarding KB4 so as to be able to move R-N3.

(*g*) Again preventing R-N3.

(*h*) Now White threatens to maintain a knight at KB5, after which the infiltration of the queen on the black squares will decide quickly.

(*i*) To guard his KN2 and also clear the rank for a flight of the king to the queen-side. But it is too late! The ensuing queen-sacrifice pulls the king into a mating net.

Game 3. The Accumulation of Advantages

White	Black
K. Gilg	S. Tarrasch

	White	Black
1	P-Q4	N-KB3
2	P-QB4	P-K3
3	N-QB3	B-N5
4	N-B3 (*a*)	N-K5 (*b*)
5	Q-Q3	P-KB4
6	P-KN3	P-QN3
7	B-N2	B-N2

8	0-0	NxN
9	PxN	B-K5 (c)
10	Q-Q2	B-K2
11	N-K1 (d)	BxB
12	NxB	0-0
13	Q-Q3	N-B3
14	R-K1 (e)	N-R4 (f)
15	B-K3	Q-B1 (g)
16	P-B5	P-Q4 (h)
17	PxP e.p.	PxP
18	B-Q2	P-Q4
19	P-B3	Q-B5 (i)
20	Q-K3	Q-B3
21	Q-Q3	N-B5 (j)
22	B-B4	P-KN4 (k)
23	B-B1	R-B2
24	P-K4 (l)	BPxP
25	PxP	QR-KB1 (m)
26	P-K5	R-B6
27	B-K3	P-N5 (n)
28	Q-K2	NxB
29	NxN	QxP (o)
30	QR-Q1	P-KR4
31	R-Q3	Q-B2
32	R(Q3)-Q1	B-N4
33	N-N2	Q-B6 (p)
34	Q-N5	R-B7
	Resigns (q)	

NOTES

(a) A poor move. Natural and good is Q-B2, avoiding a doubled pawn.

(b) Black alertly seizes his opportunity to reach a favorable position of the Dutch Defense.

(c) Black has imposed a lasting weakness on the White queen-side. Here he seizes the tactical opportunity to gain a tempo. The queen, in order to keep guard of the pawn at QB3, will have to block the diagonal of the QB.

(d) White has to get rid of the powerfully-posted bishop. But his own "good" bishop goes too. Black is left with a "good" bishop (supplementing his center pawns) against a "bad" bishop (the White QB is hampered by its own center pawns).

(*e*) Sooner or later White must play P-K4 to give some freedom to his pieces. He should have played it now. The preparatory move is unnecessary.

(*f*) One weakness of the doubled pawn is the difficulty of defending the forward pawn. Black now prepares to assail it, and incidentally he prevents 15 P-K4, for then would follow PxP; 16 RxP, NxP! 17 QxN? P-Q4 winning the exchange.

(*g*) Threatening Q-R3. Since White cannot bring another piece to the defense of QB4, he seeks to save the pawn by advancing it.

(*h*) Black has carefully avoided this move previously in order not to let White undouble his pawns and then move P(QB3)-B4, getting rid of the backward pawn. But now White cannot execute this maneuver. Black therefore nails down the outpost station on his QB5.

(*i*) Anticipating White's P-K4, Black brings his queen to B3 with gain of a tempo. White cannot afford to permit the exchange of queens, for the backward QBP would be a fatal endgame weakness. The White queen is forced to block the KP momentarily. (20 Q-B2 would get White into trouble through the pin of the QBP, e.g. 21—QR-QB1 threatening QxP ch!)

(*j*) At last the outpost takes his station. The attack on the White bishop cannot be ignored, for if the bishop goes the QBP is indefensible (Black can exclude a White rook from QB1 by moving B-R6).

(*k*) White evidently wanted to induce this move, else he would have played B-B1 immediately. But Black has no fear of "exposing" his king, for White is too cramped to be able to work up an attack.

(*l*) At last! But Black has had time to assure that the opening of lines will benefit him more than White.

(*m*) Voila! Black nails down the open file. Incidentally, he threatens to win a pawn by 26—PxP, for if 27 QxP?? QxQ; 28 RxQ, R-B8 mate.

(*n*) Threatening to increase the pressure by B-N4. White decides to give up the QBP at once to relieve the tension.

(*o*) Black's positional advantage yields the first material gain. Now White, in addition to attack on his king, has to evade any general exchange of pieces, which would leave him a lost end-game.

(*p*) Now White cannot move the knight or either rook without loss. He is reduced to a useless queen move.

(*q*) There are too many threats, RxN ch or Q-B6, etc. If
35 R-Q3 then QxR ch! 36 NxQ, R-B8 ch; 37 K-N2, R(B1)-B7
mate.

Game 4. The Surprise Move

	White	*Black*
	Bernstein	Capablanca
1	P-Q4	P-Q4
2	N-KB3	N-KB3
3	P-B4	P-K3
4	N-B3	B-K2
5	B-N5	0-0
6	P-K3	QN-Q2
7	R-B1	P-QN3
8	PxP	PxP (*a*)
9	Q-R4	B-N2 (*b*)
10	B-R6	BxB
11	QxB	P-B4 (*c*)
12	BxN (*d*)	NxB
13	PxP	PxP
14	0-0	Q-N3
15	Q-K2	P-B5 (*e*)
16	KR-Q1 (*f*)	KR-Q1
17	N-Q4	B-N5 (*g*)
18	P-QN3	QR-B1
19	PxP (*h*)	PxP
20	R-B2	BxKt
21	RxB	N-Q4 (*i*)
22	R-B2	P-B6
23	KR-QB1	R-B4 (*j*)
24	N-N3	R-B3
25	N-Q4	R-B2 (*k*)
26	N-N5	R-B4
27	NxBP?	NxN
28	RxN	RxR
29	RxR (*l*)	Q-N7! (*m*)
	Resigns	

NOTES

(a) A regular position of the Queen's Gambit Declined. White now embarks on a line that seeks to capitalize the "holes" on the Black queen-side, by removing the QB.

(b) The best defense is P-B4 at once, although this involves sacrifice of a pawn.

(c) This pawn must be advanced, else it will become a fatal weakness.

(d) A pointless exchange that largely gives up White's advantage by weakening the pressure in the center.

(e) The strategic crisis. The question is whether the "hanging pawns" will prove strong or weak. The normal impulse of the experienced player is to maintain them in offensive phalanx so long as possible. This voluntary advance to a defensive chain, ceding White the square Q4 for his knight, is the profound idea of a world champion. He will restrain and attack the White QNP. If White posts a knight on his Q4, then the Black QP is shielded from frontal attack.

(f) He still believes the pawns to be weak, else he would break them up by P-K4.

(g) An important move, made to relieve pressure on his QP, if necessary, by BxN.

(h) Again the clash of opinions. White believes the QBP will now be weak because it is isolated. Black believes it will be strong because it is passed.

(i) The tactical feasibility of this move rests on the fact that 22 RxP? N-B6 wins the exchange.

(j) Black wants to double rooks on the file, so as to release the knight for N-N5.

(k) The rook could have gone to B2 at once, on the 23rd move. But Black has indulged in a bit of camouflage, feigning reluctance to make this move. It gives the White knight a chance to attack the advanced pawn without loss of time, and apparently to win it. White falls into the trap.

(l) The danger of leaving the first rank unguarded, with the king locked behind his pawns, is well-known. White of course reckoned with 29—Q-N8 ch and saw that he had a sufficient defense with 30 Q-B1, R-Q8?? 31 R-B8ch and White mates next move. The Black king, too, has no outlet. But he overlooked the move that follows.

(m) A thunderbolt! It wins a rook outright. Of course 30

QxQ?? allows R-Q8 mate. Or 30 R-B2, Q-N8 ch; 31 Q-B1, QxR. Similarly 30 R-Q3 (hoping for QxQ?? 31 RxR mate) is met by Q-N8ch. Or 30 Q-Q3 (hoping for RxQ?? 31 R-B8ch) is met by Q-R8 ch. Or 30 Q-K1, QxR.

Like many other such surprise moves, Q-N7! is based on purely tactical features of the situation—a momentary misplacement of the enemy pieces. Were the White rook still at QB1, or the queen at QB2 or K1, or a king-side pawn advanced to give a loophole, Black would have nothing to show for his pawn minus.

Game 5. Blockade of a Whole Army

	White	*Black*
	F. Saemisch	A. Nimzovich
1	P-Q4	N-KB3
2	P-QB4	P-K3
3	N-KB3	P-QN3
4	P-KN3	B-N2
5	B-N2	B-K2
6	N-B3	0-0
7	0-0	P-Q4 (*a*)
8	N-K5 (*b*)	P-B3
9	PxP (*c*)	BPxP
10	B-B4 (*d*)	P-QR3 (*e*)
11	R-B1	P-QN4
12	Q-N3	N-B3
13	NxN (*f*)	BxN
14	P-KR3	Q-Q2 (*g*)
15	K-R2	N-R4
16	B-Q2	P-B4 (*h*)
17	Q-Q1	P-N5
18	N-N1	B-N4 (*i*)
19	R-N1	B-Q3 (*j*)
20	P-K4	BPxP! (*k*)
21	QxN	RxP
22	Q-N5	QR-KB1 (*l*)
23	K-R1	R(1)-B4
24	Q-K3	B-Q6 (*m*)
25	QR-K1	P-R3 (*n*)
	Resigns	

NOTES

(*a*) Contrary to his own teachings! The idea of this defense is to play P-Q3, preparing P-K4 and leaving open the diagonal of the QB.

(*b*) One of the frequent advantages for White in the QP openings is that he can make this move while Black cannot imitate it. Black's next move, cramping his own QB, is a patient strengthening of his center, unpinning the QP to make PxP possible.

(*c*) White seizes the opportunity to leave the Black QB locked behind his own pawns. But this release of tension in the center gives Black an easy game. Much better is 9 P-K4, increasing the pressure.

(*d*) A bad move that has escaped the censure of the commentators. Here the bishop stands exposed, and it will be wanted sooner or later to defend Q4 or QB3.

(*e*) Commencing a slow but steady expansion. If White plays 11 P-QR4 to stop Black's next move, he compromises his queen-side seriously. White gradually gets an inferior game for lack of a strategic plan.

(*f*) Now White has to give up his own outpost to prevent Black from establishing a stronger outpost at QB5 (N-QR4 and N-B5). To wait until the Black knight settles there, then play NxN, would open the QN file for Black and give him frontal attack on the weak QNP.

(*g*) A fine move that furthers the plan of expansion. It prevents N-R4 when Black later plays P-N5. Thus the knight cannot reach the outpost station QB5.

(*h*) The inferior posting of the White pieces permits Black now to expand on the king-side. White from now on must reckon with P-B5, which will threaten to rip open his king-side.

(*i*) Momentarily preventing advance of the KP. Black's last two moves have stalemated the whole White queen-side.

(*j*) Ignoring the hidden attack on his knight to threaten P-B5.

(*k*) Nimzovich comments that he gets two pawns, a rook to the seventh rank, and a further constriction of the White army—all for one knight. What more could one ask!

(*l*) Nailing down the file, which White cannot dispute because of the Black QB. Incidentally, Black threatens a quick win by R(1)-B6, winning at least the KNP. (B-B4 is no defense because of RxB.)

(*m*) Blocking the rank to threaten win of the queen by R-K7.

(*n*) A genial announcement of *Zugzwang*—the fatal compulsion to move. Although a piece ahead, White is helpless. He can move no piece without immediate loss of material; after his pawn moves are exhausted, he will have to hurl himself on the sword. For example: K-R2, R(4)-B6 wins the queen; so does any move of the QR (by R-K7). A move of the other rook, the knight, or either bishop loses the piece.

CHECKERS

The rules of Checkers are extremely simple, but this game has tremendous possibilties for skillful play. Checkers and Chess are thought of together because they use the same checkered board, but the pieces and the moves are entirely different. It is possible to learn rather quickly to play a good game of Checkers and to obtain a great deal of enjoyment from it. Checkers is also sometimes known by the name *Draughts*.

How to Play Checkers

The Board. The board is the same as for Chess. It is placed between the players so that each finds a black square at the left corner nearest him. The pieces move only on the 32 black squares. At his left, the player has a so-called *single corner,* and at his right a *double corner.*

In printed diagrams, the colors of the board are reversed, so that the pieces are shown on the white squares. Bear in mind that these are the black squares of the actual board, while the squares shaded in the printed diagram are the actual white squares.

The Pieces. The Checker piece is a disk from one to two inches in diameter, and about half an inch thick. All the pieces are alike. To commence a game, each player has twelve pieces, set up on the three ranks nearest himself, as shown in Fig. 22.

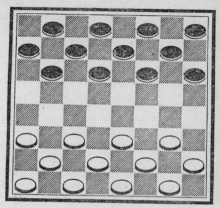

FIG. 22—Initial position of Checkers.

The Moves. Black invariably moves first, and thereafter the players move alternately. If a player is unable to move in turn, he loses the game. In fact, this is how victory is defined. The player loses who is first unable to move, either because all his pieces are gone or because all his remaining pieces are blockaded.

All pieces are initially *single men*. A single man may move in two ways. The non-capturing move is one square diagonally forward. The capturing move is a leap, diagonally forward, over an adjacent enemy piece to a vacant square just beyond it. The enemy piece leaped over is then removed from the board.

The two types of move may not be combined in one turn. The cardinal rule of play is that, if able to make a capturing move, the player must do so: he may not make a non-capturing move instead.

Furthermore, if after a capture, the piece moved is able to jump additional enemy pieces, it must do so. The piece must continue to capture—always forward—until it can no longer do so. The series of captures need not be in one line: the piece may capture zigzag.

Having a choice of which piece to move in capturing, or a choice of direction in the course of a series of captures, the player is free to use his own discretion. Only one piece may be moved in one turn.

On reaching the eighth rank, farthest from the player (the *king row*), a single man becomes a *king*. The promotion is indicated by placing a second checker on top of the first. A king has the same privileges and duties as a single man, plus the right to move backward as well as forward.

If a single man reaches the king row by a capture, it must stop there to be *crowned*—it may not continue capturing (as a king) in the same turn.

Notation. For purposes of recording a game, the 32 playing squares are numbered as shown in Fig. 23. A move is designated by the square that the moving piece occupies, followed by the number of the square on which it comes to rest. No special symbol is used (as in Chess) to mark a capture, and no typographical device is used to indicate whether a move is made by Black or White (since there can be no ambiguity). Here is a sample of the style:

11-15
22-18
15-22
25-18
etc.

A letter appended to a move, as 2-6A, refers to a note given later.

For condensation, three to six columns may be set across a page, but always read the columns down, not the rows across.

STRATEGY OF CHECKERS

General Principles. Checkers used to be an easy game—before very much was known about it. Play was guided by such maxims as "Always advance toward the center" and "Never move a man off your king row until you have to." But analysis has knocked most of the maxims into a cocked hat, by exposing their many exceptions. Today,

FIG. 23—Notation of the squares.

Checker theorists are reluctant to propound any general rule of strategy. Expert play is a matter of particulars—knowledge of many stock end positions, of starred moves and losing moves, of opening variations, of recurrent mid-game positions. We discuss these here briefly and also take up what are about the only principles of any general application concern— (a) *the move;* (b) *the bridge;* (c) *key squares* 14 and 19.

Piece-up Wins. Generally speaking, two kings can win against one, three against two, etc. Example: Black, K10, K14; White, K1. The White king is easily forced out of the double corner (else he could draw by perpetually moving 1-5 and 5-1). Thus: 14-9, 1-5, 10-14, 5-1, 9-5, 1-6, 5-1, 6-2, 14-18 (14-10 is useless because of 2-6), 2-7, 18-15, 7-2, 15-11.

Tyros are often puzzled by how to win with three against

two. When the two are united in one double corner, the secret is to sacrifice the extra piece so as to force a favorable exchange. Example: Black, K13, K14, K15; White, K1, K2. One way to win is 14-9, 1-6 (not 1-5, 9-6), 9-5, 6-1, 13-9, 1-6 (not 2-7, 15-10), 5-1, 6-13, 15-10, 2-6A, 10-14, 6-2, 14-9. A: or 13-9, 1-5, 9-13, 10-6. When the two kings are in separate double corners, the three should occupy a line between them and force a *cut* (an exchange of captures). Example: Black, K10, K15, K19; White, K9, K27. The play is: 15-18, 9-5, 10-6, 27-32 (not 5-1, 18-15), 19-23, 5-1 (not 32-28, 6-9), 6-9, 1-5A, 9-14, 5-1, 23-27. A: or 32-28, 23-27, 28-32, 9-14.

There is, however, one situation in which one king can draw against two. Example: Black, K29, K30; White, K22. Black to move. After 30-25, 22-17, 25-21, 17-22, it is obvious that 29 can never get out. Nor can Black make headway by sacrificing a piece, for then "the move" is against him.

The Move. The outcome of many end-situations is determined by *the move* (which is analogous to what in Chess is called the *opposition*). Here is the simplest case: Black, K22; White, K14. If it is Black's turn to play, he finds *the move* against him and loses: 22-26, 14-18, 26-31, 18-23. If it is White's turn to play, he similarly finds *the move* against him, but is saved because he can reach a double corner: 14-9, 22-18, 9-5, 18-14, 5-1, 14-9, 1-5, etc.

One player or the other *has the move* regardless of how many or how remote the pieces. Example: Black, 31; White, 2 (the pieces are single whenever K is not specified). Black to move has *the move* and wins by 31-26, 2-7, 26-23, 7-10, 23-18.

Calculation of which side has the move is made by reference to *systems* of squares. A system comprises the 16 playing squares in alternate files; the Black system is the four files downward from squares 1, 2, 3, 4; the White system is the four files upward from 29, 30, 31, 32. With even pieces, the rule is: Count the number of pieces in *either* system. If the number is odd, the player to move *has the move.*

Conversely, if the number is even, the player to move finds *the move against him.*

The move is changed by an ordinary *cut;* this is one of the factors that makes the move a potential rather than a winning advantage. Example: Black, K29, K30; White, K17, K18. Black to play. The move is against him, and he would lose by 29-25, 17-21, 25-29, 18-22. But he can draw by 30-25, threatening to move this king perpetually between 30 and 21. White could interfere only by getting a king to 21 or 30, but at the moment 30-25, 17-21?? permits 25-22, 18-25, 29-22, and *Black* wins. But if 30-25, 18-23 to avoid the cut, Black can forever keep White out of 21 and 30 by checking any king that occupies 17 or 26.

Exchange captures can occur in a way that does not change the move. Example: Black, K7, K22; White, K15, K23. White to play. The move is against him, and he should assure the draw by retreating to the double corner. If he moves 23-18?? Black moves 7-11, and whichever way White captures, Black retains the move and catches the enemy in a single corner.

Even-up Wins. In the foregoing sections, we have seen one way that a player may win against an equal force—he has the move and is able to bottle up all enemy pieces away from a double corner. But there are certain even-up wins against an opponent who has reached a double corner. Chief of these—and of fundamental importance—is "First Position," illustrated in Fig. 24. The White king has reached a double corner, but is betrayed by two circumstances: (a) his single man comes down into the same corner and so eventually obstructs the king; (b) Black has the move.

The beginner should learn the play of Fig. 24 thoroughly: 10-6, 5-1, 14-10, 1-5 (or 21-17, 6-9, 17-13, 9-5), 6-1, 5-9 (or 21-17, 1-6, 17-13, 6-1, 5-9, 1-5), 10-15 (not 1-5, 9-14, and draws), 9-5, 15-18, 5-9 (or 21-17, 18-22, 17-14, 1-6, 5-1, 6-2, 1-5, 22-17, 14-9, or 14-10, 17-14), 1-5, 9-6 (or 9-13, 18-22, 21-17, 5-1, 17-14, 1-5, 14-10, 22-18, 10-6, 5-1, 6-2, 18-14), 18-15, 21-17, 5-1, 6-9, 15-18, 17-13 (or 9-5, 18-22, 17-14, 1-6, 5-1, 6-2, 1-5, 22-17 etc.), 18-15 (not 1-5, 9-14, and draws), 9-14, (or 9-5, 15-10, 5-9, 1-5), 1-5,

14-17 (or 13-9, 15-10), 15-10, 17-22, 10-14, 22-25, 5-1 (useless is 14-18, 25-21, 18-22, 21-17), 25-22, 1-6, 22-25, 6-10, 25-22; 10-15, 22-25, 15-18, and the White king is finally trapped.

FIG. 24—First Position. Black to move and win.

Another way that a player may be able to win even-up, when the opponent has a king in a double corner, is by swapping off this king. Since two or three pieces are needed for this purpose, the opponent must then have a preponderance of pieces elsewhere on the board, and only some extraordinary configuration can prevent these pieces from coming to the rescue. An example is "Second Position." Though not nearly so frequent as First Position, this ending does arise from some regular openings. The typical formation is: Black, K6, 3, 4; White, K32, 12, 13. Black to play and win. The process is as follows. The man on 4 is run through and crowned. The White king cannot hold back this man, since the move is against him. The king is brought back to 11 in order to keep 12 from moving. Then the man on 3 is run through and crowned. This king is posted on 24, at which time the White king is necessarily on 32. Then

White's only move is 32 to 28, and with 11-16 Black is able to accept the cut with only two pieces, since the White man on 12 gives a backing. After 28-19, 16-23, White has the move. But Black regains it with a second cut, which can be forced through the man held on 13. Thus: 12-8, 23-18, 8-3, 18-14, 3-7, 6-1, 7-11, 14-9.

The usual way in which one side develops the preponderance necessary to rout a king from a double corner (at even-up) is by holding two pieces with one elsewhere. Example: Black, K22; White, K30, 13. The Black king holds both White pieces at bay. Even up the forces by adding any Black piece elsewhere, and Black wins because White has to give up a piece. Another example is "Sixth Position": Black, K6, K7, 3; White, K32, 12, 20. White to move and draw. What White has to contend with is that if he moves the king at once, Black will play 7-11. This king holds both White single men, and after 3 is run through to crown Black will have two kings against one in the double corner. To avert this line White has to play 20-16. Now Black will try to hold this man back and win it, but White, having the move, can just draw. Thus: 20-16, 6-10, 32-27, 10-15, 27-24, 7-2 (useless is 15-11, 24-20), 24-20, 2-6 (or 3-7, 16-11), 20-24, 3-7, 12-8, 6-2 (or 15-11, 8-3), 8-4 (not 24-20, 7-11), 15-11, 16-12, and draws.

The rule for calculating who has the move has one exception: with the count against him, a player may yet have the move in effect if he holds an adverse single man locked in the double corner. Example: Black, K3, K5; White, K4, 30. Black to move and win. The count shows that White has the move. Nevertheless: 5-9, 30-25 (the man has to head toward the double corner, since it cannot get by the king on 3), 9-14, 25-21, 14-9, 21-17, *9-6 (a star is the conventional symbol to indicate "the only move"), 17-13 (not 17-14, 6-10, and the cut gives Black the move), 6-1, 13-9, 3-7, 4-8, 7-2, 9-5 (else Black will win the man by 1-5), 2-7. Now Black in effect has the move against the White king and traps it.

Piece-down Draws and Wins. We have already noted

that one king may draw against two kings in the single corner. Essentially the same position may occur at the side of the board, with king vs. king and man. Example: Black, K18; White, K21, 13. Black to play draws by 18-22. Then 21-17, *22-18, 17-21, 18-22. Likewise we have seen that one king can trap two pieces, drawing because the opponent has to give up his extra piece. A two-for-one hold may actually give victory to the weaker side. Example: Black, K11; White, 12, 20. White to play loses, because even after he gives up a piece, the move is against him and the other piece is trapped.

Of fundamental importance is the ending shown in Fig. 25, Payne's Draw. Black to play cannot win, as White can perpetually prevent the man on 13 from advancing.

FIG. 25—Payne's Draw. Black to move, White draws.

The main line is: 14-17, *23-26, 17-21, 26-23, 15-10, *23-26, 10-14, *26-30, 14-17, *22-18, and now Black has to give up his extra piece (by 17-14, for 17-22 actually loses). Observe that the principle of the draw is to keep the piece on 22 as long as possible; Black cannot drive it away without tying himself up. White's final move 22-18 is starred because 30-26 now loses thus: 21-25, 22-29, 17-22.

The avoidance of Payne's Draw is the motif of many end-games, notably of the important "Third Position": Black, K13, K21, 5; White, K14, K22. Black to move and win. The essential idea is shown by this variation: 13-9, 22-18, 9-6, 18-22, 6-1, 22-18, 21-25, 18-15, 1-6, 14-17, 6-2, 17-14, 25-22, 15-10, 22-26, 14-18, 5-9, 10-6, 9-13, 6-10, 26-31, 10-14, 31-27, 18-22, 27-23, etc. The move 27-23 is the crux of the situation; it prevents White from bringing a king to 26 to back up 22. Black must be careful not to advance his single man to 13 until he can occupy 23 or else get the single man down to 21.

Most piece-down draws depend on holding back an adverse single man. A helpful guide is "Patterson's Rule": Count the pieces in *your own* system; if it is your turn to move, and the number is even, hold an adverse man on your single corner side; if the number is odd, hold a man on your double corner side. The rule is illustrated in Fig. 26.

Fig. 26—Illustration of Patterson's Rule. Either to move, White draws.

White to play draws by Payne's Draw, moving 19-23, 23-26, etc. With Black to play: 2-7, 22-26, 13-17, 26-31, 17-22, 19-23, 22-25A, 31-27, 25-30, 27-31, 7-10, 23-19, 10-14, 19-23, 14-17, 31-27, 17-22, 27-31, and this position is "Roger's Draw." The point of it is that if at A or any subsequent time Black plays 20-24, then 23-27 forces 24-28, and after 27-32 the other White king has a "quadruple corner" from 31 to 20, along which he can move perpetually and never be driven out.

One piece may win against two or more by blockade. Example: Black, K29, K30, 18; White, K17, K27. White wins by 17-22, 18-25, 27-23. One white King wins three Black pieces. Problems have been concocted to show how one surviving piece can immobilize twelve adverse pieces. The king-row tangle, oddly enough, is not uncommon in actual play. Here is a sample: Black, K29, 12, 18, 21, 28; White, K2, 26, 30, 32. White won by 26-22, 18-25, 2-7, 12-16, 7-11, 16-19, 32-27, 28-32, 11-16, 32-23, 30-26.

Two single men can blockade three, even in the middle of the board. Example: Black, 10, 14, 15; White, 22, 23.

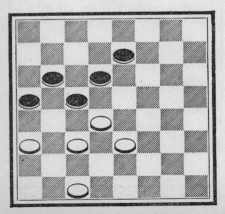

Fig. 27—White to move and win.

Black to play actually loses. Avoidance of this formation is frequently the motif of mid-game and even opening play. A surprising position is Fig. 27.

Black threatens to win two-for-one by 14-17, and if White averts this by 30-26 he runs out of moves after 7-11. But White wins by sacrificing a piece at once: 18-15, 10-26, 30-23, and after 7-11, 23-19, it is Black who is out of moves. He has to give up two pieces, leaving White one up.

Shots and Strokes. The formation shown in Fig. 27, where Black threatens to win two-for-one, is one of many in which such *shots* can occur. Others are illustrated in Fig. 28. If Black moves 21-25, thinking to run the man through, White can win two-for-one by "knocking out the middle man" with 31-26. If White moves 19-15, trying to run the man through by 15-11, Black beats him to the punch with 7-11.

Fig. 28—Two-for-one shots.

The danger that a careless move will allow such a shot is omnipresent in opening and mid-game play. The tyro, against an experienced opponent, will usually lose a piece or two within the first dozen moves. Here is the sort of thing that happens: 11-15, 23-18, 8-11, 21-17??, 9-14, and White is a piece down.

A stroke is a combination leading to a winning advantage, through a series of forced moves. It may or may not result in the gain of a piece. Analysis has brought to light hundreds of strokes that can occur in opening or mid-game play, as the result of one false move. Best-known is the "Goosewalk" or "Farmer." The crucial position can arise from the Single Corner opening as follows: 11-15, 22-18, 15-22, 25-18, 8-11, 29-25, 4-8, 24-20, 10-15, 25-22, 12-16. Now 27-24 is very inviting; it threatens to win two-for-one by 24-19, and if Black defends by 8-12 the cut by 24-19 leaves him a bad formation on this side of the board. But continue: 27-24? 15-19! 24-15, 16-19! 23-16, 9-14, 18-9, 11-22. Next move Black regains his third piece by 5-14, and this man blocks 21-17, so that Black gets a king and then brings him out. Though the pieces are even, White loses, as he cannot force his way to the king-row. The Black king is bound to gather some loot.

Another opening trap that frequently catches the tyro is the "Big Stroke," arising from the Old Fourteenth opening as follows: 11-15, 23-19, 8-11, 22-17, 4-8, 17-13, 15-18, 24-20, 11-15, 28-24, 8-11, 26-23, 9-14, 31-26, 6-9, 13-6, 2-9, 26-22. It seems natural to oppose this advance with 9-13, but this is the loser. Continue: 9-13? 20-16! 11-20, 22-17, 13-22, 21-17, 14-21, 23-14, 10-17, 25-2. Though pieces are even, White has the first king, and is able to bring it out to wreak havoc before Black can get a king.

The possibility of a stroke lurks in even the unlikeliest-looking position. Fig. 29 is an example. White appears to have the worst of it. If he makes a king, so will Black, and the White single men in the center will be in more danger than the Black men at the sides. Thus: 8-3, 23-26, 30-23, 19-26, 3-7, 26-30, and after the captures White will have to fight to save his men. If instead of 3-7, White plays 25-21, thinking then to catch 10, he is hoist with his own petard. Black makes his king and leaves it on 30 while advancing his men on the other side; if White plays 3-7, then 30-26 wins two-for-one. Or, if White moves his piece from 25 up

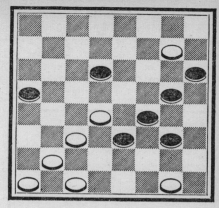

FIG. 29—White to move and win.

to 17, with intention of 3-7, Black moves his king to 25 and threatens to win a piece by 10-15. In the initial position, the possibility of a saving stroke seems to be precluded by the fact that the armies are largely past each other. White cannot press on any Black man except 10. Yet salvation is to be found in chasing this sole laggard down to a position of seeming safety! The play goes: 18-15, 10-14, 22-18, 14-17, 25-21, 17-22. Who would think that White now has a forced win! Continue: 29-25, 22-29, 30-25, 29-22, 15-11, 22-15, 8-4, 15-8, 4-18 (capturing four men). Once more the forces are even, but White has a king and Black has not. Black is bound to lose a piece.

The Bridge. The *bridge* is a formation of two pieces on the first rank: 1 and 3 for Black, 30 and 32 for White. So placed, the two pieces offer more resistance to the entry of adverse men seeking crowns than does any other formation. It is true with fair generality that a player should keep his bridge intact so long as he can (but there are exceptions even in opening play!).

To get past the Black bridge, White has to post a piece on

10 and then march other men to 2 through 6 or 7. The "keystone" on 10 cannot himself acquire a crown unless Black is induced to break the bridge. A great many endings therefore revolve around the effort to break a bridge, by forcing an exchange, or to capture a keystone. A position of fundamental importance is "Petterson's Drawbridge," Fig. 30. White can defend his keystone on 10 by keeping his

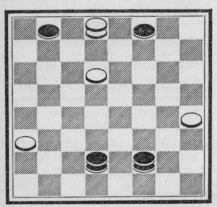

FIG. 30—Petterson's Drawbridge. White to draw.

king ready to move to 2 whenever a Black king moves to 14 or 15. But with two kings Black threatens to win 10 by posting them on 9 and 15 or 11 and 14. The pieces on 20 and 21 save White from this process by denying access to 9 or 11 except through an avenue that attacks 10 prematurely. White draws by shuttling 2-6, 6-2 or 2-7, 7-2, never moving 20 or 21 unless Black breaks his bridge.

A typical winning bridge position is: Black, K14, 1, 3; White, 6, 7, 10. Black to play and win: 14-9, 6-2 (or 7-2, 3-8 and White has to give up a piece), 1-5, 10-6, 3-10, 6-1, 10-15, 1-6, 9-13. White cannot regain his piece, and Black wins by Third Position after making a second king.

Key Squares. A White piece on 14 or a Black piece on 19

tends to cramp the adverse double corner. These two so-called "key squares" play an important part in the theory of the opening. The objective of particular moves or maneuvers is frequently to establish and maintain a piece on a key square, or to prevent the opponent from doing so. Note that from 14 a White piece is ready to step to 10 and form a keystone against the Black bridge; and 14 cannot be removed by a regular *cut* without breaking the bridge. Of course, 14 if not sufficiently defended may be *run off* by attack from Black men on 5 and 9 or 7 and 10.

The Openings. Black has seven possible first moves. All are playable. Objectively speaking, one is no stronger than another. The strongest opening is that which you know best and your opponent knows least.

White likewise has seven possible first moves, and it is now held that each of them is a feasible reply to any one of the Black openings, with two exceptions: 21-17 in reply to either 9-14 or 10-14 loses a piece without compensation. Many of the remaining 47 two-move combinations are weak for White; some are weak for Black. Four of them were formerly *barred* from tournament play: 9-14, 23-18; 10-14, 23-18; 11-16, 23-19; and 12-16, 23-19. The last is weakest of all. But "scientific draws" appear to have been established in all four openings.

Of the mechanically possible continuations by Black after the first two moves, a good many have been ruled out as known losses. But more than 150 three-move combinations have been analyzed as playable for both sides.

Many of the opening moves and formations have acquired traditional names, which are given below.

> Alma: 11-15, 23-19, 8-11, 22-17, 3-8.
> Ayshire Lassie: 11-15, 24-20.
> Black Doctor: 11-15, 23-19, 8-11, **22-17, 9-13, 17-14,**
> > 10-17, 19-10, 7-14.
> Boston: 11-15, 22-17, 9-13, 17-14.
> Bristol: 11-16.
> Bristol Cross: 11-16, 23-18.
> Centre: 11-15, 23-19, 8-11, 22-17, 15-18.

Cross: 11-15, 23-18.
Defiance: 11-15, 23-19, 9-14, 27-23.
Denny: 10-14.
Double Corner: 9-14.
Douglas: 11-15, 22-17, 8-11, 17-13, 4-8, 25-22.
Dundee: 12-16.
Dyke: 11-15, 22-17.
Edinburgh: 9-13.
Fife: 11-15, 23-19, 9-14, 22-17, 5-9.
Glasgow: 11-15, 23-19, 8-11, 22-17, 11-16.
Kelso: 10-15.
Laird and Lady: 11-15, 23-19, 8-11, 22-17, 9-13, 17-14,
    10-17, 21-14.
Maid of the Mill: 11-15, 22-17, 8-11, 17-13, 15-18.
Nailor: 11-15, 23-19, 8-11, 26-23.
Old Fourteenth: 11-15, 23-19, 8-11, 22-17, 4-8.
Orthodox: 11-15, 23-19.
Paisley: 11-16, 24-19.
Pioneer: 11-15, 22-17, 8-11, 25-22.
Second Double Corner: 11-15, 24-19.
Single Corner: 11-15, 22-18.
Souter: 11-15, 23-19, 9-14, 22-17, 6-9.
Switcher: 11-15, 21-17.
Tillicoultry: 11-15, 23-19, 8-11, 22-18.
Wagram: 11-15, 22-17, 9-13, 24-20.
Waterloo: 11-15, 23-18, 8-11, 18-14.
Whilter: 11-15, 23-19, 9-14, 22-17, 7-11.
White Doctor: 11-16, 22-18, 10-14, 25-22, 8-11, 24-20,
    16-19, 23-16, 14-23, 26-19.
White Dyke: 11-15, 22-17, 8-11, 17-14.
Will-o'-the-Wisp: 11-15, 23-19, 9-13.

EXAMPLE GAMES

The following example games are selected to show some
of the common formations that arise after each of Black's
seven possible openings.

Game 1.   Edinburgh
R. Stewart vs. R. Jordan

9-13	10-15	11-16
22-18	18-14 (a)	21-17

13-22	21-14	6-9 (d)
25-11	1-6	15-10
8-15	30-25	9-18
24-19	6-10	10-3
15-24	25-21	18-23
27-11	10-17	24-15
7-16	21-14	23-30
23-18 (b)	2-6	3-7
3-7	18-15 (c)	30-25
29-25	16-19	7-11
6-10	32-27	
25-21	4-8	
10-17	27-24	W wins

(a) Taking the key square. Note as the play progresses how this man hampers the Black development.

(b) Now 14 is secure and cannot be run off, as White can bring up defenders as fast as it is attacked. The right continuation for Black is 4-8, with a narrow draw. His actual move is a mistake.

(c) Now 14 is protected by the fact that 6-9 can be answered by 15-10. White would get the first king and keep the Black pieces out of his double corner.

(d) The answer to 7-11 would not be 14-10, which allows a draw, but 24-20, 11-18, 26-23, 19-26, 31-15, 6-9, 14-10 and wins the man on 11, as in the game.

Game 2.   Double Corner

Denvir vs. Wright

9-14	5-9	4-8
22-17	17-13	32-27
11-15	2-6	10-14
25-22	30-25	18-15 (c)
15-19 (a)	7-10	14-17
24-15	22-18	25-21
10-19	15-22	9-14
17-10	25-18	27-24 (d)
6-15	8-11	*16-20
23-16	27-23 (b)	23-16
12-19	11-16	20-27
21-17	29-25	31-24

8-11	24-15	1-19
16-7	6-9	
3-19	13-6	B wins

(a) Taking command of the key square 19.
(b) Easy ways of losing here are 27-24, 10-14 and 29-25, 19-23, 26-19, 10-15.
(c) Necessary to escape the two-for-one by 16-20.
(d) Losing by the beautiful stroke that follows. There is a narrow draw by 13-9 followed by 27-24.

Game 3. Denny

Benstead vs. Nicholson

10-14	10-14	4-8
22-17	31-26	23-19 (a)
7-10	16-20	11-16
17-13	32-28	19-15
3-7	7-11	16-19
24-19	19-16	13-9 (b)
11-16	12-19	6-13
28-24	23-7	15-10
14-18	2-11	5-9
23-14	26-23	24-15
9-18	8-12	18-22 (c)
26-23	30-26	B wins

(a) Loses. The cut by 25-22 draws.
(b) It is now too late for 25-22, for after the cut 14-18 would win a piece. White sacrifices a piece momentarily, as he will capture 19 in return. But Black gets a tempo to set up a shot.
(c) Black emerges a piece up.

Game 4. Kelso-Cross

Lieberman vs. Ginsburg

10-15	30-26	6-9
23-18	16-20	24-19
12-16	21-17	15-24
26-23	9-13	28-19
8-12	17-14	11-16

25-21	29-25	19-10
1-6	19-24 (c)	8-11
19-15 (a)	28-19	22-17 (d)
7-10	6-10	13-22
14-7	25-21	26-17
3-19	7-11	9-13 (e)
32-28	17-14	7-3
2-7	10-17	
21-17	21-14	
4-8 (b)	11-15	W wins

(a) This move is feasible because if Black takes the two-for-one, as he does, White can immediately set up a return two-for-one shot.

(b) The only move to draw is 7-10. Note that Black cannot play 6-10, in order to break loose by 9-14, because White will play 27-24 and win three-for-one.

(c) Black will run out of moves in two more turns if he does not give up his extra piece at once to eliminate the three-for-one threat.

(d) This is the killer. Black is bound to get his piece back, but this way of ceding it prevents Black from drawing by 11-15, 18-11, 9-25.

(e) Obviously forced. But White crowns first and then wins the man on 11. The Black king comes too late to make trouble. White can clear his men out of the center by the cut 14-9.

Game 5. Old Fourteenth

Analysis by J. Birkenshaw

11-15	26-23	15-22
23-19	9-14	17-13 (b)
8-11	31-26	*14-17
22-17	6-9 (a)	21-14
4-8	13-6	9-18
17-13	2-9	23-14
15-18	26-22	10-17
24-20	1-6	32-28 (c)
11-15	22-17	17-21
28-24	18-22	19-16
8-11	25-18	12-19

24-8	7-11	23-18
3-12	27-23	12-16
28-24	6-10	B wins

(a) This cut avoids several ways of losing, of which the novice's favorite is 5-9, 21-17.
(b) Loses. There is a draw by 23-18.
(c) On 30-25 or 27-23 Black moves 22-26 and gets a quick king.

Game 6.   Bristol

Wyllie vs. Barker

11-16	11-15	9-18
24-19	18-11	22-17 (f)
8-11	7-16 (b)	18-23
22-18	32-28	27-18
10-14	2-6 (c)	20-24
25-22	19-15 (d)	28-19
6-10	10-19	16-30 (g)
28-24	24-15	
16-20 (a)	14-18 (e)	
30-25	23-14	B wins

(a) The student should note that the Black formation in the single corner would be very weak were White allowed to play 24-20.
(b) But this Black formation is strong.
(c) Setting a trap that White promptly falls into.
(d) Correct is 22-18, though Black still has the better game.
(e) This move wrecks the White game.
(f) The only way to prevent the coup that follows would be 26-23. But then Black wins by 3-7, 23-14, 6-10, 15-6, 1-26, 31-22, 16-19. Then he brings the man from 7 to 16 and plays 19-24, winning two-for-one.
(g) White cannot make a king and runs out of moves. Black meanwhile can run 12 down to 32 and make another king.

Game 7.   Dundee

J. P. Reed vs. C. F. Barker

| 12-16 | 8-12 | 9-14 |
| 24-20 | 28-24 | 22-17 |

3-8	20-11	4-8 (c)
26-22	8-15	27-23
11-15	23-16	19-24
20-11	12-19	31-27
7-16	17-13 (b)	24-31
24-20	5-9	22-17
15-19 (a)	30-26	W wins

(a) The loser. 16-19 draws and so does 5-9.
(b) This move stops 2-7 or 4-8, for then White would win three-for-two by 13-9, 6-13, 22-17.
(c) The same stroke would follow 2-7. Black cannot move 14-18 because of 27-23, and if 6-9, White moves 22-17 after the exchange and Black cannot play 9-13.

BACKGAMMON

A board game for two players, Backgammon combines luck and skill in about equal proportions. The moves are governed by chance rolls of dice, but the latitude in choice of moves is sufficient so that in nine times out of ten a skillful player is likely to beat one who is inexperienced.

How to Play Backgammon

The Board. The players sit at opposite sides of a rectangular board, whose appearance is shown in Fig. 31. The outer rim of the board is raised above the surface, and so is the *bar* that bisects it—thus the *stones* are kept from sliding off the board.

The twenty-four *points* (the elongated triangles) are painted on the recessed surfaces, in two alternating colors (white and red, or white and black). In ancient times, the board was marked with twelve lines parallel to the bar; in the course of time, these lines were broken at the middle, then thickened at the base, to make the modern *points*. It may help the beginner to visualize the game to say that the *stones* move from line to line, as though they were climbing the rungs of a ladder.

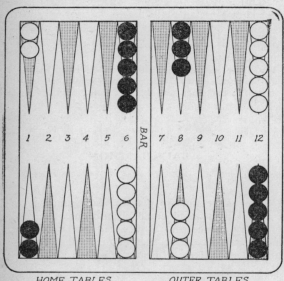

Fig. 31—Initial position of Backgammon. The captions and numbers do not appear on the board, but are added in the diagram to explain the notation.

The *bar* divides the board into two *tables,* which are called *inner* (or *home*) and *outer*. The players agree at the outset which is to be which. Custom is to designate the table "toward the light" as the inner.

The Stones. The pieces are called *stones*. A common type of folding checker board is made like a box, and is marked on the outside for Checkers, on the inside for Backgammon.

The checker pieces serve for either game. But when Backgammon boards are made separately, the stones furnished are larger and heavier than checkers.

Each player has fifteen stones of his own color. For uniformity we will call the players Black and White, and the stones accordingly, though the latter are usually white and red or red and black.

Notation. The numbers shown on the diagram, Fig. 31, do not appear on the board, but are used in the notation of the game. The points on each side of the board are numbered from 1 to 12, from inner to outer table. A point is designated by its number, preceded by W or B. The points W7 and B7 are commonly called the *bar points,* while W12 and B12 are known as the *comfort stations.*

As shown by Fig. 31, the initial posting of the stones is as follows, where the number in parentheses is the number of stones put on a single point:

> *Black:* W1 (2); W12 (5); B8 (3); B6 (5).
> *White:* B1 (2); B12 (5); W8 (3); W6 (5).

The two stones on the adverse 1-point are called *runners.*

A move is described by the point from which the stone is moved and that on which it lands. If more than one stone is moved in the same way, the total so moved is given in parentheses. Thus B12-W7 means that White moves one stone from the comfort station to his bar point; B8-B5 (2) means that Black moves two stones from his 8- to his 5-point.

Other Equipment. Each player is provided with two dice and a dice cup. The only other item of equipment is a *doubling cube,* somewhat larger than the dice, bearing on its separate faces the numbers 2, 4, 8, 16, 32, 64. This cube is used to keep track of the *doubles.* (The introduction of *doubling* in the 1920's gave Backgammon a new lease of life, and brought it from a largely juvenile arena into the adult card clubs and gambling casinos.)

Casting Dice. To commence a game, each player rolls one die. The higher number marks the first player. If equal numbers are cast, both players must roll again until different numbers are cast. The first player makes his first move in accordance with the numbers on the dice in this initial cast. Thereafter the players move alternately, and to govern his move the player rolls his own two dice from his dice box.

A roll is void if either die is *cocked*, i.e., fails to land with one face flat on the table. Players often agree that a roll is also void if either die goes outside the table in which both are cast.

Movement of Stones. The White stones move always in the direction B1-B12 on the Black side of the board, and W12-W1 on the White side. The points B12 and W12 are consecutive. The Black stones move in the converse direction: W1-W12 and B12-B1. Each player thus moves his stones around a course that ends at his own home (inner) table.

When all fifteen of his stones lie in his home table, the player may begin to *bear off*. Bearing off is in effect a continued movement in the same direction, past the 1-point to a hypothetical 0-point off the board.

The player wins who first bears off all his fifteen stones.

Rules on Moving. In accordance with the numbers that turn up on his dice, the player advances one or more of his stones in the prefixed direction, from point to point. The moves are governed by the following rules.

1. The two numbers on the dice may be applied to one stone, or to two stones separately. For example, on roll of 5-2 the player may advance one stone 7 points, or one stone 5 points and another 2.

2. *Doublets* are taken twice over. A doublet is the cast of the same number of both dice. For example, on roll of 3-3, the player is entitled to four 3's for a total of 12, and he may apply the roll to one, two, three, or four stones.

3. The player must if possible use both or all numbers on the dice. If he can use only one of two different numbers, he must if possible use the higher. If he cannot use all of a doublet, he must use all that he can.

4. If unable to make any move at all, whatever the cast, a player does not roll at all; the opponent makes consecutive rolls until he opens up a possible move to the other.

5. Any number of stones of one color may occupy one point.

6. A stone may not come to rest on a point occupied by two or more stones of opposite color. Such a point is *closed* (or *made*). When a stone makes a compound move, using two or more numbers on the dice, it is construed to rest momentarily on the intermediate points, and therefore must find suitable intermediate points *open*. For example, to apply a roll of 6-3 to one stone, the player must first move 6 to an open point, or 3 to an open point, then to the open point 9 away. If neither intermediate point is open, the compound move is impossible, even though the point 9 away be open.

7. A single stone on a point is a *blot*. If a stone of opposite color comes to rest (permanently or in passing) on that point, the blot is *hit* and must at once be removed and placed on the *bar*.

8. A stone *on the bar* must be *entered* before the owner may move any other stone.

9. From the bar, a stone must *enter* the adverse inner table. Entry is possible only when the owner rolls on one die a number corresponding to an *open point* in the adverse inner table. For example, if only the 5-point is open, the owner must roll a 5 on one die to enter his stone at all; a roll of 4-1 or 3-2 would not suffice.

10. Having several stones on the bar, a player must enter all of them before he may advance any or move any other stone.

11. A player may bear off only when none of his stones is outside his own inner table. Having begun to bear off, and then having had a blot hit, the player must enter it and bring it around to his home table before he can resume bearing off.

12. In bearing off, the player may remove any stone from a point corresponding to a number on one die; may move

within the table instead of bearing off; *must* remove a stone from the highest occupied point when one die shows a number as high or higher still. For example, on roll of 5-2, the player might use the 5 to remove one stone from the 5-point, or to move one stone from 6 to 1. If the 2-point were vacant, but any higher point occupied, he would of necessity have to use the 2 for a move within the board. With no stones at all on the 6- and 5-points, he would be compelled to use the 5 by removing one stone from the 4-point (or whatever is the highest occupied point).

Doubling. A game of Backgammon is customarily played for a basic stake, which is subject to increase as follows.

A player is *gammoned* if he has borne off not a single stone at the time his opponent wins. A gammon costs a double stake. A player is *backgammoned* if, besides having borne off not a single stone, he has a stone on the bar or in the adverse home table. A backgammon costs a triple stake.

If equal numbers are cast in the roll for first turn, the stake is doubled. Players usually agree to limit such *automatic doubles* to one or two.

Either player, in his turn to move but before casting his dice, may *double*. The opponent must either agree to continue at a doubled stake, or must resign the game and settle at the present value of the stake. Once either player has made the first such *voluntary double,* the right to make additional doubles alternates. The doubling cube is used to keep track of the value of the stake, increased by automatic and voluntary doubles.

STRATEGY OF BACKGAMMON

General Plan. It takes 167 points (on the dice) to bring around and bear off all fifteen stones, from their initial positions. If there were no obstacle to the movement of stones, the game would go by luck to the player first to roll a total of 167. A player who at any stage is notably ahead of his opponent in the race should naturally seek to keep it a simple *running game.* For example, an early roll of

6-6 gives a player a marked lead; many a player will double next turn after 6-6, almost regardless of all other considerations. Of course, it is chancy to rely on a lead established by a single roll—and therefore capable of being offset by a single roll. But the principle remains that a substantial lead in a simple running game is a good basis for a double, a psychological weapon that often induces the opponent to resign.

The precepts of the running game are brief and easy to understand: (a) Play as safe as possible; (b) Waste as few numbers as possible.

But Backgammon is more than a simple race. To carry out the analogy, it is a race in which, under certain circumstances, a runner is entitled to set up hurdles in the path of his opponent, or send him back to the starting line. The rules on closing points and hitting blots allow very few games to be won by rolling only 167. A marked lead may turn into a deficit when a blot is sent to the bar. A *prime* or a *shutout* (explained later) may force a player to waste roll after roll.

A player who is markedly behind in the race at any stage naturally strives to complicate the position, to block and delay his opponent. So long as the two armies are not entirely past each other, the possibility of momentous collision exists. Even the player with a commanding lead must reckon with the chance that a very bad roll on one side or a very good roll on the other may equalize the race or turn the tables. Therefore, it may be said that the normal course for both players is to play a *flexible game,* adaptable to all eventualities. The pure *running game* is an exception that may be essayed by a player with a large lead (and which both play perforce after the two armies are past each other).

If there is any single vital principle in the flexible game, it is to establish *lasting advantages,* as distinguished from ephemeral gains.

The exception in the other direction is the *back game,* which may be forced on a player when he is extremely far behind. The extremity normally arises only when the player has one or more *runners* trapped in the adverse home table by a fairly solid phalanx of adversely closed points. For example, if Black has made his own bar and 5-points, besides the 6- and 8-points, the White runners on B1 have very little hope of escape until the whole Black army is in its home table. The White runners could put up a better fight if there were more of them. The *back game* contemplates getting as many stones as possible into the adverse home table, to close as many points as possible to the incoming enemy, and eventually to hit blots and enforce an even greater delay upon the enemy.

The first principle of the back game is that its chance of success is proportional to the number of points held in the adverse home table. A one-point back game scarcely deserves the name; two points may serve; three points is the minimum to be striven for.

Lasting Advantages. The advantage to be sought at all normal times is to *make* (close) certain key points. Most vital of these are one's own 7-point (bar) and 5-point. Closure of either lessens the chances of the adverse runners to get by safely, and closure of both points (while holding the 6- and 8-points) makes an almost impassable barrier. Further, all additional points made around the bar provide safe landing stations for one's own stones coming down from the other side of the board, and so decrease the offensive prospects of the adverse runners.

After the bar and 5-points, the most important are one's own 4- and 3-points in that order. All points in one's own home table are good to close, but if only one point besides the 6 can be made, the value of the point ebbs as it recedes from the 6. The 4 is surely desirable; some players consider the 3-point of little value (alone), and certainly making the 2 or 1 has little significance. But after the 5 or 4 is made, any additional point regardless of number is usually worth making.

All the foregoing assumes that the opponent has at least one runner back of the points mentioned. The purpose in making such points, as has been stated, is twofold: to hold back the adverse runners, and also to save one's own army from blotting near them. But even when the runners have escaped, it often is worthwhile to close the key points, and *build up the home table*. The idea is to try to hit a blot with one's own runners, whereupon the opponent will find greatly increased difficulty in entering the blot and bringing it around.

The Prime. The closing of key points looks toward the ultimate ideal of establishing a *prime*. This is a barricade of six consecutive closed points, with one or more adverse runners trapped behind it. Patently, a prime is impassable. Once having made a prime, the player tries to "walk" it into his home board; once there, is it a *shutout*. If an ad-

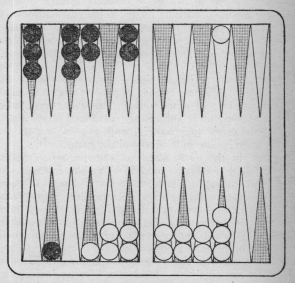

Fig. 32—The prime. A Black runner is trapped behind the White prime. White has laid a blot just ahead of his prime; when he covers it, the prime will have "walked" one step.

verse stone has been sent to the bar in the process, the opponent has no move until the prime is eventually broken perforce by bearing off.

The prime, using twelve stones, leaves three extra stones. To walk it ahead, move one of the extra stones as soon as possible to the point just ahead of the prime. Then cover it, preferably from the rear of the prime on roll of a 6. It does not matter (usually) that the stone laid ahead of the prime is a blot. If the opponent hits it, nothing is lost (usually) even if the opponent himself has a shutout. He will have to break sometime and let the blot enter—and meanwhile the prime stands intact against his runner. However, unlucky rolls can break a prime prematurely. The worst hazard is 5-5 or 4-4—these numbers usually cannot be absorbed entirely by the three extra stones. Another hazard is the trapping of one or two extra stones in the adverse home table, leaving only two or one extra stones to absorb awkward rolls that do not advance the prime in the regular way.

A prime is more deadly against a single runner than against several. A single runner is no obstacle to a regular walking tour. Two or more runners, however, may make a point. If this point is sufficiently advanced (say, on the 5-point), the prime may have to walk over it, and the runners may then escape in time to win the game.

Builders. In the early stage of a game, when nothing better offers, it is usually good to bring some stones from the comfort station down to your 9-, 10-, and 11-points. Such stones are called *builders,* because they help to make the key 7- and 5-points. Further, making any of these points in the outer table has potential value, which is considerably enhanced if you also make your bar point. A prime, when it develops, usually starts in this area.

The Runners. The two runners originally posted on the adverse 1-point are the "headache." There are various theories about when and how to bring them out. One school says, bring them out early, before your opponent has made up additional points around the bar. Another says, build

up your table and let the runners take care of themselves—
they fight better after you have prepared trouble for adverse blots. One school says, don't advance a runner until
you can bring him from the 1-point to the outer table. Another school says, advance both runners at once, keeping
them within six points of each other, so that the rearmost
can threaten an adverse blot that hits the foremost.

The best counsel is perhaps to do what disconcerts your
opponent most. Splitting the runners early, for example,
may prove good policy against a player who is hesitant to
leave blots. Against a "wide open" player who will take
risks for the sake of making key points quickly, the same
policy may be suicidal.

Opening Rolls. Under the modern rule, the first move of
a game is always made on two different numbers, never a
doublet. Certain of the combinations are "naturals," allowing a key point to be made. There is no argument about the
best way to use such rolls. Others are nondescript or
positively awkward, and here opinions differ. All alternatives worthy of notice are discussed below. They are given
for white as the first player.

6-5. A natural; move B1-B12. This is called "Lover's
Leap." There is no good alternative.

6-4. Most orthodox is B1-B11, getting one runner almost
to safety. In this connection, we may note that a blot is
easiest to hit when it is 6 away, and becomes progressively
harder as it is nearer or farther. On B11, the blot can
be hit only by a flat 2 from W12 (roll of 1-1 would not
serve); it is therefore as safe as it can be as a blot. An
alternative way of handling 6-4 is B12-W7 and B1-B5.
The idea is to try for one's bar point; if the blot there is
hit, there is good chance of making the enemy 5-point in
compensation. Holding this point in early play has good
prospects both for offense (hitting of builders) and defense
(reaching the comfort station). Another alternative is B12-
W7 and B12-W9, concentrating on making the bar point.
We prefer this to the previous alternative, for the most hazardous of all procedures is to leave two blots including one

in the adverse home table. If he can hit both, the opponent has good chances of building up a near-prime quickly.

6-3. Much like 6-4, but less desirable. The alternatives are B1-B10; or B12-W7 and B1-B4; or B12-W7 and W8-W5. The last leaves two blots within reach of the adverse runners, but they are both on key points. This is our preference, for we consider it worth one stone sent to the bar to make either key point. (Of course, such "wide open" play is appropriate when the adverse home board is still wide open, for then it is at least 30 to 1 that the blot can be entered next turn, and there is also fair chance that the blot remaining on the bar or 5-point can be covered. The over-cautious player blots only when he cannot help himself; the rational player weighs the potential advantage of blotting against the chances of quick entry if the blot is hit.)

6-2. One of the less desirable rolls. Orthodox is B12-W5, a gambit to make the 5-point. Another idea is B12-W7 and B12-W11. Take your choice, according as you value the 5-point over the bar point, or vice versa. (Even as to this preference there are warring schools of thought!)

6-1. A natural. Make the bar point by B12-W7 and W8-W7.

5-4. Let us note at once that all early 5's are awkward, since they cannot be absorbed by the runners or by the stones on the 6-point, and from the comfort station 5's go to the already-made 8-point. Hence the question with an opening roll including 5 is not what is the best move, but what is the least bad. The orthodox choice for 5-4 is B1-B10 or B12-W8 and B1-B5. The second alternative is naturally contemned by the school who frown on splitting the runners within the table (we are of that school). Most popular today is B12-W8 and B12-W9, bringing a builder down.

5-3. Orthodox is to make the 3-point by W8-W3 and W6-W3. This is our preference, but some moderns sneer at the 3-point and move B12-W8 and W12-W10.

5-2. Standard is B12-W8 and B12-W11, and scarcely any alternative is possible under the rules.

5-1. Old-time books suggest either B12-W8 and W6-W5,

or B12-W8 and B1-B2. The first is an orthodox gambit to make the 5-point. The second is the best split of the runners if you are going to split inside the board—your opponent has less prospect of gain by hitting a blot in his home table on 1 or 2 than by hitting on a more advanced point. The idea of the split is of course to make the 5-point of the bar point on the adverse side of the board. A modern idea for handling 5-1 is B12-W7, a gambit to make the bar point.

4-3. Best in our view is to bring down two builders, by B12-W9 and B12-W10. If you are of the "split the runners" school, you may prefer B1-B5 and B12-W10.

4-2. A natural. Make the 4-point by W8-W4 and W6-W4.

4-1. Two hundred years ago it was discovered that as good a prospect as any is offered by the gambit B12-W9 and W6-W5. If the blot is not at once hit, the chances are strong that it can be covered and the 5-point secured. Alternatives that have been suggested (we consider them far inferior) are: B12-W9 and B1-B2; B1-B5 and W6-W5.

3-2. This roll offers a straight choice between "building" and "splitting." Since we are of the "building" school, we recommend B12-W10 and B12-W11. The other idea is B1-B4 and B12-W11.

3-1. A natural. Make the 5-point by W8-W5 and W6-W5.

2-1. The orthodox choice is between B12-W10 and B12-W11, W6-W5. You bring down one builder, or offer a gambit to make the 5-point. But our own preference is for W6-W4 and W6-W5—leaving two blots. The idea back of this extraordinary play is as follows: If the opponent hits neither of the blots, the chances are strong of covering one or both next turn. If he hits one blot, we still may cover the other, and at worst have prospect of playing a thorough *back game.* The greatest hazard of a real back game is that the player is forced to put some of his stones out of play by moving them to low points in his inner table. The most useless stones for a back game are therefore the extra three on one's 6-point. The chance of winning by back play are increased according as these supernumeraries are sent back of the enemy lines.

Only one self-acknowledged Backgammon expert in ten understands how to defend against a thorough-going back game. The way an expert wins, nine out of ten times, against a tyro, is to strew blots *ad lib* and invite hits—if the gambits to make key points do not succeed, the expert plays a back game in which his opponent usually co-operates.

Early Doublets. The following is orthodox opinion on how to handle an early roll of a doublet, if the moves are feasible.

6-6. There is little choice when no point initially held has been abandoned. You move (as White) B1-B7 (2) and B12-W7 (2). You make your bar point, which is very desirable, and the opponent's bar point, which is not so good. The runners on B7, unless you can wait for doublets, have to run one at a time. The one left behind when they split has a maximum chance to be hit. Hence the counsel: If you have made the adverse bar point, vacate it as quickly as possible. Your runners can no longer fight against the opponent's making up his home board, which therefore only becomes better, not worse. Split your runners while the chances of entry of the remaining blot are at the maximum.

5-5. Too much of a good thing! Move B12-W3 (2). After such a roll, it is a good idea to split your runners, so as to be better able to absorb future 5's.

4-4. Many alternatives offer. The "5-point school" recommends B12-W5 (2). The "home board school" says W8-W4 (2) and W6-W2 (2). The "flexible game school" proposes B12-W9 together with W8-W4 (2) or B1-B5 (2). The latter idea is decried by a school that says "Take your runners into the outer table or leave them alone," and so favors B1-B9 (2) if the runners are to be touched. The choice is best governed by the position of the adverse stones at the time. For example, if Black has made his bar point, the move B1-B5 (2), taking his 5-point, devalues his advantage, and discourages a double. This, after all, is the primary object of play—to stave off the adverse double that puts you to a guess as to what future rolls may bring.

3-3. A natural, with a close choice between B12-W7 (2) making the bar, and W8-W5 (2) and W6-W3 (2) making two points in the home board.

2-2. The first and right impulse is to move W6-W4 (2). The question is how to take the other 2's. The best idea, in our opinion, is B12-W11 (2). The classic recommendation of Edmond Hoyle (circa 1743), B1-B3 (2), is now considered beneath contempt. Certainly better than this sickly move is to absorb the whole roll by B1-B5 (2).

1-1. The natural of naturals. Move W8-W7 (2) and W6-W5 (2), making both key points. If your opponent has already advanced his runner to make one key point, make the other and split your runners by B1-B3. It is not that this split is desirable, but that it is about the only move possible!

DOMINOES

There are many games designed to be played with dominoes. The number of players may vary from two to about nine. We describe the most interesting game for two, for three or four, for five or six, for more than six.

The Domino Set. Dominoes are small rectangular tablets of wood, plastic, etc., marked with dots like the faces of dice. The usual "double-six" set comprises twenty-eight dominoes or *bones,* as shown in Fig. 33. Each bone has two *ends.* A bone whose two ends are the same (as 6-6) is a *doublet.* The ends with no dots at all are *blanks.* One bone is *heavier* or *lighter* than another as its total of dots is greater or less.

Matching. In most domino games, including the four

here described, the dominoes are played by *matching*. They are put end to end, in a *layout* of one or two lines (though the lines are given right-angle turns as necessary to keep them from going off the table). Each end of a line is *open*,

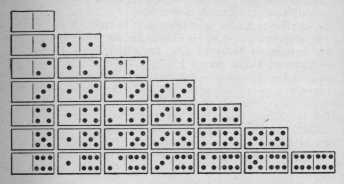

FIG. 33—The Domino set up to 6-6, comprising 28 bones.

and to play a bone the player must *match* an open end. For example, suppose that the 6-4 is laid down by the first player. The next player must play a bone having either a 6 or a 4 at one end. If he plays, say, 4-3, he abuts the two 4's and the open ends of the layout become 6 and 3.

Boneyard. To begin any game, the bones are shuffled face down, and then each player draws a fixed number of them for his *hand*. If not all twenty-eight are so drawn, those that remain are the *boneyard*. The rules vary in different games as to whether and when a player may draw from the boneyard if he cannot play in turn from his hand.

SNIFF

Best for two players; possible for three or four.

The Hand. With two players, each draws seven bones. With three or four players, each player draws five bones.

The Play. First turn to play is decided by lot. One way (not desirable) is to have each player draw and expose one extra bone; the heaviest plays first. Bones so drawn should be returned to the boneyard, which should then be shuffled. Preferable is to toss a coin.

The first player may play any bone he wishes, not necessarily a doublet. The turn to play rotates clockwise; if unable to play from his hand, a player must draw from the boneyard until he can play or until he exhausts the boneyard. After the boneyard is exhausted, a hand unable to play passes, and the turn goes to the next. Every bone played after the first must match an open end of the layout.

Play ends when any player *goes out* by getting rid of his entire hand, or when no hand can make an additional play after the boneyard is exhausted.

Sniff. The first doublet played becomes *sniff*. Alone among the doublets, sniff is open to play four ways—off both sides and both ends. Other doublets are place crosswise, but are open to play off the two sides only. The player has free option whether to play off an end or a side of sniff, and, in playing the first doublet, whether to place it crosswise or endwise. All four sides are open, whichever he decides, but his decision affects the scoring, as explained below.

Scoring. When a player causes the total of all open ends of the layout to be a multiple of five, he scores that total. For example, if the open ends show 6, 5, 4 (sniff having "sprouted" only three branches), he scores 15.

The number of bone-ends that enter into this total can vary from two to eight. The maximum is reached after sniff has sprouted four ways and each line terminates in some other doublet. Note that the *ends* of sniff (or the ends of lines radiating from them) must always be counted. For example, suppose that the first player lays down 2-2, which becomes sniff. The second player adds 2-4 on the side and the third player 2-6 on the other side. The latter cannot score 10 for the open ends 6 and 4, because the two ends of sniff (not yet played on) must be counted in; the total is 14. But of course the sides of sniff count nothing until they have sprouted. For example: first player, 1-1; second, 1-4 off an end, scoring 5; third player, 1-6 off the other end, scoring 10.

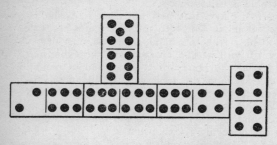

Fig. 34—Sniff. The 6-6 is evidently "sniff," since its ends have been played upon. The player who brought about this formation scores 15, the total of the open ends (2, 5, 4, 4). One side of "sniff" has not yet "sprouted," so does not show a countable end.

When a non-sniff doublet is played, necessarily crosswise under the rule, both ends count. For example, a player has just scored 15 by leaving the open ends 6, 4, 3, 2. The next hand plays 4-4, but cannot score, because the total is 19.

Tradition allows a player to call "Muggins!" and himself take a score overlooked by another player. You should agree beforehand with your opponent whether *muggins* is to be allowed. But in any event, the rule is that no player receives a score unless he claims it orally; if he overlooks that he has made the total of open ends 5, 10, 15, etc., the score is lost to him.

When a player goes out, he scores the total of all points left in the other hands. The total of each hand separately is taken to the nearest multiple of five, e.g., 12 counts as 10 while 13 counts as 15.

When play ends in a block, no player having gone out, the lightest hand wins the difference between his count and that of each other hand. Each such difference is taken to the nearest multiple of 5.

Game. A game is won by the player first to reach a total of 200 points. If he reaches 200 by scoring during the play, the deal is not played out. Settlement of monetary stakes is made on the difference of final totals.

Strategy. Scoring in play is as a rule more important than going out. Exception arises when by going out you can catch your opponent with an excessive number of bones. Playing to go out means leaving yourself at each turn with the widest possible assortment of different numbers. Playing to score means calculating which bone played will give you the best chance to score, in view of what your opponent can play. It may even mean digging into the boneyard for a desired bone, though you could play without digging.

Certain bones are intrinsically valuable because, if playable, they assure you of scoring directly after your opponent has scored. Chief of these are 5-5, 5-0, 0-0, 6-1. The first three always score after your opponent has scored, but never otherwise except that 5-5 and 5-0 score as first play. The 6-1 scores after a score if played endwise, and can also score (without previous score by your opponent) when played off the side of sniff. For example: first player, 1-1; second, 1-2 off the side; first, 1-6 off the other side, scoring 10.

Of remoter value are 6-3, 4-2, and 2-1. Each of these enables you to retort with an equal score if your opponent scores by playing a non-sniff doublet of the lower number. For example, if he scores by playing 3-3, you score the same with 3-6 because that end of the layout still counts 6.

To play for scores, save any of these valuable bones you draw for an appropriate occasion. When the boneyard is very low, and you have reason to believe it contains one of these "naturals," you may be well advised to dig for it in order to counter a score with a score. Don't overlook that you can often infer what "naturals" (as well as other bones) your opponent *does not* hold, by his failure to play them at appropriate occasions. In fact, a skillful player keeps track of *all* the bones his opponent evidently lacks and shapes his own play accordingly.

DRAW DOMINO

Good for two to four players.

The Hand. With two players, each draws seven bones. With three or four, each draws five.

The Play. Any player drawing the 6-6 plays it as first turn. If the 6-6 is not drawn, the next-highest doublet drawn is played as the *set* (first play). Thereafter the turn rotates clockwise. All plays are by matching, and all doublets are placed crosswise. The layout always has just two open ends. If unable to play in turn, a player must draw from the boneyard until able or until he exhausts the boneyard. If unable to play even then, he passes and the next hand plays.

Play ends when any player gets rid of his entire hand, or when play comes to a standstill after the boneyard is exhausted. There is always a winner—either the player who goes out or the one left with the lightest hand—unless the game ends in a block and all hands count the same. The winner scores all points left in the other hands, with no deduction for any points left in his own. If two players tie for low, they divide the winnings equally.

Game may be fixed at 50 or 100, as desired.

Strategy. With choice of play, choose the bone that will leave you with the widest possible assortment of different numbers. But usually play a doublet whenever you can, since doublets are hardest to get rid of. Watch for opportunity to create a complete block. There are eight ends of each number. If all eight of, say, the 4's, are in the layout, with a 4 at each end, no further play is possible. The hand then to play has to take the rest of the boneyard and the lightest hand wins.

BLOCK DOMINO

Best for four or five players; possible for three.

The rules are the same as for Draw Domino with these exceptions: (a) Each player draws five bones for his hand; (b) there is no digging into the boneyard; if unable to play in turn, a player must pass; (c) the player with the lightest hand (or who goes out) wins from each other hand the difference of the two. *Game* is usually fixed at 100.

TIDDLY-WINK

Best for six to nine players.

Each player draws three bones. The highest doublet drawn is *set*. Each hand in clockwise rotation must play or pass; there is no digging into the boneyard. On playing a doublet, the same hand may play again if able. The layout at all times has *only one open end*—the exposed end of the bone previously played. The sole object is to *go out*. In effect, each deal is a separate game. Monetary stakes are settled by equal antes to form a pool before each deal; the winner takes the pool.

PART THREE

Word Games and Pencil-and-Paper Games

ANAGRAMS

A "set" for Anagrams comprises from 50 to 200 cards, tiles, or blocks, each bearing a letter of the alphabet. Some cardboard sets have letters printed on both sides. There is no "standard" set and no need for any. All that matters is to have enough units for the number of players. Up to four players, use at least 200 units; with more players, use 400.

Many different games can be played with an Anagram set. Perhaps most popular is the one here described. It is excellent for social gatherings when brainy rather than hilarious amusement is sought. A duty devolves upon the hostess to fix the rules in advance and announce them to the players. The rules should be suited to the temper of the company.

The Play. The tiles, cards, or blocks should first be thoroughly shuffled, face down on the table. Appoint two or three players to shuffle, because if all join in many of the tiles may be knocked face up. After play has begun, a tile inadvertently exposed should be (a) added to the *center,* or (b) discarded, according to the rule adopted.

The hostess appoints the first player. Thereafter the turn to play rotates clockwise. It is not strictly necessary for players to keep turn, but doing so helps to keep the game going.

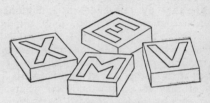

FIG. 35—Anagram blocks.

A play consists in bringing one of the face-down tiles to a space cleared in the center of the table, then turning it face up. The player should turn it outward, so that he will not see its face before the other players.

Making Words. The object of play is to make words from the available tiles. The face-up tiles that accumulate in the center are always available. On seeing the letters needed to spell a word, the player announces the word orally, then withdraws the tiles to a row in front of himself. For example, suppose the letters successively turned are M, X, R, Q, G, E. When the E appears, someone cries "GERM" and collars the four letters for himself.

The game is won by the player who first gets a prefixed number of words, usually five or ten.

Stealing Words. A player may claim all the letters of a word held by another, if with the help of at least one letter from the center he can rearrange the letters to form a longer word. For example, GERM can be stolen with a I to make GRIME. A player may add to his own words in any way, to make them harder to steal. But all changes must lengthen the original word.

Rules. All of the following points should be covered by some agreed rule, whether our suggestion or another is adopted.

1. The shortest valid word comprises four letters, excluding plurals of three-letter words made by adding *s*.

2. All words must be good English, and not obsolete. Any challenge to the validity of a word is settled by the hostess, preferably by reference to a dictionary kept at hand. When a dictionary is used, only the hostess may consult it.

3. To steal a word, a player must make some significant change in meaning or sense. Mere addition of *s* to make a plural or of *d* to change the tense of a verb is barred.

4. A player may make any addition whatsoever to his own word, so long as the longer word is still correct English.

5. When several players call simultaneously, the longest word has priority. Among words of equal length, the first-called has priority. If no precedence in time can be determined, the tied players toss a coin.

6. If a player calls a word that cannot in fact be made from the available tiles, he must return to the stockpile the last word he got. Any tiles he has taken erroneously from the center or from another player are restored.

7. Any player who has at least one word in his possession may challenge the validity of a word called by another. If several challenge at once, the first at the left of the challenged is deemed the challenger. If the word is ruled invalid, the player must restore the tiles taken from the center or from another player, and must then return his last previous word (if any) to the stockpile. If the word is ruled valid, the challenger must return his last previous word to the stockpile.

8. A reasonable time must be allowed between turns from the stockpile. Before turning a tile, a player must ask "Ready?" and must wait on demand from any player. But the hostess may curtail delays at any time and require the next play to be made.

Excessively slow play is the bane of Anagrams. Rarely

can a strict time limit be enforced. The best antidote is a hostess with gumption.

Strategy. Apart from a wide vocabulary and active imagination in anagramming, the chief requirement of the game is instant response to stimuli. For example, suppose that the first letters turned are C, J, B, R. On appearance of the R, the experienced player sets up some automatic responses: if an A is turned next, he will shout CRAB; or if the next is U, he will cry CURB. Similarly, when any word is made, all players including the owner calculate the letters necessary to steal it or hold it. For example, if the word is REAP, a player may establish in his mind: T means TAPER; S means SPARE; C means PACER; and so on. As the play progresses, the player may accumulate a dozen such responses in his mind—but he must be sure to delete those that become impossible by the withdrawal of available letters. It is more fatal to respond incorrectly than not to respond at all.

The ideal words to get are those that can virtually never be stolen: BUZZ, QUIZ, ONYX, JACK, etc. It is scarcely worthwhile to try for such a word as REAL—let someone else get it, then steal it. But then watch out that you don't lose it. We have seen REAL change hands four times, through LEARN, RENTAL, LATRINE, INTERNAL. Inveterate Anagram players know many series of such enlargements.

WORD SQUARES

Any number may participate in this round game. It is therefore a natural for social parties, provided that the temper of the occasion inclines toward word games.

The Play. Provide each player with paper and pencil. To

prepare for the game, each player draws a large square, divided into 5×5 smaller squares.

Then each in turn names any letter of the alphabet, until twenty-five letters have been named. When a letter is called, each player writes it in any cell of his square that he chooses. The object is to make good English words along the horizontal rows and vertical columns.

After the twenty-fifth letter is called, all squares then being filled, they are scored: for a word of five letters, 10; for a word of four letters, 5; for a word of three letters, 1. The player having the highest total score wins the game.

Before a player calls in his turn, he should ask "Ready?" Anyone who has not yet placed the previous letter should speak out, for the basic rule is that every player must commit himself to the placement of a letter before the next is announced.

Only one word may be counted on a line. For example, GRATE counts as a five-letter word, but it may not also score for its components RATE and RAT and ATE. Any question as to whether a word is admissible should be settled by reference to a dictionary, kept at hand.

Strategy. The tyro is prone to attempt too much. He tries for four or five words each way, horizontally and vertically, and ends up with something like this:

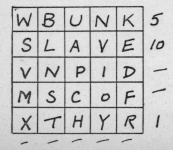

FIG. 36—A candidate for the booby prize.

The way to escape the booby prize is to plan the whole box in advance. Fill your whole box with letters, written lightly, in some such arrangement as the following.

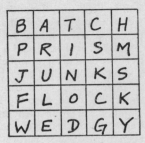

FIG. 37—Planning for a high score.

As each letter is called, write it heavily in its pre-assigned cell. When letters are called that you cannot use, such as X, Q, Z, put them all on one row, chosen for the sacrifice because it is the least advanced toward its prefixed target.

The *desiderata* of such a plan are:

1. It should aim for a maximum of five-letter words;
2. It should concentrate all the long words one way (horizontal or vertical), making crosswords the other way as the occasion arises, but sacrificing nothing for this purpose;
3. It should contain each vowel once, and once only;
4. It should offer the widest possible variety of consonants, by minimizing repetitions.

The reason for 3 is that vowels are sparse, in "fast company." Usually, eighteen or nineteen consonants are called before someone "breaks down" and calls a vowel. Therefore plan your words to require no more than one vowel each, relying for length on consonant combinations as in the above sample. (By the way, if you think WEDGY isn't a word, look it up!)

The reason for 4 is that you don't want to have to sacrifice more than one row for letters not in your plan. Be prepared to handle as many different consonants as possible.

What letter to call in your turn depends on how far your plan has been filled, without need for change. You would like, of course, to call a letter useful to yourself and to no one else. The logical course is to call a letter needed in your own five-letter word nearest completion, unless you can count on that letter to be called later by someone else. Until the last half-dozen turns, you should assume that every vowel will be called once, also R, L, N, T, and S. Having B-TCH, don't waste your turn on A, but having BAT-H, call C. Watch especially for chances to call a consonant that has been named once before—repetitions are sure to be embarrassing to some of the other players. On this account, your advance plan may well include repetitions of a few of the less-common letters.

The fine art of play consists in modifying the original plan so as to absorb without sacrifice letters that it did not originally contain. For example, if the first player calls V, you might change your intended word BATCH to VETCH. If two N's are called, you might absorb the second by heading from PRISM to PRINT, PRINK, BRING, or from FLOCK to FLANK, FLINT, FLING, FLOWN.

SALVO

Known also as "Battleship," Salvo is a game for two players, combining both skill and luck.

Equipment. Each player must have a pencil and a sheet of paper ruled into squares. Simplest is to obtain what is called "quadrille" paper, marked in manufacture with vertical and horizontal lines. The size should be either four or five lines to the inch. Lacking quadrille paper, the players may draw the necessary boxes on plain paper.

Each player marks out two boxes on his paper, each box enclosing 100 small squares in a 10×10 square. One box represents the player's own *battle zone;* the other is the opponent's battle zone. For reference, the vertical columns of each box are denoted by the letters A, B, C . . . to J, and the horizontal rows are numbered from 1 to 10.

The player also marks out four areas representing the opponent's *ships.* These areas comprise respectively five, three, two, and two small squares.

The Play. To commence a game, each player marks out his own *fleet* in his own battle zone. The fleet comprises four *ships:* a *battleship* of five squares, a *cruiser* of three

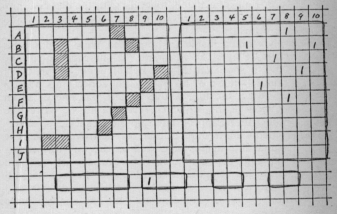

FIG. 38—Salvo layout. The square at the left is the player's "own battle zone"; at the right, the "enemy battle zone." The rectangles marked out below represent the enemy ships; they are used for keeping track of the hits. The player has just fired his first salvo of seven shots upon the squares marked "1" in the enemy zone, and has been informed that he hit the enemy cruiser with one shot.

squares, and two *destroyers* of two squares each. The player may dispose his fleet as he sees fit, within the 10×10 zone, but the squares comprising any one ship must be adjacent in a straight line, on a row, column, or diagonal. An optional rule is that no two ships may touch each other.

First turn to play is decided by lot. Suppose that the players are A and B, and that Player A draws first turn. He delivers a *salvo* of seven *shots* upon B's battle zone, by writing the figure "1" (for 1st salvo) in any seven squares he chooses. As he writes in "Opponent's battle zone" on his sheet, he announces the squares verbally, as "B2, D3, C5 . . ." etc. Player B writes the figure "1" in each named square of "Own battle zone" on his sheet. After the salvo is finished, B announces "You hit nothing," or "You hit my battleship once," or whatever is the case. The number of actual *hits* must be stated, together with the class of ship, but the player does not reveal which shots were hits and which were misses.

The salvos on each side are numbered, from 1 up. On his second turn, Player A will write "2" in each square he chooses for a shot, and Player B will write "2" in every corresponding square of his own battle zone. Thus when a hit is registered, the firer knows that it was one of seven (or less) shots in the salvo. To record a hit, he writes the salvo number in the appropriate ship on his sheet, representing the enemy battleship, cruiser, or destroyer. When he hits the same ship again, he is well on the way to locating it. For example, suppose he hits the cruiser with "2" and with "5". On his "Opponent's battle zone" he looks for all places where a 2 and a 5 stand on one line, adjacent and with an empty square adjacent, or with one empty square between them.

The game continues by alternate salvos, each player striving to sink the other's entire fleet. A ship is *sunk* when every component square has been hit. The game is won by the player first to hit every component square of all four enemy ships.

The allowance per salvo is seven shots so long as the

player has lost no ship. Loss of his battleship reduces his allowance per salvo by three shots; loss of the cruiser, by two; loss of a destroyer, by one.

Strategy. The largest ship is the easiest to find, and sinking it most cripples the enemy offensive power. The prime objective is therefore to sink the enemy battleship. If the first hit chances to be on the cruiser or a destroyer, it pays to continue search for the battleship, instead of to try for additional hits on the first ship.

There is of course a good deal of luck in finding an enemy ship, and each player has his pet plan. Our recommendation is to limit each of the first four salvos to a different quarter of the zone (if necessary), so that when the first hit is scored on the battleship its location can be fairly narrowed down. Once it is hit, the ensuing salvos should be concentrated in that quarter until the battleship is sunk.

The natural pattern for an exploratory salvo is to separate the shots by a Chess knight move (see page 148). This touches upon a maximum of different lines. For example, here is a typical first salvo: A2, B4, C1, C6, D3, E5, F2.

The only useful advice that can be given as to how to dispose your own ships is to vary your style from game to game. If, for example, you repeatedly put one ship near each of the four corners, your opponent will probably discover the fact and sink you in a hurry. Try to guess what he will guess *you* will do—then do something else.

QUADRANGLES

Quadrangles is a contest between two players, using pencil and paper. Though played by children throughout the world, this game has not hitherto received the recognition that is its due. It does not even have a generally-accepted name. It is known as "Squares," "Angles," the "Dots Game," and in European books it is referred to by various fanciful titles, such as the German *Käsekasten* (cheeseboxes). We have chosen the title Quadrangles as fairly descriptive, but avoiding ambiguity with other "square" games.

How to Play Quadrangles

Equipment. The paper is preferably of the kind known as *cross-section* or *quadrille*—ruled into squares by light horizontal and vertical lines. For children, we recommend the size with four squares per inch; adults may prefer five to the inch.

In lieu of quadrille paper, unlined paper may be used by marking rows of dots with the point of a pencil. The dots should be fairly well aligned horizontally and vertically, to represent the corners of small squares. (From this juvenile makeshift comes the name "dots game.")

The "playing field" is an aggregation of small squares, forming a large square or rectangle. Neither the shape nor size of this field affects the character of the play. But too large a field makes a tedious game. We suggest the use of a square field of 25 or 49 cells.

In using quadrille paper, start by outlining the field of agreed size. Do not draw lines right on its outer boundaries, for these lines must be supplied later during the course of play; make some kind of enclosure *outside* the boundary lines. (See Fig. 39.)

The only other equipment needed is one or two pencils, preferably of soft lead so that the lines drawn will stand out distinctly from the field.

The Play. Determine by tossing a coin who is to play first. Each player in turn then draws a line on the field, marking one of the sides of any of the small cells. The player at all times has free choice where to place his line.

During the early play, each player takes care to supply no more than two sides to any small cell. But presently a stage is reached when every cell of the field is marked on two sides. The in-turn player is then compelled to supply the third side of some cell. His opponent can thereupon draw the fourth side, and this act makes the cell his property.

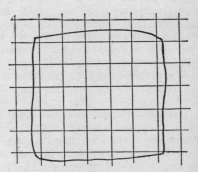

Fig. 39—Quadrangles. A square field of 25 cells is ample to test your ingenuity to the utmost.

On winning a cell, the player writes his initial inside it. Simpler is for one player to use X and his opponent O, in the same way as in the very familiar game Tit-Tat-Toe.

The play is governed by three rules:

1. The player wins a cell by supplying the fourth side; if this line also supplies the third side of an adjacent cell, the same player may play again and capture the latter cell by supplying its fourth side. In this manner the player may continue his turn so long as he captures a new cell with every new line. His turn ends only when he makes a non-capturing move.

2. It is not compulsory to capture when able. The player *may* refrain from completing a cell if he wishes.

3. On capturing a cell, the same player *must* play again.

The game is won by the player whose mark of ownership shows in a majority of the cells, when all the cells have been filled. The field should preferably comprise an odd number of cells, to avoid ties.

STRATEGY OF QUADRANGLES

As far as the author knows no analysis of possibilities in the game of Quadrangles has been made in the way in which the mathematical aspects of Chess and Checkers have been studied. However the author's own investigation has uncovered some useful principles of strategy for play in Quadrangles, and these principles follow.

Circuits. We will denote by K the stage at which the in-turn player can find no move that does not cede his opponent a cell.

The play prior to K partitions the field into one or more *circuits*. A circuit is a chain of cells so connected that a play upon any point will allow the opponent to capture the whole chain. For example, Fig. 40 shows K reached with three circuits: a circuit of 2 at upper right, one of 10 at upper left, and all the other 13 cells in one circuit at the bottom.

In Fig. 40, it is the turn of F (the first player), since an

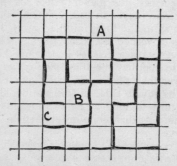

Fig. 40—Circuits. The "K stage" has been reached, with three circuits. Now the players must necessarily commence ceding squares to each other.

even number of lines (32) has been drawn. One might think that S (the second player) is destined to win the game by 15 to 10, thus: F *breaks* the circuit of 2, which S takes; S then breaks the circuit of 10, after taking which F has to cede the circuit of 13 to S. But this simple alternation in the capturing of circuits is not forced, for reasons explained below.

The Gambit. The vital rule, usually overlooked by the tyro, is that *capture is not compulsory*. Let us see how F can profit by this rule, in Fig. 40. He duly breaks the circuit of 2; S takes the 2 and breaks the circuit of 10, say by a play at A. (The point of break does not matter.) F proceeds to take eight of the cells, ending at B; but now he abandons the last two, playing at C. As this line completes neither of the last two cells, the turn passes to S, who is therefore compelled to break the final circuit of 13. Thus F wins by 21 to 4!

Observe that the *gambit*—the sacrifice of the end-cells of a circuit, to change the move—is perfectly legal. More, it is the soul of the game.

The gambit cannot be worked with a sacrifice of less than two cells. (Certain formations require the sacrifice of four.) It is feasible only in a circuit of three or more cells, not in a circuit of two or one. Hence we have an important dichotomy of circuits into *large* (three or more cells) and *small* (two or one).

We must note that the gambit may be permitted in a circuit of two through an adverse mistake. In Fig. 40, suppose that F were to make the mistake of breaking the smallest circuit by a horizontal line (top boundary of the field). Then S could complete this horizontal without capturing either cell, and so change the move. Of course the right play by F is to supply the vertical partition between the two cells, whereupon S cannot gambit.

The Critical Point. We see that there is a critical point beyond K (though it may coincide)—the stage at which the in-turn player has to break a *large* circuit. We can say with certainty that:

The player to move at the critical point is bound to lose the game.

For, his opponent can gambit in every large circuit, sacrificing usually two (possibly four) cells to win the rest, including the last circuit entire. It is demonstrable that the total of sacrificed cells can never reverse the win.

With correct play, the small circuits are bound to be won alternately; hence we can say:

The player to move at K is bound to lose if the number of small circuits is even, or win if this number is odd.

However, it must be noted that the number of circuits *may or may not be fixed* at stage K. Configurations are possible in which the player has choice of making two circuits or one.

The Rule-of-Thumb. Whose turn is it to move at stage K? The answer depends on the number of lines already drawn: if the number is even, it is now F's turn; if odd, S is to play. What determines whether this number is odd or even—the caprice of the players or the size and shape of the field itself?

Here we can give only a contingent answer. The field itself determines a relationship between the number of circuits and number of lines at K, which *usually* applies. There is, however, at least one formation (and there may be more) that *exactly reverses* the formula as between odd and even. It remains to be discovered whether a player can prevent the establishment of any such formation, and also whether he can control the number of circuits to the extent of oddness or evenness.

Where the formula is valid, we can lay down the rule-of-thumb:

F should strive to keep the number of large circuits odd or even in the opposite sense of N (where N is the number of cells in a square field).

If N is odd (as it should be to avoid draws), F should therefore try to make an even number of large circuits. Note that this rule is stated in terms of the large circuits, not the small, although the latter govern the passage from K to the critical point. The above-mentioned formula also fixes a relationship between large and small circuits.

S should of course strive for the converse. When N is odd, he should try to make an odd number of large circuits.

The Locked Circuit. We have said that there is at least one formation that exactly reverses the formula. This is shown in Fig. 41. This *locked circuit* has two oddities. First, to gambit in it means the sacrifice of all four cells, not two. If the horizontal line A is added, the gambit is possible

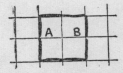

Fig. 41—The locked circuit. Any wholly-closed rectangle such as this exactly reverses the formulas as to odd and even.

only by continuing the horizontal at B, capturing no cell. Second, the existence of one locked circuit in the field exactly reverses the rule-of-thumb for F and S. This fact should be utilized to try to escape an otherwise sure loss. In a field sufficiently large to accommodate two or more locked circuits, this number might be worked into the general formula. It certainly should be taken into account in practical strategy.

Which of these popular new Permabooks do you want?

(Continued on next page)

New titles are added monthly. See your local dealer for these and other new Permabooks.